AMERICAN EDUCATION

Its Men

Ideas

and

Institutions

Advisory Editor

Lawrence A. Cremin
Frederick A. P. Barnard Professor of Education
Teachers College, Columbia University

The Beginnings
of Yale
1701-1726

Edwin Oviatt

ARNO PRESS & THE NEW YORK TIMES
*New York * 1969*

88599

Reprint edition 1969 by Arno Press, Inc.

*

Library of Congress Catalog Card No. 70-89214

*

Reprinted from a copy in
The Free Public Library of Newark

*

Manufactured in the United States of America

Editorial Note

AMERICAN EDUCATION: *Its Men, Institutions and Ideas* presents selected works of thought and scholarship that have long been out of print or otherwise unavailable. Inevitably, such works will include particular ideas and doctrines that have been outmoded or superseded by more recent research. Nevertheless, all retain their place in the literature, having influenced educational thought and practice in their own time and having provided the basis for subsequent scholarship.

Lawrence A. Cremin
Teachers College

The Beginnings
of Yale
1701-1726

The Granting by the Deputies of the Collegiate School Charter, October 1701

THE BEGINNINGS OF YALE

(1701-1726)

BY EDWIN OVIATT

Illustrated by Theodore Diedricksen, Jr.

NEW HAVEN: YALE UNIVERSITY PRESS
LONDON: HUMPHREY MILFORD
OXFORD UNIVERSITY PRESS
MDCCCCXVI

THE HERBERT A. SCHEFTEL
MEMORIAL PUBLICATION FUND

The present volume is the second work published by the Yale University Press on the Herbert A. Scheftel Memorial Publication Fund. This foundation was established January 12, 1915, by a gift to Yale University by Mrs. Herbert A. Scheftel, of New York, in memory of her husband, a member of the Class of 1898, Yale College, who died September 12, 1914: "in recognition of the affection in which he always held Yale and in order to perpetuate in the University the memory of his particular interest in the work of the Yale University Press."

PREFACE

A surprisingly small number of books on Yale University are accessible to us. President Clap's quaint "Annals" of 1766 can now be consulted only in the few rare copies that have survived; Ebenezer Baldwin's dry compilation of 1831 has long been out of date; President Woolsey's fine Anniversary Address of 1850 is no longer in general circulation; the late William L. Kingsley's monumental "Yale College" was published as long ago as 1879. These old-time books, together with a few chapters in Bagg's "Four Years at Yale" (now out of print), and Professor Dexter's brief epitome of the University's history, together with such other narratives as may be found in periodicals and in American college history compilations, comprise practically all that has appeared in book form regarding Yale history. Much fresh material concerning these bygone days has come to light, of course, since 1879. Professor Dexter's researches, for instance, have brought out new facts and revised old statements. Delvers into Yale's past must needs become acquainted with his numerous papers in the publications of the New Haven Colony Historical Society, with his exhaustive collection of facts in his "Yale Biographies and Annals," and with his "Documentary History of Yale University," to be published this year. Anson Phelps Stokes' "Memorials of Eminent Yale Men," published in 1914 by the Yale University Press, has brought together a great amount of hitherto scattered information regarding a number of graduates of the early days. Colonial town records have become much more accessible during these thirty-five years; letters and diaries have been discovered and published; new treatment has been given the whole Colonial period by numerous scholars, including our own Professors Fisher, Andrews, and Walker. As a result, much that had previously been accepted as true (as stated by such supposed authorities as Clap and President Quincy of Harvard and his school of followers) has had to be revised. The present writer has spent many an off-duty hour poring over these original sources, ransacking town-record offices and town and church histories, and visiting the scenes where Yale had its beginnings. Where considerable portions of this book give the modern understanding of certain epochs in Yale history, I presume that these latter-day corrections of the old views are responsible. Where I have given perhaps a new interpretation to certain other movements in this history, no one may be called to account but myself. Mr. Diedricksen's illustrations for this book should form not the least interesting and useful feature of it. Most of them have been drawn from ancient woodcuts and photographs; where an imaginary reconstruction has been attempted, only myself may be blamed for such anachronisms as may have crept in.

It has been my plan to treat the several Colonial periods covered by these chronicles in such a way that one might first renew his acquaintance with the broad events of the times, and then follow the participants of the several acts of the drama in a perhaps more intimate way against that background. These three main periods are: the Davenport epoch, during which New Haven was founded as a Separatist church-state and attempts at a college were made; the Pierpont period, during which the Collegiate School was founded and carried on at the modern Clinton and the old Saybrook; and the Andrew-Cutler-Edwards era, during which Yale College was established and took root at New Haven. It is a coincidence, but a happy one, that this book on these beginnings of Yale appears at the time of the two-hundredth anniversary of this latter event.   That these easy-going pages may serve to give something at least of that new realization of how Yale's beginnings came about which the author came to have in writing them, is the cordial hope of the writer.

EDWIN OVIATT.

Ogden Street, New Haven, September 4, 1916.

CONTENTS

PART I

JOHN DAVENPORT AND HIS NEW HAVEN COLLEGE

PART II

THE FOUNDING OF THE COLLEGIATE SCHOOL

PART III

THE COLLEGIATE SCHOOL AND YALE COLLEGE

ILLUSTRATIONS

PAGE

as Greenwood's drawing has it, has been adopted for this representation. On the other hand,—accepting Mr. Isham's decision, made after close study by him of all available sources, that "Greenwood probably sat down before this building and drew it 'just as it really was,' "— all of the other details of the traditional sketch have been retained in this new representation. Says Mr. Isham: "From my examination of the Greenwood engraving it seems to me that, apart from the fact that it is inaccurate and wrong in many ways in proportion and perspective, it is correct in important items." As to the drawing in this book Mr. Isham says: "It is a good interpretation of the Greenwood engraving, and is as near as anyone can ever get to the building as it was in 1718, though the element of conjecture, of course, will largely come in in any modern reconstruction." Later contemporary sketches of this building are entirely at variance with each other, from the correctly-elongated plan in Brown's Map of 1724, and the high and short elevation in Wadsworth's Map of New Haven "with all the buildings in 1748" (which gives it six entries and a hip roof), to the views in Honeywood's sketches printed in Stiles' "Literary Diary." The fact, however, that it had three entries, is fully established both by Greenwood's sketch and by the rough pen drawings in President Clap's manuscript College "Account Books" in the University Archives, wherein he assigned the rooms to the students

PART I

JOHN DAVENPORT AND HIS NEW HAVEN
COLLEGE

The Davenport
Arms

CHAPTER I

JOHN DAVENPORT

I

N the latter days of the reign of the good Queen Bess, the quaint little city of Coventry, famed for its ancient procession of the Lady Godiva and for its wooden-headed Peeping Tom, was still the considerable rural community that it had been for two centuries of English history. Around it still ran that great city wall,—three miles long and nine good English feet in thickness,—which, with its thirty-two towers and twelve fortified gates, had done good service for the rebellious Warwick against Edward VI and which, a half-century later, was to defy Charles I and, still later, be demolished by his son. It was, in 1600, a community of some twelve hundred houses, built for the most part of great timbers filled in with the plastered brick of the early 15th Century style, the upper stories of which projected over the narrow paved lanes below. Through it then, as in William Dugdale's day, still flowed the river Sherbourne, to join the Avon a few miles out in the country and then meander through pleasant woods and meadows to Warwick and Stratford-on-Avon, where William Shakespeare was shortly to end his days, and, come a few years, John Harvard to be born.

Difficult it would have been to imagine, when John Davenport was born in 1597 in this ancient walled English city, that the seed was there to be planted that later, in the

career of this famous son of Coventry, was to come to
flower in the New World church-state of New Haven, and,
two generations later still, to bring forth that institution
whose beginnings are again to be traced in the following
chapters.

Yet the occasion was forming, for the England of Elizabeth's day, as we will recall, was at the parting of the
established ways of the English centuries. The forty years
of Elizabeth had seen the highest development in Tudor
history of the power of the Crown; on the other hand, of
the most generally contented public under the traditional
English monarchy. Yet the underlying movement for what
we now know as the modern era was rising steadily. With
the tactless opening acts of James I's reign, it was shortly
to sweep up through the two decades of that grotesque
period, and end, at the close of the civil wars of Charles I,
in carrying Cromwell's Puritans over the decapitated body
of the King into Whitehall, and, when that furious religious-
political wave had subsided, in the beginnings of modern
England.

Coventry, as all Warwickshire, had been a storm-center
of this hardly-understood popular movement throughout
the half-century before John Davenport was born. During
his grandfather's later years, Elizabeth being queen, the
Protestant refugees who had scurried to Geneva during the
brief days of Bloody Queen Mary had returned to their
homes. They since, throughout rural England, had been
growing in numbers and influence; had come to assume high
offices in Church and State, and now, during the last years
of the 16th Century, were the predominant party among the
middle-class Englishmen, both in London and in the provincial cities. In Warwickshire, the Protestant movement
had been especially strong ever since the Lollard days.
Warwick men had been famous martyrs to the popular

Church reform under the earlier Tudors, and Coventry friends and neighbors of Davenport's family had gone to the stake for the new religious principles. So that, I fancy, the majority of the people among whom John Davenport was to grow up as a serious-minded and ambitious boy, were prepared by the year 1600 to cast their lot with the new party and to add to the rapidly growing public feeling throughout England against the petty despotisms of the divinely appointed James and his impositions of Church ceremony. In 1565 the young Queen Bess had visited Coventry and had been received with that genuine show of loyalty which was life itself to her. Ten years later she was again entertained, and the famous old Coventry play of "Hock Tuesday" performed for her benefit. But twenty-five years more, and the good Coventry townsfolk would have stood silently in their narrow paved lanes had Elizabeth visited them again, in strong aversion to the type of English life and court morality which the Queen and her royal favorites had come to typify for them.

Coventry in 1600

This change, which made the Coventry of John Davenport's youth a different place from that of his father's, had, of course, permeated the whole of England. We may recall how it had been coming. The introduction of the Bible as a popular book had been reacting on the social as well as the religious conditions of the people for a century previous. The New Learning had come in with the Italian Renaissance and had brought with it the philosophy and poetry of the Greeks and Latins. A broadened intellectual horizon had thus come to Englishmen. The new sense of individualism that grew out of the free study of the Bible had worked to produce that swelling tide of popular learning and that new sense of personal liberty which were shortly to lay the broad foundations for our modern intellectual and political democracy.

The Coventry people had long been taking part in this new popular change. The great-grandfather of John Davenport could have bought suppressed translations of the Bible at the Coventry Corpus Christi Fairs from itinerant missionaries, just as his father probably did buy, surreptitiously, the "Martin Marprelate" attacks on the Elizabethan episcopate from discreet neighboring tradesmen in the Corpus Christi Fairs of his day. In fact, the "Marprelate" printers at one time had taken refuge from the Bishop of London and the Primate in friendly Coventry, and had secretly issued their anonymous and revolutionary pamphlets from the very houses where, doubtless, Davenport's father was a frequent visitor. The final suppression of these pamphlets, with the execution of one of their authors, was no doubt a determining factor in the religious zeal with which Coventry people, as Warwickshire folk generally, supported Cartwright, the master of the hospital at near-by Warwick, in his attempt to introduce his more or less Presbyterian scheme of church discipline and organization of classes and synods as a rival system to the established Church. Mid-England, and London as well, were thus—by 1600—preparing for the movement which, as we know it in Puritanism, was shortly to rock the nation to its very social and religious center, and bring about new times.

So that John Davenport's religious and political surroundings, as he grew up to boyhood in the ancient walled city of Coventry, were decidedly revolutionary. The opening acts of the coming Puritan period were well under way by the time that he first appears as a scholar at the Free Grammar School of his old city. This school building, famous among the great English public schools that sprang up throughout the country during the Reformation, four centuries previously had been the home of the Coventry Hospitallers of St. John, and had been granted, during Henry VIII's sweeping suppression of the monasteries, to

Coventry Free School

one John Hales, who, a New Learning follower, had given it to the town as a Free School. One of the original aisles of this ancient hospital, and the schoolroom of young Davenport's boyhood, now a parish room, may still be seen by the inquiring visitor. It was in this tiny, high-peaked, stone-buttressed building, with its mullioned windows, that young John Davenport went to school, there to learn his grammar, to drone out his three music lessons a week, to recite his Latin verses, and, no doubt, boy fashion, to hack his initials in the old oak prior's stalls as did the famous antiquarian, Dugdale, before him. The father of John Milton's Cambridge tutor was later in charge of this school, and Dr. Holland, a renowned classical translator and drill-master of the day, was a youthful usher there when John Davenport began his schooling. John Davenport's lifelong fluency in classical study, and his various attempts to build his New Haven Colony education on it, very likely began in the many long boyhood hours that he spent in this quaint old Coventry Free School under the encouraging eye and rod of the scholarly Holland.

It was during these school years of Davenport, and just before he went up to Oxford, that Coventry had that first serious clash with King James over religious matters which was to become in time an important factor in the establishment of his Puritan commonwealth. Throughout Elizabeth's reign, and up to this time in King James', the popular feeling of the growing Puritan element in the Church had steadily been gaining ground for a repression of the many English-Church ceremonies which the liberated English mind connected with the Church of Rome. In addition to the giving of a ring in marriage, for instance, the Puritan element objected to the traditional custom of kneeling to receive the sacrament of the Lord's Supper. Coventry people, following the rebellious Cartwright, had come to relinquish a number of these ceremonies. But nonconformity in anything was to James I not only an evidence of disloyalty to the established Church, but to the Crown itself, and Coventry, in 1611, received a letter from the King's own hand soundly rating the Mayor and Corporation for permitting such revolutionary acts. John Davenport was fourteen years old when the uproar broke out upon the receipt of the King's summary commands, and it could hardly have escaped affecting him, as it no doubt had its part in unconsciously determining him in his own course some few years afterwards. The townspeople doubtless gave in, as the old records of Coventry show that King James made a formal visit there five years later, with a great train of nobility, to be received in humble loyalty. The houses and town gates were painted black and white in his honor on this occasion, there was a great procession of the Mayor and Corporation, and a massive cup of pure gold was presented as a peace offering to his Majesty and put among the royal plate. Two years later young Davenport went up to Oxford, to fit himself for the Church.

Davenport's Oxford days are obscure and bear little on what was to follow. Whether he went to Merton College and thence to Magdalen (as Wood, the Oxford chronicler, says) or matriculated at Brasenose (as says Mather, who had Davenport's private papers before him when he wrote his biography in the "Magnalia" many years later) we do not now know. At any rate, he entered Oxford as a "battler," or beneficiary for his tuition and board, at the expense doubtless of his relatives in Coventry. It was probably two years later that he was forced to leave Oxford, his degrees ungained for want of means to continue his study for them. Yet he had made a small mark there, even in that short time, if we may accept the word of a later enemy, one

Stephen Goffe,—a most disreputable individual, by the way, and brother, as it happened, of that regicide whom Davenport was to befriend many years later in New Haven. Goffe says that Davenport had made a name for himself as a speaker and writer at Oxford,—natural gifts which were to make him one of the foremost preachers of his time.

Oxford at that day was far from its earlier character as a "nest of Papists." It had passed through a tremendous religious excitement due to the incoming of the New Learning. Yet, when Davenport was there, it was probably less intellectually rebellious than its sister university and in a few years was passively to accept King James' authority, as Coventry had done. This very passiveness may have had its usual effect in Davenport's mental training, and have driven in still deeper the sense of personal freedom in religious matters with which he had come up to the University from Coventry. Yet I imagine that those two early years of Davenport's at Oxford were years of acquisition rather than of religious rebellion, as would be apt to be the case in a sixteen-year-old youth who had his chosen career before him. The opportunities in this way were unusual, even for Oxford. Sir Henry Saville, the renowned classical scholar, was Master of Merton then; John Hales, a descendant of the Coventry Hales, was Royal Professor of Greek; Dr. Thomas Holland, "an Apollos mighty at the Scriptures," had been Regius Professor of Divinity at Balliol, was now Rector of the Puritan school at Exeter, and later was to be one of the six Oxford scholars who were to translate the prophets for the King James Bible. Christopher Angelus, a Christian Greek who had been forced to leave his own country, had just arrived from Cambridge to teach elementary Greek and vaingloriously to impress his scholars,—so the story goes,—with the marks that he carried of Turkish persecution.

Magdalen College Tower

Yet Oxford in John Davenport's day was partially rebellious. Balliol College was a Puritan center then, Robert Abbott leading in the new movement, to the mounting anger of William Laud, then President of St. John's. This latter brilliant Churchman, later to be the sincere if cruel tool of the Stuarts in suppressing Puritanism and to have a determining effect on John Davenport's career in the Church, was even then attracting incipient Puritan fire and brimstone. The Oxford students of that day—Davenport among them—could hardly have escaped excitement over the situation in the University which resulted from such fierce public attacks upon him as when Abbott, thundering in Balliol pulpit, cried: "What art thou? Romish or English, Papist or Protestant? a mongrel compound of both." So that, if Oxford in 1616, when Davenport left it, was officially passive in the King's hands, there were professors and preachers in it who must have opened the eyes of the students to the coming struggle between the Church of James and the people of England.

John Davenport's Oxford knew probably little of that other intellectual world, literary London. Shakespeare, having written "The Tempest" and "A Winter's Tale" during these formative years of young Davenport's life, had died comparatively unknown on the Avon in the year that the latter had left Oxford to begin his career in the English Church. Spenser had finished "The Faery Queen" when Davenport was two years old; Thomas Dekker and Ben Jonson were coming on for the last stage of the declining Elizabethan drama. But all of this magnificent crest of the first great English literature had passed by such earnestly religious youths as John Davenport, and was doubtless little noticed by them. It is worth recalling something of this, as the cultural lack which we cannot fail to sense in the community that John Davenport later led to the New World, and its absence in the intellectual life of the early days of the college his successors were to found, goes back, in very large measure, I doubt not, to this separation.

I do not need to do more than pass rapidly over the well-known facts of Davenport's career in the next few years. We trace him through a minor chaplaincy near the historic church of Durham to a small position in St. Lawrence Jewry in London, and then suddenly to the vicarage of one of London's most influential churches, St. Stephen's in Coleman Street,—a position which in itself is the best evidence that we can have of his inherent powers and capacity. Here John Davenport found himself suddenly in the midst of the fullest public life of his time, and in touch with the leaders on all sides of the great public questions. He went up to Oxford now, to pass his examinations for his degrees, and, returning to London, seems to have launched himself full upon the troublous waters of the day.

These, we hardly need again to recall, were troublous enough. It had now been some sixty years since the first small voluntary congregation of Separatists from the Church of England had been broken up in London and most of the members unceremoniously marched off to jail. It had been some fifty years since Robert Browne's pioneer Congregational church had been formed and, in its extreme revolt from traditions, had angered the Puritan element in the established Church as much as the Church dignitaries themselves. It had been but a generation since, to the hilarious amusement of the Court and of the university men in London, that one of their members, John Barrowe, the Cambridge graduate, turned Puritan. The Separatist movement, fanned by the extremists who had fled to Holland and Geneva and returned, was now rapidly gaining. James, shivering and gibbering over the fear that the Scottish presbytery would follow him into England, had, immediately upon his accession, demanded conformity of the English Puritan clergy and laymen, and begun that tense religious struggle which was at once to become a political one, with the results we now know. William Brewster, at Scrooby, had organized his Separatist congregation, and had attracted to it the William Bradford who later, as the first Governor of Plymouth, was to become a leader in the New World settlement. The Scrooby Separatists' church had been stopped by the public prosecutors, and the members had fled to Leyden in Holland. But the Puritan movement was under way.

II

All of which was the beginning of a new era in English history. And other factors were coming in as well. During the latter years of this period, English trade had established itself across the Atlantic in successful dispute of Spanish appropriations, and joint-stock companies of English capitalists had been formed to colonize the New World's eastern coast and benefit from the great trading possibilities that were imagined to lie in that direction. The story is well known: how, in 1607, one of these companies settled Jamestown, Virginia; how in this way the attention of the London Puritan refugees was directed to the possibility of emigrating under one of them; how these so-called Pilgrims, under Brewster and Bradford, sailed across the ocean and, by a fortunate miscalculation, landed in what is now Massachusetts and settled Plymouth. And familiar is the story of how John White, the Puritan rector of Dorchester, saw in this pioneer emigration the chance to "raise a bulwark against the kingdom of Anti-christ," and thus to establish a Puritan refuge in a new England. This scheme, once broached, appears to have met with immediate favor among the leading Puritans. Salem was settled with Endicott as

Governor. The enterprise of "The Governor and Company of Massachusetts Bay" was then begun, the charter for which Charles had unsuspiciously granted in the same week that had seen his dramatic ending, for eleven years, of popular Parliament in England and his clapping of the democratic Eliot into the Tower of London, there to end his noble days. In 1629 John Winthrop had ridden to Boston in Lincolnshire to consult with Thomas Dudley regarding this Massachusetts scheme. A month later the famous Cambridge "Agreement" had been drawn up, and then Winthrop had sailed to become Governor of Massachusetts, where, in the next few years, over a thousand Puritans settled about the new Boston in New England.

John Davenport was in his second year in his first London parish when the Brewster party had founded Plymouth, and he contributed £50 to this new Winthrop emigration. This gift, however, had been anonymous. He did not wish to come too prominently, at this time, to the notice of William Laud, now Bishop of London and rapidly becoming a power in the Church. The curious interest of that implacable enemy of nonconformity had for some time been turned in the direction of the young and brilliant preacher in Coleman Street; envious tongues had been wagging; no doubt, like other Puritan leaders, he was discussed gaily at Ben Jonson's "Devil's Tavern" in Temple Bar; his popularity in London, which had come to fill St. Stephen's Church each Sunday, considering the unsettled state of the public religious sentiment, was a suspicious matter. Meeting charges of nonconformity he seemed to have proved to Laud that he had conducted himself with at least full outward semblance of the strictest conformity to the Church ritual, even insisting on that kneeling upon which Laud set such importance. He did not escape so easily, however, in another matter. He had joined with a number of serious Puritan churchmen in a sort of home-missionary society, formed for the purpose of supporting, with purchased parish impropriations, a better grade of ministers for the country towns than Laud's party in the Church had been willing to have. This philanthropic effort had been stamped out by Laud as soon as he discovered it, and the culprits—including Davenport—had all but been haled into the courts on criminal charges. The moment, therefore, was not propitious for a public avowal by him of his interest in the Massachusetts Bay Puritan emigration. To be seriously suspected of private inclinations toward "Doctrinal Puritanism" was to invite exclusion from the Church, suppression, and even imprisonment. And so, during this period, John Davenport found himself one of a very large number of earnest folk, both clerical and lay, who were tending toward Puritanism, yet attempting what finally became to them an impossible reconciliation between their outward acts and their private opinions.

It was at this time, when he was under suspended indictment for his share in the "Feoffees" incident, that John Davenport seems to have proceeded methodically to investigate his own mind on the subject. In a voluminous personal notebook that has come down to us, is contained the exhaustively argued account of his own intellectual change at this time from conformity to nonconformity. That this was brought about by outside influences, also, we now can have no doubt. In London were then in concealment two famous nonconforming ministers, whose cases were the subject of considerable public excitement. These two men, the later careers of whom were to be closely intertwined with John Davenport's, were John Cotton and Thomas Hooker. Both were university men and famous preachers, and both were friends of Davenport. Cotton had just been driven out of St. Botolph's in Boston by Bishop Laud, and Hooker had been silenced for nonconformity in his preaching in the little country village of Chelmsford in Essex. Cotton had come to London in disguise, and was now in hiding under Davenport's protection. The latter seems to have set out to change Cotton's mind, and reclaim him for the Church, as he had his uncle in Coventry. But the long argument that ensued appears, instead, to have unsettled John Davenport's own mind. Cotton escaped to New England, to join the Boston settlement. Davenport remained away from the communion services of St. Stephen's for the next few months and, when his old friend and protector against Laud suddenly died on August 4, 1633, and it became known that Laud was to be elevated to Canterbury, left London for the country, remained in seclusion there for three months, and then, "in a gray suit and an overgrown beard," took passage to Holland, a refugee from that Church in which he had planned to spend his life.

London Spires

OHN COTTON and Thomas Hooker had emigrated to the Massachusetts Bay Colony with large parties of their followers during this crisis in John Davenport's life, and the final few groups of the great Puritan emigration, which were to follow them, were now being formed.

The last of these was now coming together in London, led by one Theophilus Eaton, an established London merchant of wealth and reputation. Eaton was a parishioner of Davenport's in the Coleman Street Church, and had been a boyhood friend in old Coventry. He was a good representative of the well-to-do middle class of the day who had become Puritan in their Church connections. Though not a university graduate, he was a man of parts, traveled, versed in Roman law and the classics, and of an attractive personality which had permitted him to cut a good figure in the small London society of his day. He had at one time been employed, while abroad on his own affairs, as an agent of King James in Denmark. As subsequent events were to prove, Eaton was a man of unusual solidity and ability. Like Davenport, he had had a hand in the formation of the Massachusetts Bay Colony and had subscribed to it, though his purpose in this was probably more commercial than religious. He had married, as his second wife, the widow of David Yale, a provincial gentleman of Denbighshire, North Wales, whose estate was but a few miles away from his father's church in Great Budworth, whither the Eaton family had removed in the early days from Coventry. This David Yale was the son of a distinguished Churchman, the vicar-general of Chester, and had settled in London, where he had recently died. His widow brought to Theophilus Eaton a "fair and large house" in the Coleman Street parish, and two grown sons, Thomas and David Yale, both of whom joined the Eaton party. David Yale, at this time well established in London business on an extensive patrimony, was in time to become the father of Elihu Yale. Edward Hopkins,—who had married Theophilus Eaton's step-daughter by the latter's marriage to the widow Yale,— also a merchant in the city, likewise joined the London party.

That the exile in Holland of John Davenport must have had a good deal to do with this decision of Theophilus Eaton to emigrate to New England, and that, during the two or three years that now elapsed while the many details involved in preparing for the change were being worked out, Eaton must have corresponded with Davenport from London about it, is highly probable. The religious impulse toward such a change was in itself a determining one to most of the London folk who now gathered about Theophilus Eaton to embark upon it. The latter's brother, Samuel, a silenced nonconforming minister, was at this time in hiding and prepared to follow a colleague who had already left for New England. But Theophilus Eaton was a business man as well as a Churchman, and, from what later was to happen, I imagine that we may couple commercial ambition with religious fervor as the factors that made him the leader of the party, and that attracted to him that considerable group of other well-to-do London Puritan tradesmen who joined him. Under his leadership several other groups, made up from the countryside about London, were now added to the new emigration. The Reverend Whitfield of Ashford had been leading a Separatist church movement in the diocese of Canterbury over which William Laud now presided as head of the English Church, and had been facing arrest and silencing; hearing of the new emigration he seems to have thrown in his fortunes and those of his Kentish parishioners, who followed him, with it. The Rev. Peter Prudden of distant Herefordshire, near Wales, added his little group, though they were not to sail with the original party. A third section, from Yorkshire, were under the leadership of their own nonconforming minister, the Rev. Ezekiel Rogers.

II

John Davenport had now spent three miserable years in Holland, where, in spite of the fact that he seems fully to have expected at first to return to good standing in the established Church, he had engaged in strenuous controversies with other English refugees, and had tried, with unhappy results, to conduct Separatist services on his own account. Letters from John Cotton in Boston, and doubtless from Eaton in London, apprising him of the proposed emigration, would appear to have finally settled his mind. He slipped back again across the channel early in 1637 and, when the Eaton party sailed from London late in April of that year, had been accepted as the joint leader of it with Eaton, and as its spiritual pastor. A "covenant" was drawn up between the various groups of the Eaton party before the ship "Hector" weighed anchor off English shores,— an agreement of some sort defining the purposes of the emigration and the rights of the shareholders in it, much the

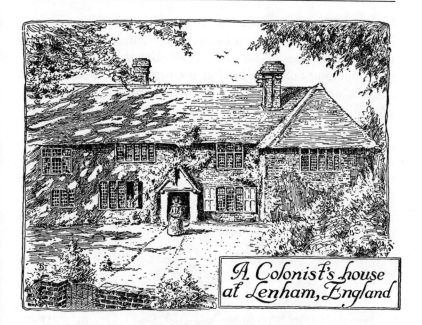

A Colonist's house at Lenham, England

same in purpose as the Cambridge agreement of Mr. Winthrop's party. Considerable obscurity surrounds this episode in the coming New Haven history. But I fancy that we may rather clearly see in it, viewing it from the advantage of later events, the informal preliminary foundation on English soil of that Separatist Church-State which eventually was to be built on the Quinnipiac.

Much more importance surrounds this new emigration than usually has been accorded it, for it was to be a unique enterprise. The original Plymouth congregation had had no intention of separating themselves politically from the old country; nor had the Massachusetts Bay settlers such a purpose. Both were English colonies of Puritan church folk in New England, remaining, in the New World, in touch with English affairs and contentedly, for a time at

least, amenable to the Court of High Commission.
Whether Theophilus Eaton at first had intended to go
further than that we do not know. But that John Davenport, thinking out the situation for himself in Holland, had
come to an extreme position in his own mind concerning the
possibilities involved in the new emigration, there can be no
doubt. We have many indications of this, in Davenport's
own thoroughgoing contemporaneous study of what such a
commonwealth should be, as well as in the original papers

The "Hector"

of the New Haven Colony itself. And we may well imagine
that the personal relations of Davenport to the English
Church, and especially to its primate Laud, had much to do
with this decision for an independent church congregation
in the New World. For such it was to be. William Laud
had had, to be sure, his share in forcing the previous Puritan
parties out of England. But, when Davenport's party was
forming, he had come into autocratic power as the head of
the Church. As such, this great tool of Charles I was now
expending all of his force and power to demand conformity
among the Puritan clergy, with the end in view of eventually
reuniting the Church of Rome with the English Church, for

his own and Charles' purposes. As a result, a new period of severe repression of nonconformity had come in. Moreover, the English Church was forcibly being swung by Laud toward Catholicism in both doctrine and ceremonies. So that John Davenport, but a few years previously one of the most promising clergymen of London, now that he had taken the irrevocable step of fleeing from Laud's domination, was his implacable enemy. "My hand will reach him there," Laud had angrily said when he heard of Davenport's escape from England. Under such circumstances, Davenport not only had every reason to attempt to find a place for his settlement in the New World where Laud could not reach him, but to find a place where he could build his own church-state, independent even of the Puritan congregations in Massachusetts that had preceded him. It was with this unique Separatist purpose in mind that the leaders of the Eaton-Davenport party landed in Boston harbor on June 26, 1637.

III

The primitive Massachusetts Bay Colony, to which John Davenport was now welcomed by his old friend John Cotton and by John Wilson, received the newcomers—including as they did so considerable a number of wealthy Puritan laymen—with every desire to have them settle there. And a number did so.

But, even if the Boston of 1637 had not been under the distant eye of Laud, other circumstances would have kept Davenport from remaining there. The famous Antinomian controversy was just then at its height, and the ravages which the valiant Mrs. Anne Hutchinson and her brother-in-law, John Wheelwright, were making in the Boston church, as well as the trouble that had just been settled by the exile of Roger Williams, showed clearly that Massachusetts was no permanent home for a new group that had its own independent religious purposes to work out. Yet we may imagine that it was not entirely easy to carry out the plan of settling elsewhere. Several towns offered free land to the Davenport settlers if they would join the Bay Colony. Theophilus Eaton was made a Massachusetts magistrate in the expectation that he would remain there. A college had just been founded by an act of the Colony legislature with a public endowment of £400, and, just after John Davenport landed, the General Court had appointed twelve of the leading men of the Colony to establish it. Davenport, as the most distinguished new addition to the university-bred leaders of the Colony, was appointed to be one of these, serving with John Cotton and John Wilson, Governor Winthrop, Stoughton, and Thomas Dudley. I imagine that that famous journey of the Bay Colony leaders across the marshes and river to Newtowne, to choose a site for the school that the next year was to be named "Harvard College" in the new "Cambridge," may well have had its important part in giving to John Davenport that idea of a similar academy in his own colony which he was later to urge throughout his life and which finally was to be instituted by his successors. Not only in these ways did the Boston folk draw the newcomers into their most important affairs, but they named Theophilus Eaton's younger and scapegrace brother, Nathaniel, to be the first superintendent of the infant Harvard College, and its first instructor, with what amusing results Harvard's early history tells.

But, in spite of these agreeable amenities, the Davenport party persisted in proceeding with that first determination to establish a new colony of their own. We do not need to do more than outline the familiar events which thereupon occurred. The redoubtable Captain Stoughton, returning in 1637 from his chase of the remaining Pequot Indians over the southern Connecticut marshes, had brought glowing tales of the excellent harbors to be found in that new country and of its climate and other possibilities. To investigate these stories, and the particularly rosy account of the harbor of the Quinnipiac Indians, Theophilus Eaton sailed in August with a few of his hardiest followers around into Long Island Sound, past Roger Williams' forest home at Providence, the newly fortified English post of the younger John Winthrop at Saybrook, and into the broad, low mouth of the Quinnipiac. Adopting the wooded and fertile plain between the two cliffs that the Dutch had called the "Red Rocks" as a most desirable location for John Davenport's enterprise, Eaton left a few men for the winter and returned to Boston to recruit his colony. On the assumption that Quinnipiac was included in the land rights of the little Puritan colony of Connecticut that Thomas Hooker had but two years previously settled at Windsor and Hartford, Eaton sent his son-in-law, Edward Hopkins, to Hooker to secure a title for the new site. So far as we know, nothing came of this except the decision of Hopkins to cast in his lot with Hooker rather than with Davenport— a decision which, as time was to show, was to prove of considerable importance in our narrative. Not hearing from Hopkins, the Eaton party, leaving behind at Boston such members as elected to stay there, and adding others who wished to leave Salem and Plymouth and Boston under the new leadership, set out for Quinnipiac in March, 1638. On April 10 they had rejoined the pioneers, whom they found living in mere earth cellars and half starved, and John Davenport preached his first sermon on his own soil, finally safe from the persecutions of a Laud, and free to build his own church-state, unattached to the English Church and Crown and unentangled with any of the Puritan congregations then on New World soil.[1]

The First Quinnipiac Winter

IV

It is a point worth noting that the Calvinistic society that John Davenport now founded on New Haven soil differed much more from the neighboring democratic commonwealth that Thomas Hooker had begun in the Connecticut Colony than it did from Massachusetts. The Massachusetts state and church were all but identical. The leaders there had clung to the old English idea of a government of a Christian church by Christians. And they had the old English social

---

[1] The traditional site of this landing of John Davenport at New Haven is the northeast corner of College and George Streets. The creek to this spot, up which the New Haven settlers sailed from the harbor, was a navigable stream far into the 18th Century. Fairly recent excavations have unearthed ancient boats and crude docks used by Davenport's successors.

feeling for an aristocracy. In that Colony the tendency was toward strong governmental centralization in the Governor and Council—the counterpart, to them, of the King and Commission at home. None but church members had the franchise, though there was taxation for everybody, whether communicant or not. As a result, there had grown up, in the brief decade since its settlement, a somewhat undemocratic condition in Massachusetts. Influential non-church members who had joined the Colony and yet retained their allegiance to the established English Church, had a social dominance and standing quite out of proportion to their legal status in the community. Out of this, much trouble was later on to come. In the original settlement of Plymouth, however, non-church members were given the franchise. This was in full sympathy with the far-sighted views of that most distinguished of New England settlers, Thomas Hooker, who, therefore, in founding his Connecticut Colony at Windsor and Hartford and Wethersfield, broke away from the Massachusetts theory and, following the Plymouth idea, made no distinction, so far as the suffrage went, between church and non-church members.

This fundamental question was not decided by the New Haven colonists for a full year. When it was determined to adhere to the Massachusetts plan, it was the decision of the entire body of colonists, and therefore of those who had separated from the Church of England and those who had not. This was decided at the famous meeting in Mr. Newman's barn[1] in June, 1639, where the whole plan for the government of New Haven was adopted in public meeting. At this meeting (a full report of which has been preserved) John Davenport spared no pains to have it known how he felt about the matter, and how he emphatically stood with

[1] This was on Grove Street, at about the foot of Hillhouse Avenue.

John Cotton and John Winthrop on it. Indeed, he had set this forth in an essay, which he had written during that first year of general discussion of the policy to be pursued, and which, as a treatise on "Civil Government in a New Plantation whose Design is Religion," he afterwards published. The opposition to his plan from among the considerable number of New Haven planters who had not yet left the English Church, was led by Theophilus Eaton's brother, the Rev. Samuel Eaton, who, while a nonconformist in England, had not left the Church and in fact was to end his life years later still a clergyman in it. There was a prolonged debate. The "rules held forth in the Scripture" being first unanimously adopted as the only laws of the new colony, the franchise problem was finally decided (Samuel Eaton alone dissenting) by agreeing "that church members only shall be free burgesses, and that they only shall choose magistrates and officers among themselves."

This was a momentous decision for the Colony of which Theophilus Eaton now became the Governor and John Davenport the pastor, and for the generations of their successors. It differentiated, at the start, the purposes of New Haven from those of the Connecticut Colony. It set John Davenport's New Haven Colony in fundamental harmony, so far as its religious framework went, with Massachusetts. It went even further than that. It produced a unique independence, religious and political, for its citizens. Creating a church-state as it did, wherein there was little or no distinction between the two, and where the Mosaic Law was the only legal court, it led, as we shall see, to a society that was under obligations to perpetuate itself and that, to meet those obligations, had to adopt methods, particularly in education, which are to be of much significance in our chronicles. It was to lead to a situation where the conservatives of another Connecticut generation were to find themselves on the side of a similar party in Massachusetts and to hark back to the fundamental principles of this religious organization of John Davenport's New Haven in their renewed efforts for orthodoxy.

CHAPTER III

THE NEW HAVEN CHURCH-STATE

I

 F the ambition of John Davenport had thus been satisfied to found a church-state of his own, the ambition of his fellow colonists to establish a New World trading metropolis was now to be met. It had been for this purpose that Eaton's London colleagues had decided with him upon Quinnipiac, with its wide harbor spreading southward into the Sound. John Brockett, a young London surveyor who had followed Eaton in the hope of making the fair daughter of one of the settlers his wife, now staked out the town with Eaton's large plan in view.

West of the modern Meadow Street and east of State, when the settlers arrived, were two broad, navigable creeks, the one running to beyond where College Street now intersects George, and the other paralleling the present State to Elm. The lovelorn Brockett based his boundaries on these creeks, laying out the town in a half-mile square subdivided into nine equal squares or "quarters," the innermost of which, now the Green, was to become the "Market-place" of the future metropolis. Cellars dug on the western creek's inner banks and covered by rough-hewn planks and leaky sod, with a few log cabins and barns, did for houses for the first few months. It was doubtless in one of these that the infant Michael Wigglesworth (that "Little Feeble Shadow of a Man," as Cotton Mather called him, and later lurid poet of "The Day of Doom") nearly caught an early death from exposure. Very likely that "easiest room in Hell," which later he was sympathetically to set aside for unbaptized infants in his verses on the Hereafter, may have had its origin in a remembrance of this early New Haven home of his father. But this was in 1638. Within a few years the settlement had come to be a village of perhaps a hundred comfortable houses, sprinkled over the eight outside squares, about which were the burned and cleared meadows or uplands, protection alike against prowling Indian or Dutch and the packs of wolves that infested the neighborhood. The central square, or "Market-place," a sloping tract of woodland at first, was early cleared of most of its wood for the Meeting-house, the schoolhouse, and the public fences, and remained a sandy waste, dotted with stumps and a few remaining ancient trees, except at what is now the Church Street side, where there was a swamp out of which trickled a brook to the State Street creek. Across this bog, at the present corner of Chapel and Church Streets,—then "Mr. Thomas Gregson's corner,"—was built a footbridge, and two log causeways led over it to the Meeting-house and schoolhouse from the "Mill Highway," now Church Street. This Meeting-house, a rude, square structure, with a hipped roof on the apex of which was a square watchman's turret, stood in probably the precise center of the Market-place. On this turret the broad-brimmed town drummer lustily beat the community to church on Sabbath days, and on occasions of Dutch or Indian alarms sentries stood there all day and all night, ready to fire the signal for the town watch. North of the Meeting-house was the schoolhouse. On the modern College Street side, about opposite the present Phelps Gateway to the University, were the town stocks and pillory. Here also were the town gaol and the watch-house, the latter a great-chimnied, one-story building, wherein the watch not infrequently fell asleep and were haled ingloriously before the Colony Governor and magistrates therefor. About the primitive Meeting-house, by 1650, a few graves had been dug for the early victims of the rigorous change from the mild English winters.

Little as we perhaps are apt to realize it, this ancient New Haven was a fortified town, as well protected against its enemies as was John Davenport's Coventry from Charles I's tyrannical soldiery. About the entire plantation was probably a stockade[1] of sharpened palings, or "palisadoes," set close together and perhaps seven feet high, through

---

[1] I am adopting Levermore's statement on this open question. It is not precisely known whether New Haven had such a stockade or not. Branford had a five-mile outer fence, and Milford was stockaded. As to New Haven, the Colony Records of 1639 have a vote: "Ordered that gates shalbe made att the end of every streete att the outside of the Towne, wth all ye outside fences." This outer fence, or "Town pale," appears to have been kept up at public or common expense, whereas the "Quarters'" fences were privately maintained. Barber, in his "Antiquities of New Haven," recalls an ancient gate across West Chapel Street six rods west of York, which may have been a last survivor of this pioneer palisade. The question is an open one, but the small evidence available points perhaps to the fact of such a stockade. A second stockade was erected in 1676, when the Indian wars became serious.

which great chained gates led into the open farmlands and woods without. Each of the eight "quarters" was fenced off from the streets by a paling, doubtless of rough-split logs five or so feet high, while, in a year or two, the house-lots themselves were separated by high "rail" fences, built of three or five broad planks laid against heavy posts. The passer-by on the cleared sandy lanes of this primitive New Haven may well have thought himself in a fortified maze, able, as he must have been, hardly to look over the house-lot stockades into the gardens, within which, among their fruit trees and under their virgin-forest oaks and button-woods and elms, nestled the weather-beaten clapboarded houses of the planters.

William Hubbard, New England's quaint contemporary chronicler, was a youth when Davenport's Puritan Separatists settled New Haven. Passing through the village a little later, he was astonished at the size and architectural excellence of some of the houses. "Fair and stately," he reported these to be, "wherein they at first outdid the rest of the country." Hubbard thought that the London immigrants at Quinnipiac had spent too much on these houses. But the New Haven settlers had been London tradesmen or farmers in comfortable English villages,—some of them well-to-do men,—and they built their new homes as closely as possible after the English town and village style to which they had been accustomed. Among these were a few log cabins, no doubt, and numerous small, one-room houses, steep-roofed for sleeping lofts above. But there were a number of larger houses, two stories high, with second floors projecting a little over the first as was the fashion in English towns. And, as in the old country, so in Davenport's New Haven, the windows of these houses were generally diamond-paned, while the doors were in two parts, opening outward from the narrow front stair entry. Huge

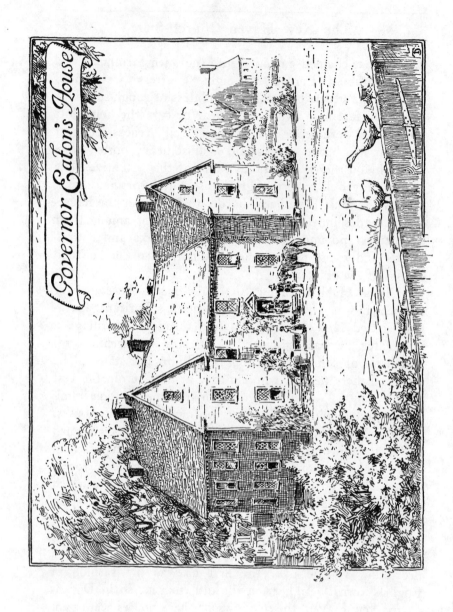

Governor Eaton's House

stone chimneys stood in the middle of these larger houses, on either side of which were the "hall" and kitchen, and the "parlor." In all of the gardens were well sweeps, and nearly every householder had his small thatched barn.

There were, however, several very large houses in this early New Haven. Four of these,—Governor Eaton's, Mr. Davenport's, Thomas Gregson's, and Isaac Allerton's,—were probably unequaled in any of the other three New England Colonies. Mr. Davenport's, which faced north on the present Elm Street, below Orange, was built in the form of a cross, and had, so tradition later said, thirteen fireplaces. Mr. Allerton's, which was built later and just below State Street, was similar in shape, with "four porches" or doorways in the four ells.[1] Governor Eaton's, which faced Mr. Davenport's nearly across Elm Street, had at least ten fireplaces, not counting more in the attic rooms. This was a famous house for those days. It was in the not uncommon English country style of a capital E, its two ells forming a small court facing the street. The front door opened directly into a great "hall," furnished with an immense "drawing" table and forms, at which the family probably met for meals, and about which the Colony General Court no doubt sat, in front of a yawning stone fireplace, for its frequent sessions. In the west ell was a "parlor" or state guest-chamber for distinguished travelers, and, in the rear, a library or "office." Here the Governor of the little republic held his daily prayers with his numerous family and relations (Elihu Yale's father, David Yale, lived with Eaton until he removed to Boston in 1649), and here

[1] There is a good account of these early New Haven houses in Lambert's history of the Colony, and an exhaustive study of the Eaton house in the "Early Connecticut Houses" by Isham and Brown. The drawings in this book of Davenport's period have been modeled on Isham's studies of contemporary Connecticut Colony houses, which were not essentially different, he thinks, from New Haven's.

he received his callers on public business and for the numerous demands that were made on him to settle private quarrels and correct the wayward of the village. In the east ell were the kitchen and buttery or milkroom, back of which were his gardens and fruit orchards and hedged flower beds.

The inventories of this early day show that many of the people lived in a very fair degree of comfort. Probably few were as impoverished as one planter who, in selling his house, could trump up only a bedstead and trundlebed, "a pair of vallance, a piece of blue charnix, a malt-mill, a well bucket and chayne, two loads of clay," and his fences to sell with it. Governor Eaton's belongings were of a high order. He had "round" and "short" tables, "green cushions," "sideboards," a "great chair with needlework," low and "high wyne" stools, books, a globe and map, tapestries on his walls, and "Turkey carpets," which had just come into fashion in England, and which were used either for floor coverings or on the tables. His "great hall" was filled with heavy pieces of old English-made furniture, and was ornamented with much silver plate, a wall-clock, and with the silver basin and ewer which Mrs. Eaton had years before been given by her husband's colleagues in his Baltic Sea adventures. In this great house, in which, it was said, there were thirty people altogether, Governor Theophilus Eaton was accustomed to spend most of his day, reading and at his private devotions, or receiving the people of his Colony and dealing out, as English squires did in their own halls, the magisterial justice that devolved upon him, which in his case meant settling matters by the Mosaic law.

II

We may get a very good notion of how John Davenport's colonists lived, by poring over the wills and inventories of the time, and the musty pages of the Colony Court records, open to us in the cramped but still legible handwriting of Secretary Thomas Fugill. The life within the town stockade was a drowsy one, enlivened only by the military training-days and elections, visits of trading vessels or travelers from the Bay, frequent searches for lost cattle, Sabbath-day meetings, and the numerous public punishments of malefactors at the town pillory and stocks. Inside the great paling the village was compact and fortified; outside, there were the commons and allotted farms and fenced-in pasture lands for oxen and cows, the town pound (which was at State and Chapel Streets), the fenced-in lot for "straingers' horses" (which was about where Hillhouse Avenue joins Grove Street), and the distant wigwams of the Indians in East Haven. The streets were not named, except that north Church Street was known as the "Mill Highway," leading as it did to the flour mill near East Rock, and north State Street the "Clay Pitts Way," leading to the Quinnipiac meadows where the settlers very early had discovered clay deposits for their brick. The block on Elm from Church to State was known as "Mr. Eaton's Street"; that on Chapel opposite the Market-place as "Mr. Goodyear's"; the modern prosperous Chapel Street, near State, began as a neglected ditch road, known merely as "the lane that leadeth to Zuriel Kimberley's house"; the street intersections were known as "Mr. Perry's corner," or "Mr. Evance's," or "Mr. Tench's." There was a landing place far up George Street near High,—just a step beyond where the settlers had first set foot on Quinnipiac soil,—and another on State at the foot of Chapel, opposite the pound. The main landing for larger vessels, however, was outside of the village itself, on the present Water Street bank of the harbor, and at the old Indian "Oyster-shell Fields," where the water was rather higher than it is today. Here the

Bay ships unloaded their supplies of cattle and meat and the latest English fashions, and here the great people of the Colonies stepped upon John Davenport's New Haven soil from the shallops or lighters that at long intervals carried passengers back and forth from Hartford and Saybrook, Milford and Stamford, and across the Sound to Southold. Visitors on horseback came into the town from the east over the "Neck" bridge at State Street, and from Milford way over the West River bridge. There appear to have been few horses in the early days, but later these were numerous and occasioned many squabbles between rival claimants. The Colony eventually ordered each town to maintain two or more horses, with saddles and pistols, for travelers on public business.

The New Haven people of these early times were not so solemn a folk in their everyday life as we sometimes imagine them, or as the renegade Peters described them to ready-eared English readers after the Revolutionary War. Despite the rigid laws and religious regulations and beliefs under which they lived, the citizens of Davenport's small republic were not entirely depressed by them. Now and then there were gay times after the good-night drum, and late tipplers would feel their way home in the dense blackness by the "quarters' palings" to escape the watch; there were "watermillion" moonlight escapades by the young people in this or that Goodman's garden, and youthful "dalliances" and what not. But the routine life of the plantation was not very exciting. Out from the ancient records step the vigorous-bodied and dignified planters in their square-cut doublets and "mandillions" and their broad-brimmed sugar-loaf Puritan hats, in their shapely half-hose and laced shoes, their waist girdles, and their cloaks of white, red, or black stuffs. Quaint replicas of their fathers are the youngsters of the village, in their stiff little knee-

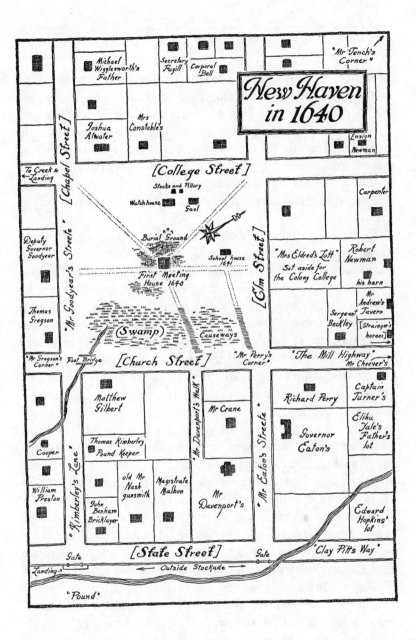

breeches, double jackets, broad hats and laced shoes. Not too garish in dress were the matrons and maids of Davenport's colony, in their high hats and broad white collars and quiet-colored gowns, over which they wore their many-pocketed aprons, though now and then one of these good wives would wear green stockings or a scarlet cloak, or would trade her beeswax or "pease" for the latest fashions in embroidered colored petticoats that the traders brought from the Bay.

But it is at their work and public duties that we may best recall these sturdy pioneers. Houses and fences were to be built, and so there was at first great felling of trees on the Market-place and streets and in the house-lots, and then in the forests outside the town, where farmlands had to be cleared for corn plantations and for cattle pastures. Boats and canoes were needed, and small sailing vessels; chimneys of stone, now and then brick-topped as the workmen began to use the Quinnipiac clay pits, were necessary; hay and straw, grain, pork and beef had to be stored against the long and famined winters. And so, as the years slip by, we see the men and grown boys in Thomas Fugill's ancient pages at work building and repairing the bridges and palings and houses, planting that corn which Winthrop wrote to his wife made a Paradise of New England, working in their fruit tree orchards (the New Haveners were great fruit growers) or gardens or in the fields outside, harvesting, tending the cattle and "haunting" the hogs, and cutting wood in the surrounding forests where today a broad, modern city crowds the whole plain between the two great Rocks. Planters, joiners, plasterers, bricklayers, ships-carpenters, tanners, coopers, mowers, cattle-herds, thatchers,—were these first settlers. Twelve hours was a man's day's work in summer and eight in winter, while the women and girls managed the households, taught the little chaps their letters, spun wool and flax in the special rooms set apart for these gossipy occasions, tended the geese and chickens and bees, and made the woolen and leathern clothes for themselves and husbands.

And now comes the watch, that had to keep a martial eye open for invaders of the calm of the little stockaded republic, to look out for chimney fires at night, to see that each householder kept his ladder against his thatched or shingled roof day and night and a "fire hook" handy, to corral late wayfarers along the high-walled lanes, and to apprehend cheerful sailors or servants who might have had too many "strong watters" at Mr. Andrews' or Mr. Harriman's ordinary. The drummer beats at sundown for the watch to prepare; the master of the watch goes to the watch-house, and an hour after sundown the six watchmen have to follow, arms complete with pike and sword and musket. In pairs these watchmen then patrol the village all night, up and down the lanes and inside and outside of the town paling, so go the orders. They are to shout "Fire!" or "Arms, Arms, all the Town out!" as necessity dictates, and lug to the watch-house any suspicious persons for appearance before Governor Eaton the next Colony Court day. The great public business of the colonists, however, is the training-day on the Market-place. This comes on "Quarter-days." Two hundred men formed this military company, each settler over sixteen years of age having his obligatory share in the maneuvers. A martial sight it is, no doubt, as we visualize it from the old Court Records. First come the town drummers and the company secretary, to take their places near the Meeting-house, where the roll of the assembly drum brings the soldiers from all quarters. And now out troop the companies,—"squadrons," as they are called,—headed by the sturdy Captain Turner, veteran of the Pequot wars, sword in hand, his cloak, lined with scarlet,

Training-Day on the Market-Place, New Haven

thrown martially over one shoulder, his eye fired perhaps by remembrances of the recent Indian battles over Pequot way. Then comes Lieutenant Seely with his "partison," and the Ensign with the Colony colors. The "squadrons," with their sergeants and corporals, round the sandy public square to the beat of the two company drummers. Terrifying they may look to the wide-eyed Quinnipiac Indians who have slipped quietly through the great clanking gates of the stockade to witness these astonishing maneuvers of their white-faced invaders. Boldly the "squadrons" troop about the square, each private in his best yellow buckskin breeches, high hat, iron breastplate and flowing cloak, armed with musket or pike, with dangling sword, his "bandaleer" carrying his powder and bullets and round of "swan-shot," and on special occasions wearing the thick "cotton-wool" coats that the town has ordered the women to quilt for their husbands' and sons' protection against Indian arrows. Grouped about the open Market-place, under the few old trees that have been left standing, these proud dames and damsels are no doubt as frightened as are the scampering Indians when the "Quarter-day" parade ends with the explosive firing of the three "great guns," the volleys from which shake the wooden houses and echo over the surrounding woods to the distant hills. Then come feats of agility and strength among the younger soldiers (for the village bucks were mighty proud of their muscles and the turn of their calves),—when they play at cudgels or "back-sword," and leap and "wrastle" as the Colony orders have it, and the great day ends. A few years later a horse troop (when the Dutch became bothersome) was formed, there was an artillery company, and, still later, a Colony dog pack to hunt wolves and track Indians.

But it is in the Sabbath-day ceremonies at the Meeting-house that we seem best to visualize the people of these early Puritan times, long sleeping under the modern Green or in the Grove Street burying ground, in devout belief of their rise to join Christ's second coming. The roll of the second drum is reverberating through the quiet gardens and up and down the sandy lanes, vigorously pounded in the Meeting-house turret by that jovial Robert Bassett who later was to entertain some itinerant sailors at his home with so hospitable a decanter that he was fined five pounds and later left for Stamford, there to lead in mutinous outbreaks against the Jurisdiction. Walking sedately across the Market-place from their homes and those "Sabbath-day houses" that the country people built for their Sabbath noons in New Haven, come these pioneer Puritans of New Haven. Captain Turner, sword in hand, waits at one of the low, square doors of the first Meeting-house, to place the guard for the day within and the sentry without. And now come the shadowy forms of the planters. Ezekiel Cheever, in broad flowing cloak and high hat and starched neckband, comes up Church Street with his wife and boy from his cabin at Church and Grove Streets. Governor Eaton, supporting his now aged mother, moves majestically, as becomes the first magistrate of this New World republic, up Elm Street and over the made causeway from "Mr. Perry's corner," his numerous family and servants, and the future father of Elihu Yale behind him. Then come the other settlers: from the Clay Pitts Way Magistrate Malbon, once a prosperous London merchant and now expecting great things from New Haven trading enterprises he is financing, from his large house on State Street fronting the not far-distant harbor; old Thomas Nash, once a Puritan refugee in Leyden, and now the official Colony gunsmith; Anthony Thompson, Lenham village merchant; John Benham, brickmaker and town-crier; Goodman Kimberley, poundkeeper; Deacon Gilbert, from his spacious house at Church and Chapel Streets; Nicholas Augur, the town dispenser of physic; the impecunious William Preston, whose large family of children are mostly kept alive by his wife's earnings in "dressing" the Meeting-house. Then come Deputy Governor Goodyear, former London trader, and Thomas Gregson, now one of the Colony's most energetic business men, from their adjoining houses on Chapel Street opposite the Market-place; young Joshua Atwater, late of Kent, and now treasurer of the Colony, from his great mansion where Osborn Hall now stands; tottering old Edward Wigglesworth, with his small son Michael the coming poet, from Chapel Street near the present High; Thomas Fugill and Corporal Bell, Ensign Newman and William Andrews the tavern keeper, and Goodman this and Goodwife that, until all of the small community are

grouped about the Meeting-house door, on the broad nailed
panels of which the latest bans of marriage and notices of
estates that are before the Colony Court have been put up
by the Secretary. And now the Rev. William Hooke, the
Teacher of the church, in his flowing ministerial gown,
comes alone down through the footpath under the trees from
the College and Chapel Streets corner of the Market-place,
his thoughts, perhaps, as much on his great cousin Cromwell's possible patronage if he should return to England,
as on the two-hour prayer he is to make that morning. And
then the people turn their faces across the open square to
"Mr. Davenport's Walk," that has been fenced off for his
use between two Church Street open lots where the present
City Hall stands. The once famous preacher of the London
church in Coleman Street comes slowly out from his
"Walk," across the log causeway that has been laid over the
bog for his comfort, and to his waiting flock, unspoken to by
anyone on this great day of the Colony week. Slowly he
walks, in gown and small black skullcap, Bible in hand.
Through the silent ranks of his congregation he passes in
through the rough-hewn door and up the broad center aisle
of his crude new church, to the raised pulpit under the
sounding-board of the day. Mrs. Eaton and the Governor
follow, the congregation troops in, each man wearing his
hat except when the opening prayer is pronounced, the important families take their benches in order of Colony rank,
men on one side and women on the other, and the children
scatter to the pulpit stairs or sides of the bare room (where
they make so much trouble that officers have to be appointed
to keep them in order) and the Sabbath-day services begin.
Mr. Hooke expounds a chapter from the Scriptures. The
hourglass on the high pulpit may be turned once or even
twice before the central event of the Colonists' week, the
sermon by John Davenport, is over. Mr. Hooke then

The First New Haven Meeting-House

prays (and the prayers of those days were nearly as long as the sermons), "bills" are put up for the sick and the absent, and a long psalm follows, the pastor reading each line before it is droned out by the congregation. The short noon hour over, the Meeting-house is filled again for the afternoon service. Mr. Hooke now preaches, and Mr. Davenport prays, there is one more long psalm, and the wearied and not infrequently half-frozen people return to their candle-lit homes and firesides to meditate on the great words they have heard during the day, and the children to repeat the heads of the preacher's discourse from memory.

III

An earnestly pious people were these New Haven settlers, believers in the all-sufficiency of the Scriptures for human needs, individual and political, building their church-state on the Mosaic law as it was interpreted by the Colony magistrates and deputies. The "Moses" of New Haven, Cotton Mather called Governor Eaton. But it needed another Solomon to manage the affairs of this new republic, and Theophilus Eaton was one. Before his Colony court came an extraordinary number of matters to settle, for the Colony officers did not hesitate to manage even the smallest details of the planters' lives. A settler could not leave the Jurisdiction without written permission; if a shoemaker was not giving good leather he was haled before the court to answer for it; if the town storekeeper (a Mrs. Stolions) overcharged, she had to explain and cut her prices; if a man's fence was down, he had to stand trial for damages his cattle and hogs did to his neighbors' gardens in consequence; if a settler "took tobacco" in the streets or outside of his house, he was brought before the court to pay a fine; if a soldier came to training without his full equipment, if a watchman slept on his rounds, if a laborer broke the Sabbath, if a good wife slandered another woman, if a ladder was not in its place against a house,—Governor Eaton's court decided the penalty. And these penalties were severe ones. Hubbard wrote that the New Haveners were very "vigorous in the execution of justice, and especially in the punishment of offenders." The town stocks and pillory were a busy place for a few days after each court meeting, and many a careless planter and servant and visiting sailor cooled his legs and neck on the board platform next to the watch-house on College Street to the gaping entertainment of the villagers. For more serious offenses there were public whippings of both men and women, and these were so severe that one unlucky malefactor vowed he would rather "fall into the hands of the Turks" than be whipped again. And they had other agreeable little methods of making an incorrigible reform. Halters were hung about these fellows' necks, and locks put on their legs; the tongues of slanderers or profane persons were bored with hot irons or put into cloven sticks; not a few offenders against the comparatively few capital laws of the Colony were publicly hung. The laws were the laws of the Hebrew God, and alack for him who transgressed them. Even the Deputy Governor was fined on one occasion for having permitted the sale of liquors by an elected tavern keeper who had not yet taken office.

To us of today, the church discipline of these pioneer times undoubtedly seems the most exacting. Yet there was good reason for this, considering the peculiar religious republic that John Davenport had founded. The New Haven Jurisdiction churches, separate as they were from all other New England churches, were the New Haven state. The towns and Colony political organizations were but the machine by which this church-state was supported. None

The Town Watch

but the regenerate could vote in town meetings, or for the
Governor and magistrates and deputies to the Colony Court.
Church members ruled the New Haven state, and noncon-
formity to the churches was treason to the state itself.

And so we find John Davenport extremely alert for any
infringements of his religious authority and for any backsliding from the obligations of church membership. He
and his New Haven flock were believers in witchcraft, and
in the second coming of Christ. It is said that they expected
Christ to make New Haven the seat of his second em-
pire,—so the Colony's theological lamp must be kept
trimmed. So serious was this motive in the New Haven life
that as important a member of the community as Governor
Eaton's good lady fell into difficulties with Davenport and
was publicly punished therefor. So earnest was John Dav-

enport in this conception of his duty toward a pure church membership that he became, in time, renowned through New England for his severity in church discipline, and was said by Cotton Mather to "use the golden snuffers of the sanctuary overmuch." The more lively of his parishioners in this orthodox New Haven, thus ecclesiastically snuffed out as occasions arose, doubtless endorsed this sentence. For they were brought up sharply for very small misdoings. The Colony Court would settle a case of profanity with dispatch and unction. Some unlucky visiting sailor, for instance, had admitted saying a round "by God." The New Haven church and state were shocked. Governor Eaton, facing the astonished culprit across his great table, vowed that it was a manifest "piercing of the name of God in passion," whereas the rule of God was "let your words be yea yea and nay nay." The unlucky sailor's tongue was bored for his crime, and he was sent out of the Colony to warn others not to be profane in it.

From time to time, in the old Colony papers, we find the citizens of this too ideal republic breaking forth into exasperate opposition to this kind of discipline. It is an enlightening scene that the old Court Records describe, when a Mrs. Moore is apprehended for a theological eccentricity. She had, it appears, "pished" at the statement that there were "2 sorts of angells, some sperits, some in flesh." Mrs. Moore thought "angells" were the only "sperits" and had privately given it forth as her opinion that the officers of the New Haven church were going beyond their rights in claiming to be "angells" of God "in the flesh." Governor Eaton rebuked her severely. "Christ," he said, "was indeed with his apostles in their worke through all their travells, & they travelled farr, yet could not goe into every part or country of the world. Probably [he said] they were never in this lardge tract & part of the World, called America."

Therefore Christ had to be represented in New Haven by "angells in the flesh," which office Mr. Davenport and the church elders had humbly succeeded to. Mrs. Moore was not, however, satisfied, and went out of the Governor's house "in a great rage," announcing, with a fling of her independent head, as she passed through his great gate to the street, that "she would goe to none of the church officers for any truth of *her* salvation." The case made a mighty noise in the Colony. Others had from time to time burst their church bonds, and some had "pished" at Mr. Cheever's teaching, and even at Mr. Davenport's business ability, and not a few had been "sermon sick." But no one until Mrs. Moore had openly flaunted the right of the church elders to call themselves "angells." A growing number came to do so as time passed, however, and that final day was to come when the whole question of the divine authority of the inner church membership in the Colony was to become a serious one, and with it the question of the fundamental soundness of John Davenport's great church-state scheme itself.

A Guilford House in 1660

Early New Haven Wharves

CHAPTER IV

THE DAVENPORT EDUCATION

I

ON leaving Boston for the Quinnipiac in 1638, John Davenport had brought with him a young professional schoolmaster in the quaint and energetic person of that Ezekiel Cheever whom we have mentioned, and who, in later years, was to become one of the most famous of colonial pedagogues.

This able gentleman was at this time twenty-three years of age. He was a Londoner by birth, and for several years had been a private tutor among the Rev. John Wilson's flock in Boston. Tradition pictures him vividly as a tall, thin young fellow, whose pointed beard became a sort of animated barometer to his wary scholars; when he stroked this beard to its point, the story goes, his pupils cocked an eye for trouble. And this frequently came (as Cheever was of an irascible temperament) from unexpected causes; for not only did the first New Haven schoolmaster use the alder and birch rods that he ominously cut as he crossed the swamp to the schoolhouse of mornings, but he also had the salutary habit of licking the good boys for not exerting their influence over the obstreperous ones. Cheever was an excellent Latin scholar,—a bit of a pedant, perhaps, if the truth were known,—and during his eleven years in the rude New Haven settlement wrote his famous "Short Introduction to the Latin Tongue." This, as the famous Cheever "Accidence," ran through twenty editions before 1785 and emerged, for the last time, to the astonished chagrin of still another generation of American youngsters, as late as 1838, when it was succeeded by others,—Bullions, etc.,—no less formidable. Through this Latin grammar ploughed very nearly all of the college-bound youths of Massachusetts and Connecticut during the first century of Harvard and the first half-century of Yale.

Ezekiel Cheever had arrived in Quinnipiac with £20 and two dependents, and one of the earliest businesses of his fellow townsmen, after the raising of the square Meeting-house on the Market-place and of the great mansions of Davenport and Eaton, appears to have been to build a small cabin for him. This was set up at what is now the south-east corner of Grove and Church Streets, and here Cheever seems to have begun to teach New Haven's first school. In that quaint account of his own life that Michael Wigglesworth left to a laxer and more critical posterity, he says that, having escaped death in his father's dug-out cellar on the banks of the creek in New Haven, he was sent to school in 1639 to Ezekiel Cheever, "and under him," says he, "profited so much through the blessing of God, that I began to make Latin & to get forward apace." This was probably in Cheever's own cabin on Grove Street.

It was on Christmas Day, 1641, that John Davenport secured a town vote to establish the Colony's first public school.

I fancy that we may set this date among the large events in New Haven history. Such a public school had been set up in Boston, hardly had the Winthrop party arrived there. The year following, 1636, one had been established in the primitive settlement at Charlestown. The Rev. John Fiske had become the first teacher of a similar Salem school in 1637, and in 1639, when Cheever had begun to teach in his own house in New Haven, a public school had been begun at Dorchester. The Cambridge public school was to be established a year later. In several of these cases, the school had even preceded the church organization itself, so anxious were the Puritan colonists that there should be no interruption in the upbringing of the next generation in their church.

And we may now see the necessity for this immediate beginning of youthful education in the colonies. The public school and the grammar school were no novelty to the New England settlers. The Londoners in the New Haven Colony had long been accustomed to it; their forefathers had known it ever since Dean Colet had opened his grammar school beneath St. Paul's in 1510. Even the immigrants from such English rural villages as Ashford or Lenham, a number of whom, as we have seen, were in the New Haven party, had had their free schools at home. Among the settlers of Massachusetts were some sixty Cambridge University graduates and about a third as many Oxford men, and these men,—now the leaders in their new communities,—naturally looked upon the immediate beginnings of a New England school system as an imperative matter, nearly if not as important as the institution of the churches themselves.

But the movement in this direction had an even deeper significance. The great guide to conduct of the Puritan element in the English Church for a hundred years had been the Bible; and, as the Puritan interpretation of religion was individualistic, so the reading of the Bible was a matter of individual duty. It was to bring about this general ability to read the Bible that those numerous Puritan foundations had been established throughout old England from which the public-school system, leading in many cases to the advanced grammar school with its study of the Latin commentaries and of the Greek originals of the New Testament, had grown. Yet the English school system was sporadic and privately endowed, as in the famous Hales Free School of Coventry, which we have seen John Davenport attending when a boy.

The Dutch church-school system, on the other hand, which the Plymouth colonists and John Davenport had become acquainted with when in exile in Holland, was of a different nature. There a state educational system had for some time been established. This was a compulsory public-school system, supported by municipal or parish taxes instead of by private donations as in England. This novel and democratic notion of public education could not but have made a strong impression upon John Davenport when he was in Rotterdam. And, during his short stay in Boston, he had seen the new plan being attempted, though perhaps in no very definite way at that time, in the first of the Massachusetts public schools. The general principles of the Dutch idea were now incorporated in Davenport's scheme for his New Haven commonwealth, superimposed upon which was his own notion of a graded system from the common school up through the grammar or Latin school to a sort of Puritan "college" similar to the Harvard which he had had a hand in planting.

II

Fully to realize the departure which John Davenport thus made in beginning, in 1641, the New Haven Colony public school, and agitating almost as immediately his plan for a "college," we may recall what had been done in schooling matters in this country before his arrival. The Virginia Cavaliers, for example, living a patriarchal existence on their great tobacco plantations, had no such community life as had the New England townsfolk. They had brought over with them the customary English idea of secondary and higher learning for the youth of the upper classes only. They had founded no common schools, as, indeed, their manner of life called for none. They had contented themselves with importing private tutors from Cambridge or Oxford for the favored sons of the ruling classes; for the poorer children they had begun industrial schooling on the plantations. The Virginia public sentiment, in fact, was against a free public education. The colonists there were good Church of England communicants, and, even at the comparatively late date of 1692, when William and Mary College was chartered, their purpose in it was to afford a colony higher education for the sons of the upper classes alone. In Dutch New Amsterdam, on the contrary, the parochial school system of the old country had early been established, though probably of the elementary type in Holland. In Puritan New England, both the stern necessity of the churches for raising the new generation strictly after the religious principles of the settlers, and the community life which was at once begun, centering about the church, led to a third type of school, the purpose of which was, at least at some public expense, to bring the Bible into the lives of the second generation and thus to continue the Puritan commonwealth in all of its original purity of character.

The First Schoolhouse

It was with one of the earliest examples of this last type of colonial schools that John Davenport now began that New Haven educational history, which, for generations to come, was to be built up about a central religious interest and in support of the orthodoxy of Calvinistic church and state.

It was in accordance with this fundamental purpose of the New Haven education that, in 1641, there was now laid down, in John Davenport's language, that phrase which did duty for the New Haven Colony schools for the next half-century and which, in its statement of the intention of the school "for the better trayning upp of youth in this towne, that, through God's blessing they may be fitted for publique service hereafter, either in church or commonweale," was to find its refrain in the intentions of Yale's founders some six decades afterwards.

By 1644 the schoolhouse itself had been erected, and Ezekiel Cheever moved his Latin books and his birch rods into it. It was a one-story slab cabin, this first New Haven school, with a rough stone chimney, and was likely enough furnished (as were others of its day) with the same kind of backless plank seats that helped to rivet the older generation's attention on the weekly worship at the Meeting-house, a few rods further south on the Market-place. This schoolhouse probably stood just northeast of the present United Church. A rough cart road, which has since become Temple Street, traversed the public square from schoolhouse to Meeting-house, but on the north side, where now is Elm Street, there was a better road, flanked by the high palings of the first Elm Street gardens. Here, until 1649, Ezekiel Cheever propelled the first New Haven Colony youngsters through his Latin grammar, and, in good old English schoolmaster style (which held that every cerebral impression had to be pounded in through the epidermis), held the noses of unwilling smaller chaps to their elementary English composition and Catechism by rod and cuffings.

III

As events were to show, this was the single prosperous period in John Davenport's large plans for his New Haven school. Cheever prepared at least a half dozen New Haven youths for Harvard during these years, giving them a fitting that was unexcelled throughout the colonies. The oldest son of Governor Eaton was one of them; the son of Isaac Allerton, that wealthy Mayflower Pilgrim who had difficulties at Plymouth and who had settled in New Haven and was later to lose his whole estate there, was another; Michael Wigglesworth received his first lessons under Cheever, as we have seen, and went up to Harvard, there to go through a fervid religious awakening and, dropping his "selfish" desire (as he writes) "for honor & Prefermt & such Poor Beggarly ends, learnt to study with God & for God," and change his ambition to become a chirurgeon to study for the ministry. Nathaniel Brewster, the son of the Francis Brewster who was to be lost on the famous Lamberton ship from New Haven, prepared for Harvard at this little log-cabin school of Ezekiel Cheever's, and grew up to take a degree at the University of Dublin and to accompany Oliver Cromwell's son to Ireland in 1655 as a Puritan minister in the fateful colonization of Ulster. A John Davis also went up, whose Harvard College accounts in 1650 show that he paid for his board and tuition in wheat, and once with "3 pecks of pease," no doubt shipped by sailing vessel from his father's farm lot in New Haven.

Sadly enough, however, Ezekiel Cheever was scholar first and theologian afterwards. The flowing-robed Aristides and his Athenian democracy may very likely have seemed to him a better human society than that of the black-gowned John Davenport and his New Haven theocracy. The details of the trouble are ʾlost to us, but by 1647 Cheever had come into open and violent collision with the New Haven church (having apparently criticised some instances of public church discipline) and was called before it for "his contradictory, stiff and proud frame of spirit,"—an eccentricity that John Davenport vigorously chastised in everyone who showed it. As a result, the ecclesiastical head

of Ezekiel Cheever was unceremoniously snipped off by the
golden snuffers of the sanctuary, as that of Governor
Eaton's good wife had been three years before. Two years
later Cheever departed in high dudgeon for Massachusetts,
to become the schoolmaster at Ipswich, and then at Cambridge and Boston,—there to train probably the largest number of boys for Harvard of any pedagogue in that colony.
He died at an advanced age, the scourge and yet the single
largest factor, perhaps, in the lives of many of Massachusetts' earliest church and state leaders. Though the records
are scant as to his work in New Haven, we know what
results he got elsewhere with such precocious students as
John Leverett, the later president of Harvard, and with
Cotton Mather. Cheever had brought Cotton Mather, by
twelve years of age,
to excellent work in
Latin composition,
and to the point
where he "conversed with Tully, Terence, Ovid, and Vergil,
and had gone through his Greek Testament, and entered
upon Isocrates, Homer, and his Hebrew Grammar." If
he did not do as much for any of John Davenport's New
Haven youths, it was doubtless their fault and not his.

It was a serious blow to Davenport's educational plan for
New Haven, that so remarkable a man as Ezekiel Cheever
was forced to leave the infant Colony. A very different
story might have been told, I imagine, of the after developments of the New Haven school had Cheever remained at
its desk. Higher education in New Haven now had a long
hiatus; it was thirteen years before another New Haven
youth was prepared for Harvard. Founded as an ideal
human society in 1639, and to be conducted as such by the
combined theological and worldly wisdom of Davenport and
Eaton, the rift in the lute that the coming New Haven

metropolis was to play among God's orchestra on earth, was shown thus early in Ezekiel Cheever's case, as it had been, a few years previously, in Edward Hopkins'. However much we may see in this Puritan leader that is remarkable, the fact remains that, in leading his flock out of England, Davenport, as others of his generation in New England, set up quite as intolerant a persecution in the New World of those who would not agree to his religious despotism as he had himself escaped from at home. I imagine that John Davenport's plans to control and develop his peculiar church-state permitted no further usefulness, as a factor in it, to anyone, regardless of position, who differed from him.

But if Ezekiel Cheever's withdrawal interfered with the school, other and still larger matters had an even more lasting effect. Circumstances, both within and without the Colony, were by 1649 rather suddenly to precipitate a situation out of which the Colony itself was barely to escape with its life.

IV

We have seen how a portion of the London group in the Eaton party had joined it for business reasons quite apart from the religious purposes of the others. To the soaring plans for a pure and undefiled Puritan Utopia which John Davenport had in mind for New Haven (and good old Thomas More's book came over with him, properly enough) these Roundhead London tradesmen had added the supposedly very practical scheme of a New World commercial center. Built up about the religious-political structure of Davenport, there was thus to be founded a Puritan trading metropolis, protecting the former from financial disaster and incidentally bringing in quite an earthly revenue of its own to the elect.

The New Haveners, hardly had they arrived at Quinnipiac, and hardly had either church or school been established, made their first efforts in this alluring scheme. The historian Hutchinson says that vessels were early built here for foreign voyages, and the town records show the crazy commercial schemes which were now to be attempted. The end of the Puritan immigration to New England, with the New Haven parties, had resulted in few, if any, large ships sailing into Quinnipiac harbor from London. What indirect trade Eaton's mariners therefore had with England was through the port at Boston, whither the small home-built New Haven shallops, pinnaces, and ketches now began a precarious trade, carrying to Boston the beaver skins and other furs of the Quinnipiac woods, and bringing back Massachusetts cattle and merchandise and English stuffs landed at Boston. Some small business was also begun with the Virginia farmers, and, for a while at least, the New Haven traders seem to have stopped at New Amsterdam on their way home, and sold Virginia tobacco to the Dutchmen there. A few even more adventurous voyages are recorded in the early colonial papers. Several New Haven ships went to the Bermudas and the Barbados in these first few years, and even to the Azores. Captain Lamberton had a trim little vessel called the "Cock," the first seagoing vessel owned, if not built, in New Haven; the town records tell how, in 1640, an attempt was made by three miscreants to steal it, and how they got a sound public whipping and leisure to repent in the town stocks.

So I suppose that for the first two or three years, this trading, while not as promising in large returns to the Colony as had been expected, was fairly prosperous.

But in 1640 the first serious mistake was made. An agent was in that year sent to the Delaware River to find a suitable site for a trading post, and most of the leading and wealthy

New Haven men formed "The Delaware Company" and took shares in it. All might have gone well, had it not been that, in the year following, the New Haven Colony voted its political jurisdiction over the new settlement, and sent a considerable body of people, in Lamberton's "Cock," to it. Anchoring off New Amsterdam, the Dutch Governor held up the enterprise until the promise was made of allegiance to him in the new territory, which was on Dutch soil. Matters naturally not turning out as William the Testy had desired, two Dutch ships sailed from New Amsterdam in 1642, successfully attacked the New Haven traders, burned down their log cabins, arrested the settlers, and confiscated the land.

The result of this sudden disaster was the loss of some £1,000 to "The Delaware Company," as well as the emergence of a new danger in the now aroused Dutchmen.

I take it that this fiasco, and the threatening troubles from New Amsterdam resulting from it, had a good deal to do with what otherwise would appear to have been a curious political move that the New Haven folk now took,—a move which, unless it partly arose from these circumstances, would appear to have been a reversal of the original plan for complete disentanglement from the other New England colonies. Until the year 1643, the several New England colonies had existed as independent commonwealths. The first alarms of coming Indian wars, however, were now sounding throughout Massachusetts; the Frenchmen at the north, with their war-painted Indian allies, were a possible menace, if a remote one at that time; and now New Haven had got into trouble with the Dutch on the western frontier. The proposal resulted, in Massachusetts, of a protective confederacy of the English Puritan Colonies against these dangers.

Facing the unexpected end of all of their commercial plans (as the Dutch, at New Amsterdam, could easily close up that end of Long Island Sound to New Haven vessels sailing to Virginia) the New Haven folk seem to have been keenly interested in this proposal. To join such a confederacy, however, the New Haven Colony and its loosely connected outside plantations at Milford, Guilford, and Stamford, had first to settle their own political organization. From this necessity the so-called "New Haven Jurisdiction" arose. This was begun in April, 1643, a month before the United Colonies of New England was formed at Boston, to consist of Massachusetts, Plymouth, Connecticut, and New Haven. It was completed the following October, when Milford,—which, under the Rev. Peter Prudden, had not conformed to the church-membership franchise restriction of John Davenport's New Haven,—compromised on that issue, and was admitted. To this "Jurisdiction," with legislative headquarters at New Haven, the towns of Southold, L. I., and Branford were later added. From then on these six towns formed a republic, and, as such, a component part of the first union of American commonwealths.

And now, in 1646, the newly formed New Haven Jurisdiction took another step in its relations to the outside world, which again, unless we understand its relation to the necessities of the case, would appear to have been a step backward from the original independent conception of its founders.

The trading purposes of the voyage to England of Captain Lamberton's "Great Shippe," under the auspices of a new commercial company, "The Ship Fellowship," were important enough. It was the first attempt at a large trading undertaking of the New Haveners. It was said that nearly all of the remaining free capital of Davenport's people,—some five thousand pounds,—had been invested in

A New Haven Street in 1650

it as a final effort to recoup the Colony fortunes lost on the Delaware. Governor Eaton, Captain Malbon, Lieutenant Governor Goodyear, and Thomas Gregson,—the important men of the community,—were back of it. In it sailed, to conduct the sale of the hides and planks, the beaver furs and the "corn and pease" consigned by the planters, seventy of the best blood of the Colony,—Goodman Gregson and Captain Turner among them. But "The Great Shippe" foundered at sea.

This sufficiently completed the financial ruin of the once promising and ambitious colony to make it the most serious event in the first decade of New Haven's history. But, I take it, the errand upon which Gregson went in it is even more important. This was no less than that of securing some form of recognition of the New Haven Colony from the English government,—very likely charter rights to the land and legalization of the political organization which was now a part of the New England Union, and the only part not so equipped, in one form or another, with colony powers from England.

This was a far cry from the political high horse that Theophilus Eaton and John Davenport had ridden so gallantly when they formed their independent church-state at Quinnipiac only nine years before. Not only had that independence been given up in New Haven's joining the New England confederacy; the Colony was now compelled to seek further outside aid against impending trouble with the Dutch and Indians by turning to England for a charter.

But allegiance to the English Crown had become a different matter in the thirteen years since John Davenport had escaped from the Archbishop Laud of the early days of Charles I. The Puritan movement in the meanwhile had rolled up in a mighty wave over Strafford and Laud and the King himself; the Long Parliament of 1640, with the great Puritan, Pym, as leader of the House of Commons, had swept from Charles' court all of the enemies of the rights of the people; Laud had been sent to prison; the Army Plot had failed in its plan to restore the royal power; Strafford had been beheaded; the old Cartwright principles of Davenport's early Coventry days had come into wide popularity; the Bishops had been excluded from the House of Lords, and King Charles had left London for Oxford (where his artillery trained in Davenport's old college park), to muster a royal army to quell the Roundhead uprising, and to enter upon that civil war which, with the rise of Cromwell as the champion of the new popular movement, had ended in 1645 at Naseby with the wreck of the Stuart reign and the beginning of the Roundhead Parliament. In far-off New Haven, it was now possible, in 1647, for Governor Eaton to announce that "The Kinge's Armes are cutt by Mr. Mullyner for the towne and set upon a post in the highway by the seaside." With the King absent, and the appeal for such a charter as was now asked by New Haven (and doubtless backed by the other members of the Confederacy) coming before more friendly officers, the reason for this otherwise peculiar act of John Davenport's people may easily be seen. Cromwell, a relative through his wife's family of William Hooke, John Davenport's assistant minister, might be expected to see that the appeal should come before the right officers and be granted. The foundering of the Lamberton ship, with the New Haven messenger in this effort aboard, ended that possibility at the same moment that it plunged the townspeople into the lowest depths of their rapidly ebbing commercial fortunes. No further effort to secure a legal title for John Davenport's colony was ever made, with what results we shall later see.

V

From this date onward, until the first Puritan generation
had passed off the stage and new times came, John Davenport's colony seems to have had a very hard time of it.
By 1650, it might well have seemed that the end had come.
It was now but a decade since they had escaped from the
mounting persecutions of a Laud to settle a new Puritan
commonwealth on the Quinnipiac. Yet the whole scheme
for their great Roundhead trading emporium in the New
World had fallen with a crash, at the very moment when
their old friends and neighbors in England had fought
through their struggle with the Crown and English Church
and were coming out of it victors. The despair of the New
Haven folk was complete. They seem to have looked about
elsewhere for a new settlement, even considering the possibility of recrossing the ocean and beginning a new Puritan
home in Ireland. Davenport had been vigorously urged by
his old friends at home to abandon his dream-city and return
to England and take part in the popular uprising, but had
not gone. He had been invited, in 1643, to become one of
the clergymen of the Westminster Assembly, and had refused. The Protectorate now began, and Cromwell, no
doubt interested in the New Haven Jurisdiction through
Hooke, offered the people a new site in Jamaica, which he
was intent upon building up as an English bulwark in the
West Indies. For some reason or other, John Davenport
and his New Haven congregation did not accept this offer.
Possibly they were too impoverished to consider any large
and new undertaking; possibly the chief leaders were now
passing the age when such a thing was easy. They remained
to make the best of a bad bargain on the Quinnipiac. Only
Reverend Hooke left the ruined Colony and went back to
England, where he became Cromwell's private chaplain.

It was at this low juncture that Ezekiel Cheever had left the settlement, and that, with no schoolmaster in charge and no financial support likely from his ruined flock, John Davenport, turning his back on the alluring offers from the new English government, began over again to build his shattered educational edifice and his church-state.

Interior of Schoolhouse

John Harvard —

CHAPTER V

DAVENPORT'S NEW HAVEN COLLEGE

I

UP to this time the New Haven people had been forced to turn to Harvard for the only higher education open to their sons. It had been in a very neighborly spirit that they had done this, and that they had gone even further, in contributing to the general support of Harvard. A town order of 1644, passed but five years after New Haven had been settled, had established annual voluntary gifts in the country pay of the times for this purpose. These gifts,—called "the College corn,"—had been asked of everyone "whose heart is willing thereunto, a peck of wheat or the value of it" to be used "for the relief of poor scholars at the college at Cambridge." Collectors were appointed to receive these gifts, which amounted to forty bushels of wheat in the first year after the order had been passed. Three years later, however, the New Haven public interest fell off in the matter. The purpose of the Harvard support had been "that children being fit for learning, but their parents not able to beare the whole charge, might the better be trayned upp for publique service." In 1647, however, Governor Eaton had to urge this collection upon his people, "considering the worke is a service to Christ, to bring up yonge plants for his service, and besides, it wilbe a reproach that it shalbe said Newhaven is falne off from this service." Three such admonitions had to be given by the Governor. But public interest had subsided. With Ezekiel Cheever's departure this finally died out altogether.[1]

In the meanwhile John Davenport had begun a public movement for a college of his own.

It is worth retelling this well-known story of John Davenport's efforts thus to found a second Harvard in New Haven, inasmuch as, had they succeeded, Yale College, under quite a different name, would have been established before 1650 in New Haven, instead of under very different conditions some fifty odd years later, and elsewhere.

A start had been made toward this end as early as 1641, when the town school had been set up. In the original layout of the village, John Brockett had marked off some forty or more acres between the modern Olive Street and the harbor shore, which was called, from the Indian middenheaps found there, "the Oystershell-fields." The rent of these fields to various townspeople for farming purposes

[1] The purpose of this was "for the reliefe of poore schollars att the colledge att Cambridge." A Reverend Shepherd of the Cambridge church was a Bay delegate to the meeting of the United Colonies at Hartford in 1644, and appears to have suggested this assistance. Both Connecticut and New Haven undertook to give it. The New Haven boys at Harvard were from the wealthier families and received no public help to go there. The "College corn" was a general contribution to help support poor boys from other colonies. The scheme did not succeed, largely because of the poverty of the western colonies. Joshua Atwater, Anthony Thompson, Corporal Bell, Roger Alling and others were among the New Haven collectors.

was ordered to be used, later on and when the occasion arose, to support a "college." So that this "college" appears to have been one of the original projects of John Davenport.[1] It was now proposed, in 1647, to proceed with the plan.

It had been in January, 1646, that the New Haven folk had followed their ill-fated vessel out on the harbor ice, through which they had sawed a channel for it to the open Sound, and had there prayed a fervent God-speed for it with their minister. Returning within the year, as they anticipated, with a Colony charter and increased fortunes for the townsfolk, the Lamberton venture was to bring about the long-delayed prosperity of which they had dreamed in their London counting-rooms. Awaiting that day in high hopes, John Davenport now proposed to start the "college," the second step which was to give New Haven the educational advantages of the older Boston.

And so, the old town records tell us, the town-lot committee was requested to "consider and reserve what lot they shall see neat and commodious for a college, which they desire may be set up as soon as their ability will reach unto." Three acres on what is now Elm Street, facing the Market-place, was chosen for this purpose by the town-lot committee. This was land that had been originally allotted to a Mrs. Eldred, who for some reason or other had not joined the Eaton party as she had planned, and whose allotment

---

[1] Hutchinson says of New Haven's early college ambitions: "They made many attempts all along, from the first to the last of their being a distinct colony, even such as were above their strength to promote learning by public schools. Yea, it was in their hearts to set up a college and there were sundry provisions made and some land laid up in order thereto, in which desires, though they in issue failed, yet there is an honorable testimony of their good will to learning and liberal education of youth and may have its acceptance, in proportion with David desiring to build a temple, though it was effected by his son."

was therefore now at public disposal. It was about where
Elm Street now crosses Temple, and thus opposite Ezekiel
Cheever's schoolhouse, and practically in the center of the
village.

But nothing came of this public action. It was early in
1647 that this step had been taken. By the end of that
year the New Haven people had given up all hope of the
return of the Lamberton expedition, and had sorrowfully
settled the estates of the settlers who had been lost in it.
The financial loss thus sustained seems to have settled the
"college" project for the time being. It was to recoup this
loss by a third commercial venture, that another expedition
was now sent to the Delaware. This was even less suc-

The Dutch Arrest New Haven Traders

cessful than the first. The waiting Dutchmen peremptorily arrested all the party and sent them ignominiously packing back to New Haven, followed down the Sound by explosive threats of what would happen if a New England Puritan party ever tried again to settle on Dutch soil. This was the end of New Haven's repeated efforts to establish itself as a commercial metropolis. Three years later, to be sure, there was a sudden renewal of the Delaware enthusiasm, and New Haven even sent messengers to Massachusetts to recruit settlers for a final attempt to force the Dutch. But the scheme did not materialize.

II

But five years later John Davenport again boldly brought forward his college project. This renewed agitation appears to have been of a most determined character, surprisingly so when we consider the low ebb of the Colony's finances at this period. It may well have been that this very poverty operated to make the cost prohibitive to individuals who wished to send their sons to Harvard. But another reason had an even larger share in the matter. In a town vote shortly to be passed, the New Haven magistrates set down that "in some respects this seemes to be a season of some disturbances being at present at the colledg in ye Bay concerning the dismission of President Dunster." It is interesting to find this reason given in connection with Davenport's efforts to found a New Haven college. A Harvard situation, as we shall see, was again to have its large part in Yale's beginnings. President Dunster had been having a hard time of it at the infant Harvard, of which he had been the first president. He had just petitioned the Commissioners to the seminary that the original building was in poor condition, that the library was defective in law, philosophy, and some other things, and that his own salary was paid out of "stipends from the scholars" and not too punctually paid at that. But President Dunster had himself fallen from grace; good Puritan that he was, he had come to disbelieve in infant baptism, and had neglected to present one of his own children for the traditional rite. The Massachusetts Puritan doctrines rested so firmly on the universal acceptance of infant baptism as the only means to salvation and upbringing in the orthodox path of the fathers, that Dunster's action, however valuable he himself had been to Harvard, could have had but the one result of his dismissal.

I imagine that the rising disturbance at Harvard over this event (which took place in 1654) had its considerable effect on the minds of the New Haven leaders in the three or four years just before it. Davenport, some fourteen years Dunster's senior at Magdalen College, Oxford, had little liking for the theological training that his New Haven boys might receive under so prominent an opponent of one of his fundamental church rules. However that may be, the opening act of 1647 in Davenport's efforts to found a New Haven college was followed, five years later, by a general agitation of it throughout the plantations of the New Haven Jurisdiction. In the town records of Guilford, in this later year, we find an entry concerning the matter.[1] The Guilford people were ready to do their share toward establishing such a "New Haven Colledge," providing so powerful a neighbor as the Connecticut Colony "do joyne,"—a proposition of which we hear nothing, so far as I can discover,

---

[1] "The matter about a Colledge at New Haven was thought to be too great a charge for us of this jurisdiction to undergoe alone; especially considering the unsettled state of New Haven Towne, being publiquely declared from the deliberate judgment of the most understanding men to be a place of no comfortable subsistence for ye present inhabitants there." The Guilford people, however, "desire thanks to Mr. Goodyear for his proffer to the setting forward of such a work."

from any other source. But the New Haven people were
pressing, and several of their leaders enlisted themselves in
the plan. Stephen Goodyear, second to Theophilus Eaton
in public standing among the laymen of the little stockaded
village, was one of these. While the town records of the
next year are lost, we find in a later remark of John Davenport's that Stephen Goodyear, then Deputy Governor, had
offered his house and lot on Chapel Street (about where the
Taft Hotel now stands) for the president's house. Nothing
appears to have come either from the Goodyear offer, or of
Guilford's proposal that Connecticut join in the college plan.

Two years later, however, the college scheme was again
advanced by the energetic Davenport.[1] The New Haven
planters were agreed in favor of the project of educating
their sons at home, but, their commercial dreams finally
stripped of all fancies, now wanted to be assured of the
financial side of it.[2] They very practically wanted to know
how much would be subscribed. In 1655, therefore, the
General Court cast up accounts and discovered that New
Haven was prepared to give some £300 in cash in addition
to its two lots of land already appropriated, that Milford

[1] In May, 1654, the town "was informed that there is some motion again
on foote concerning the setting up of a Colledg here at Newhaven, wch, if
attayned, will in all likelyhood prove verey benificiall to this place, but
now it is onely ppounded to knowe the townes minde and whether they are
willing to further the worke by bearing a meet pportion of charge if the
jurisdiction, upon the pposall thereof, shall see cause to carry it on. No
man objected, but all seemed willing, pvided that the paye wch they can
raise here will doe it."

[2] May, 1655, the town records have it that "it is now intended to be
ppounded to the gen: court; therefore this towne may declare what they
will doe by way of incouragmt for ye same, and it would be well if they
herein giue a good example to ye other townes in ye jurisdiction, being free
in so good a worke. Mr. Davenport and Mr. Hooke were both present
upon this occasion, and spake much to incourag the worke." A committee
was thereupon appointed "to goe to the seuerall planters in this towne and
take from them what they will freely giue to this worke."

was ready to advance £100, but that the other towns wanted more time to look into the matter. New Haven now asked the General Court to bring the affair to a conclusion, and so collectors were sent around among the smaller towns of the Colony to raise the local contributions to the amount desired. It is probable that they had little success in this effort, if indeed they made it with very great enterprise. But £240 more was raised in this canvass. But the £640 thus promised seems to have been sufficient to make a beginning at the long-talked-of project, and a request was made for but £60 a year more, to be used to pay the "president."

This whole proceeding, in the light of local conditions in New Haven in 1655, was a bold one. The "college" appeared to be now a certainty, in spite of the financial depression that still hung over the Colony. The New Haven General Court would seem to have understood the matter as concluded. So far as it was concerned, a "New Haven College" had been established "for the education of youth in good literature" and "to fit them for public service in church and commonwealth," quite as surely as the Massachusetts General Court, in 1636,—the much bewigged Sir Harry Vane presiding in his courtly robes,—had established what had since become Harvard College. John Davenport so looked upon it, and, awaiting its successful beginning, renewed his efforts to maintain the grammar school which was to prepare his town youths for it. But nothing appears to have happened, the outside towns being but little interested and New Haven being financially unable to carry out the project alone.

III

In spite of all the great plans for it, during these few years the town school had practically dropped out of sight. The small children, both boys and girls, were still required

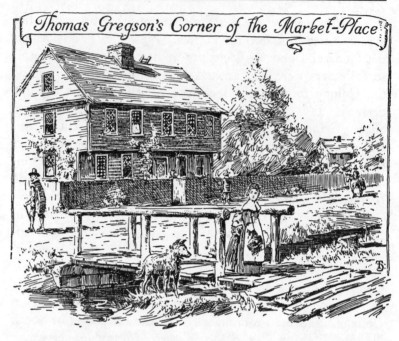

Thomas Gregson's Corner of the Market-Place

to learn their letters and to write, at home, and impoverished females were encouraged to set up "Dame schools" for this purpose. The few boys whose fathers could afford it continued to go to the town school, and there to proceed into Latin. But the first flush of enthusiasm for this important part of John Davenport's church-state scheme now appears to have faded away. After one unsuccessful attempt to fill Ezekiel Cheever's place in the little log-cabin schoolhouse on the Market-place, the Rev. John Bowers had become the schoolmaster. This Bowers was a young Harvard graduate, a native of Cambridge, and the classmate of two later Presidents of Harvard—John Rogers and that Urian Oakes whose philanthropic later life, to quote Cotton Mather, " 'twas like a Silkworm, he spent his own Bowels or Spirits, to procure the Garments of Right-

eousness for his Hearers." But the youthful Bowers had
at once found himself in difficulties, both educational and
financial. His boys were sent to him as unprepared as ever
in their English reading and grammar, and unable "to
understand the main grounds and principles of Christian
Religion necessary to Salvation,"—an interesting suggestion
of the troubles that John Davenport was having in his own
pulpit. Nor could Bowers collect tuition. The famous
New Haven School code of 1656 was very likely drawn up
by Davenport and Bowers to meet these difficulties. Six
years previously, a compulsory school law had been framed
to meet a similar situation in Thomas Hooker's Connecticut
Colony, no doubt as a result of the educational interest
begun there by young John Alcock. This young Harvard
graduate, three years Bowers' senior and the nephew of
Thomas Hooker, had been so successful in his efforts in
the Hartford school that, in 1649, supported by this law,
he had sent four Connecticut Colony boys to Harvard, the
first thus to go in the thirteen years of that Colony's history.
New Haven was now forced to enact a similar law.

Curious it is to realize that, before 1650, so soon after
the promising founding of these two idealistic Puritan
commonwealths and in spite of their basic differences in
political and church organization, both Connecticut and
New Haven were facing disaster in their educational
schemes. Yet a similar difficulty had been the experience of
the Massachusetts towns. Doubtless it had been expected
that the religious zeal of the settlers would insure the voluntary education of the rising generation. But, sad to relate,
this had not been the case. Quite the opposite is true of the
commonly accepted tradition that these first Puritan New
England schools were successes. The "one chief project of
that old deluder, Sathan," had always been to keep men
from the knowledge of the Scriptures. The old deluder had

been working in Massachusetts, as well as in Hooker's and
Davenport's Utopias, with a vengeance. Compulsory educational laws were everywhere required. The acts that the
Connecticut and New Haven ministers and their magistrates
now found necessary were passed by their respective General
Courts, "that Learning may not be buried in the Grave of
our Forefathers in Church and Commonwealth, the Lord
assisting our endeavors." The Connecticut Colony school
law commanded that each town should see that there was
no "Barbarism" allowed any longer "in any of their families, at a penalty of twenty shillings for neglect." The
New Haven code, now following, was quite as strict. All
the "Children and Apprentices" were to be taught "to read
the Scriptures, and other good and profitable printed books
in the English tongue, and in some competent measure to
understand the main grounds and principles of Christian
Religion." The New Haven Court followed this with a
general order that every plantation in the Jurisdiction
should "set up and maintayne" a school and pay a third of
the schoolmaster's salary. To help matters along, the New
Haven General Court three years later freed from payment
of personal taxes all those who studied diligently; if they
ceased doing this, the rates were imposed again.

But, so low were New Haven's financial affairs, even
these paternal legislative acts had little influence upon the
rebirth of the town Free School. Master Bowers, in 1660,
finally had to appear before the Court about it. If the town
wanted a school, said he, and him for the schoolmaster, the
proper thing was to show that they did, and do something
beyond passing laws which evidently were given small attention by the townspeople.

We may imagine the perplexities of the town fathers as
they received this upstanding communication from their
young Harvard schoolmaster. Doubtless there were many

waggings of heads under the broad-brimmed hats of the day and pullings of noses and dubious suggestions of the state of the Colony and the disproportionate cost of the higher education for so poor and long-suffering a settlement of disappointed tradesmen. But the other plantations of the Jurisdiction were having similar difficulties in supporting their enforced Free Schools. The question had become a broader one than New Haven's school troubles alone. Whoever made the suggestion, we do not know (very likely it was Davenport), but the Court decided to meet the situation by turning the New Haven Free School into a Colony Grammar School and to admit boys who wished to "make Latin" from all of the six towns in the Jurisdiction to it. The businesslike John Bowers resigned at this point, going first to Guilford and then to Branford, where he was later to succeed the elder Abraham Pierson[1] in the village church. The Colony School, successor to that pioneer town school on the public Market-place, now promised, as did the sleeping college project, the first fruits of John Davenport's two long decades of struggle to found a well-rounded educational plan for his New Haven church.

IV

And we may suppose that the old Puritan leader (for John Davenport was now sixty-one years old) now felt that there was but one more stumbling-block in the path of his cherished plans. This, as was the case generally throughout New England in educational matters, was financial. The New Haven college needed money from without the Colony if it were to succeed. And so we find John Davenport

[1] Abraham Pierson the younger, now just graduating from Harvard College and later to appear at the forefront of the personages in these pages, had come to New Haven from his father's Branford home during these years of John Bowers' teaching, and had been prepared by him for Harvard.

writing a letter in the book-lined study of his spacious house
overlooking the harbor, to his old friend Edward Hopkins,
and enclosing with it, no doubt, a supporting word from
Governor Eaton over the way, step-father to Edward Hopkins' wife, who had been a Yale, and his chief on the
original emigration.

Edward Hopkins, whom we left at the settlement of New
Haven removing to Thomas Hooker's Connecticut Colony,
had led an eventful life there until 1653, when he had returned to England upon the death of his brother, warden
of the fleet under Oliver Cromwell. In Connecticut, Hopkins had been a useful planter, occupying the Governor's
chair for seven annual terms and acting in large Colony
matters as one of its first citizens. He had been the chair-
man of the Connecticut Commission that had treated with
George Fenwick, in 1644, for the absorption of Saybrook,
its fort and its "two demiculvering cast pieces, with all the
shot thereunto appertaining, one murderer with two chambers, two barrels of gunpowder, bandoleers and rests," etc.,
"and all the housing within the pallisado." Three years
later he had headed a second commission, with Captain
John Culick and others, to rearrange the money terms of
this transfer. He had several times represented Connecticut in the meetings of the New England Union. During the
Dutch and Indian troubles he had been an energetic leader
in the Colony's defense, and, when he had returned to
England, was the spokesman for the Connecticut agent who
had been sent to Lord Cromwell, Parliament, and General
Monk, to secure English military aid against the New York
Dutch. He had, it was said of him, "conducted the affairs
of government with great wisdom and integrity, and was
universally beloved." He seems to have been looked upon
by his contemporaries as the Theophilus Eaton of Connecticut. His charities were "great and extensive; besides the

relief he dispensed to the poor [I am quoting from Benjamin Trumbull] he gave considerable sums of money to others, to be disposed of to charitable purposes." Unlike his former colleagues in the New Haven Colony, Edward Hopkins had added to rather than lost his original fortune, and had gone back to England a comfortably-wealthy American colonist. Though he had expected to return, and, in 1654 had been reëlected Governor of Connecticut in that expectation, his reception by Cromwell had been so hearty that he had remained there, at first succeeding his brother as First Warden of the English Fleet, then as Commissioner of the Admiralty and Navy, and finally becoming a member of the Second Protectorate Parliament.

It had been in either 1656 or 1657 that John Davenport had written to Hopkins outlining the facts regarding the New Haven college project. Afterward restating these in a public statement he said "that, sundry years past, it was concluded by the said General Court, that a small college, such as the day of small things will permit, should be settled in New Haven, for the education of youth in good literature, to fit them for public service, in church and commonwealth, as it will appear from the public records." He asked Hopkins for a money contribution to it.[1] The latter's reply was as follows: "Most Dear Sir, The long continued respects I have received from you, but especially, the speakings of the Lord to my heart, by you, have put me under deep obligations to love and a return to thanks beyond what I have or can express." He then added what Davenport wanted: "That which the Lord hath given me in those parts, I ever designed, the greatest part of it for the furtherance of

[1] In the light of the gift by Elihu Yale, some fifty-six years later, it is worth noting how in 1657 his aunt's wealthy husband was at the point of forestalling him in a first considerable endowment to the New Haven "college" which might have resulted in a Hopkins College instead of Yale.

the work of Christ in those ends of the earth, and if I understand that a college is begun and like to be carried on, at
New Haven, for the good of posterity, I shall give some
encouragement thereunto."

But Fate would have it otherwise. And it was in such
an incident as this that we may read clearly the natural
penalties that were inherent from the beginning in the great
Davenport social scheme. For had Edward Hopkins
chosen to remain with the New Haven colonists in 1638 he
would at this moment have made his gift to the Davenport
Colony college. That he had chosen, instead, to join the
more liberal Connecticut people could hardly have been for
other cause than that he preferred their religious and political system to the narrow theocracy of New Haven. And
so, where we cannot but believe that John Davenport's
political ideas had driven Edward Hopkins to Connecticut
in the first place, we now may see where, from that incident,
and others like it, was to result that chain of events which
in the end was to be the undoing of the Davenport scheme
of things.

For Hopkins, when his sudden death occurred a year
after he had thus agreed to give substantially to the New
Haven college, did not do it, but, instead, left a will dividing
the money that Davenport had asked for, between New
Haven and his own old Colony of Connecticut.

From this act a long train of results was to follow. The
estate, which consisted of Connecticut property in large
measure, both real and personal, came to £1,324 "and a
negar," and Hopkins named as cotrustees for its collection
and distribution his two old New Haven friends of the
early London days,—Davenport and Eaton,—and two
Connecticut men, that Captain Culick who had served with
him on various Connecticut commissions, and William
Goodwin. Had this large estate been left to John Daven-

port's Colony alone, the proposed New Haven college would have been established by 1660 at New Haven.

Not only, moreover, was the Hopkins bequest made to the two colonies, but under the terms of the will it was to be used for "both grammar school and college." So that, even if the New Haven share of the estate had come at once, it would not all have been at the disposition of the projected higher institution. But even that was not to be. Governor Eaton had died before he could act under the will, and John Davenport met the Connecticut trustees and agreed (as we may read in his elaborate statement of the case to the New Haven General Court in 1660) to divide the legacy equally between the two colonies, after £100 had been given to Harvard.[1]

Yet, in spite of these unexpected reverses, John Davenport might well have anticipated, in 1660, that half of the Hopkins gift was now to come, and that, even if part of it would have to go to the grammar school, the remainder, with what had been promised in the Jurisdiction, would be sufficient to begin his long-cherished college plan. This would very likely have been the fact, had not circumstances now come about which were to throw the whole college project to the four winds and end in an entirely unexpected way for John Davenport's church-state itself.

[1] In 1659 the Hartford church was split into two warring factions over matters of church organization, and the dissatisfied faction, led by Mr. Goodwin, the Hopkins trustee, had moved to Hadley. When the final settlement of the Hopkins estate was made, therefore, one half of the Connecticut share went with Mr. Goodwin to Hadley, where a Hopkins Grammar School has continued to this day on the foundation.

CHAPTER VI

THE DOWNFALL OF THE NEW HAVEN REPUBLIC

I

IT had been in 1660 that John Davenport, acting as the surviving New Haven trustee of the Hopkins bequest, had turned over to the General Court of the New Haven Jurisdiction all the papers concerning the trust, and his own proposals concerning its use. The success of the New Haven College plan was now assured, in popular fame. Davenport ordered that the town should accumulate from then on the rents of the old "Oystershell-fields" that had been set aside for the purpose in 1641, till they should be needed when "the college" should be set up. "Mrs. Eldred's lot" on Elm Street was ordered to be used for the site both of the coming college and the grammar school which the Hopkins money was to bolster up. And the townspeople were again commanded to keep their sons "constantly to learning" against the time when the new college should "train up" the youth for "public serviceableness." According to these instructions the Colony itself was to settle £40 annually for "a common school," and add £100 for a schoolhouse and a "library"; the original £40 a year to be paid by the other towns for a Colony grammar school was now to be settled upon some town, presumably New Haven, and a schoolmaster engaged to teach the Latin, Greek, and Hebrew tongues. In relinquishing this trust Davenport ordered that a committee of church members should be chosen to consult "in emergent difficult cases that may concern the school or college," over the acts of which he desired a veto power for himself. To keep the trust papers, a "convenient chest with two locks and keys" was to be kept in the house of the Governor of the Colony (at that time William Leete of Guilford) "till a more public place (as a library or the like) may be prepared."

These various orders of John Davenport undoubtedly were intended to establish at once a grammar school, the "College," though still in view, to be postponed until the time was ripe for it, which of course was to be at once. The famous New Haven Hopkins Grammar School dates from this public action by John Davenport. For we find the Governor, Deputy Governor, one freeman, and the two ministers of the New Haven church, meeting on June 28, 1660, and deciding to engage the Rev. Jeremiah Peck, then the schoolmaster at Guilford, to come to New Haven with his wife and take charge of the new school which we now know by that name.

This new schoolmaster was a Londoner by birth, and was now twenty-seven years old. He was to receive the £40 salary appropriated by the General Court and "to keep school" and "fit the scholars for the College" shortly to be established. His first act was to secure £10 more salary, and a house, besides the board and fees from the scholars who came into New Haven from the neighboring towns to the new school. While this young man remained but a year, and then left to be the minister at Saybrook,[1] under him John Davenport's educational machinery seemed finally to be in motion. All that remained for its permanent success was the receipt of the Hopkins money.

This, however, was not forthcoming. Connecticut interposed unexpected obstacles to the division of the estate as planned, the General Court appointed an administrator, this officer stopped all collections and managed to lose track of some of them, and for the next five years the whole affair was held up, for reasons which we shall shortly describe.

All of which was undoubtedly enough to dishearten the most vigorous of Puritan fighters in Christ's service. And John Davenport was disheartened enough. To add to his troubles, his New Haven people again held back from supporting the new school. The Colony Grammar School had been established, the town had the Hopkins trust papers, a schoolmaster had been found, "oratory" had been added as a curriculum attraction and the opening hours accommodatingly moved forward a full hour until eight o'clock of winter mornings. But nobody seemed to want it. In 1661 only five or six boys were again coming for instruction, and the disheartened new schoolmaster unceremoniously departed. A year later, the General Court, concluding that, "considering the distraction of the time" and probable further costs, "the end is not attained for which it was

[1] Jeremiah Peck was probably the second instructor of Abraham Pierson, the Collegiate School's first Rector, who was then fifteen years of age and preparing for Harvard College. Peck later returned to Guilford, emigrated with his father-in-law, Robert Kitchell, with the Branford party of the elder Pierson to Newark, and later preached at Waterbury, where he died in 1699.

settled no way proportionable to the charges expended," voted point-blank to give up the whole enterprise. For a year or two, one George Pardee of the town, an old pupil of Ezekiel Cheever's, was engaged to teach English and writing to the handful of boys who still attended the town school, and "carry them on in Latin so far as he could." But this was apparently a very little way. The great school project of Davenport, and with it the immediate prospect of his "college," had again,—and, as it was to turn out, finally,—collapsed.

II

The withholding of New Haven's share in the Hopkins bequest by the Connecticut General Assembly was not, as we may now look at it through the perspective of two centuries and a half, as badly advised as John Davenport and his New Haven supporters naturally considered it. For events were shaping themselves on a new and broader scale throughout New England, and in these Connecticut and New Haven had their share.

The Restoration of Charles is a landmark in the history of the relations between New England and old England, as it is in the history of Puritanism as a political factor in England itself. Charles II ascended his father's throne on May 25, 1660. Ending, as this did in one swinging blow, the ascendancy of the Roundhead party at home, the most eminent of that party's leaders were at once blacklisted (among them that early friend of Harvard, Sir Harry Vane, whose head was enthusiastically chopped off by the new government at the first opportunity). The effect of the change was immediately felt in the New England colonies, where the news of it was received with dismay by the dominating orthodox Puritan leaders. If Massachusetts was at once to find herself in serious political complications with the new Royal government, New Haven, one of the four confederated New England colonies, was in an even worse plight. Unlike Massachusetts, New Haven had no charter from the King, or any patent to its land titles from any-one,—in fact had deliberately settled in the New World without it, and, as we have seen, had never acquired one afterwards. Its leader, Davenport, had been a particularly strong anti-Royalist, and was considered to be among the chief, though distant, surviving supporters of the Cromwell régime. And New Haven, as Massachusetts, was in especially bad odor with the King because of its strict measures against the Quakers, whose persecutions the politic Charles II, intent upon theological toleration for quite untheological purposes of his own, at once undertook to stop.

To add to their long list of mistakes, the New Haven people now took a step of hardly concealed hostility against the new English ruler. This, as matters turned out, was a decidedly serious one. The young Governor John Winthrop of Connecticut had secured, on March 14, 1660, the passage by his legislature of a fulsome proclamation of the new King. As the immediate future was to disclose, this was a highly politic act, as it brought the little Connecticut Colony to the gratified attention of the King hardly had he ascended his throne, and, very possibly, gave him his first knowledge that there was such a place. New Haven did not do this. In fact, John Davenport's people proceeded in quite the contrary direction, ostentatiously hiding William Goffe and Edward Whalley, the Regicides of the King's father, while perspiring and exasperated Royal officers were hunting for them. It is said that old John Davenport even secreted the two Cromwellian soldiers and judges in his own house on lower Elm Street, and that he preached a highly independent sermon to the English posse on the unequivocal text, "Hide the outcasts."

It was at this juncture that Connecticut sent young Governor Winthrop to England, with £500 for "expenses," to see what he could do for his Colony with the new King. Evidently fearing that New Haven's interests might not receive equal attention with Connecticut's, the New Haven General Court now rather tardily drew up a document for Winthrop to take with him,—which document, while it finally proclaimed the restoration of Charles, did so in such a grudging manner that it had better not have been done at all. The New Haven Colony, said this paper, had not received any formal notification of the accession of Charles II, yet had "thought fit" to acknowledge him to be "their sovereign." This diplomatic effort was little calculated to excite King Charles' enthusiasm for the weak and independent Cromwellian settlement on the Quinnipiac, lorded over, as it was, by so well known a Roundhead as the fanatical John Davenport. Moreover, New Haven sent no "expense" account with it, as had Connecticut, to see that it reached the King.[1] What happened might have been expected. Though Winthrop, for many years a close friend of Davenport, had verbally agreed to the contrary, he sent back in 1662 a new Connecticut charter, under which his legislature immediately claimed New Haven's inclusion.

[1] Whether John Winthrop had to bribe his way to the King is not fully established. It was a pleasant little habit of the times. Winthrop had a good friend at Court in old Lord Say and Sele, a member of the august Privy Council and of the Council for Plantations. Saybrook was named partly for him under the patent that included it, and Winthrop had been Saybrook's first Governor. But Winthrop was a polished man of the world, and had, so Professor C. M. Andrews writes, "great tact and an attractive personality." Cotton Mather relates that at the right moment in these negotiations over this charter, Winthrop gave to Charles II a ring that the King's father had given his own father when the latter was Governor of Massachusetts.

A great deal has been said on this matter of Connecticut's arbitrary grabbing of the New Haven Colony, and the Connecticut leaders have more than once been pilloried by historians for their action. And one may hardly deny that the act, in itself, was decidedly aggressive and, in many respects, unfair. A restudy of the contemporaneous documents would seem to bear out this interpretation,—particularly the very feelingly-written letter which New Haven's General Court asked John Davenport and his assistant minister, Mr. Street, to draw up and which was not finished in time to avert the absorption. This letter, entitled "New Haven's case stated," now in the archives at Hartford, states plainly the New Haven leaders' claim of complete legal title to their land and of independence. Against the "unjust pretences and encroachments upon our just and proper rights," it sets forth that the original New Haven settlers had chosen Quinnipiac, proposed to buy land there from the "natural proprietors," the Indians, and so "signified to their friends in Hartford in Connecticut Colony." They had received "a satisfactory answer," had so informed the Massachusetts Colony, "and with their consent began a plantation" on land "which they did purchase of the Indians." This land they had "quietly possessed about six and twenty years, and have buried great estates in buildings, fencings, clearing the ground, and in all sorts of husbandry, without any help from Connecticut or dependence upon them." They had done all this "upon such fundamentals as were established in Massachusetts," a copy of which the Connecticut Winthrop's father (then the Massachusetts Governor) had sent to them. Connecticut had never questioned all this, nor had made any difficulty over the erection of the "New Haven Colony." Nor had the up-river Colony "objected against our being a distinct colony." The New Haven letter also set forth that when

Thomas Hooker's Hartford house

the Dutch (in 1648) had "claimed a right to New Haven," New Haven had "caused the King's arms to be fairly cut in wood, and set upon a post in the highway by the sea-side," without asking Connecticut's permission; that in 1643 the New England Confederation had been established, in which New Haven had been accepted as one of the four distinct members, on an equal basis with Massachusetts, Plymouth, and Connecticut; that, in 1644, being without a legal patent to their land from the King, New Haven had, with Connecticut's approval, dispatched one of their magistrates in the Lamberton ship to solicit a charter from the first Charles [then, however, not in power], but that the ship had been lost at sea, and the attempt had not been repeated owing to "the troubles in England." And that the New Haven Colony bounds had been established on the Dutch frontier in 1650 with full consent of Connecticut.

All of which rather went to ·prove that, until this occasion, the Connecticut leaders had considered New Haven to be a separate and independent commonwealth, though without charter right to that independence from the King. "Whereby," says the Davenport letter of 1664 to the new generation of Connecticut leaders at Hartford, "the difference of times, and of men's spirits in them, may be discovered. For then the magistrates of Connecticut with consent of their General Court, knowing our purposes, desired to join with New Haven in procuring the patent. But now they seek to procure a patent without the concurrence of New Haven, and contrary to our minds expressed before the patent was sent for, and to their own promise, and to the terms of the confederation, and without sufficient warrant from their patent, they have invaded our right, and seek to involve New Haven under Connecticut jurisdiction."

Which, we may believe, was quite true. And the uncomfortable fact was that Governor Winthrop had been asked by letter "not to have his hand in so unrighteous an act" and "was pleased to certify, in two letters, that no such thing was intended, but rather the contrary," and that New Haven was to be left free to join with Connecticut or not as it saw fit. That Winthrop so intended matters to turn out, was, I fancy, quite the fact. For, before he had returned to Connecticut, Winthrop had written to his leaders at home to let New Haven alone; that they did not follow his advice was very likely not his fault. By the time he did return, matters had gone so far that there was no further chance of stopping them, and the arbitrary inclusion of New Haven had become a fact.

III

Yet I imagine that we may not lay all of this sudden and, on the face of it, bad turn of events to Connecticut alone, or lay too much stress on the unfairness of that Colony's acts. Matters in both the New Haven church and state had not been progressing smoothly throughout all these years,— the ship of state had been bumping along on as rocky a bottom as had the educational system that I have been telling about. The fact was that John Davenport's idealistic community had not been proving the success that he had planned it to be. From internal uprisings against the system laid down in that famous meeting in Mr. Newman's barn, it was nearing its wreck regardless of interferences from without. The fundamental policy of the Colony, that church members alone should have the franchise, had been largely responsible for this. We have seen how Connecticut

Governor Leete's Guilford House

had been settled on the Plymouth plan and had worked out that plan into the first broad modern democracy of New England history. New Haven was now reaping the harvest of a narrower plan, quite as Massachusetts herself, after a prolonged argument with the new King and his successor, was to reap her harvest. Leading this new generation was a new group of men, to whom the church-state scheme of the original settlers (among whom John Davenport and old Abraham Pierson of Branford now stood as the nearly sole survivors) was no longer the desirable political organization that Davenport had dreamed it was to be. These new leaders in the outlying settlements of the Judisdiction, such as Guilford, Stamford, and Southold, L. I., had come to be in the majority against the autocratic church-rule emanating from New Haven. Without regard to what Connecticut had in mind in her new charter, these towns were now almost unanimously in favor of leaving New Haven and joining the older colony. This spirit had come to a head in Guilford in 1663. When the controversy between New Haven and Connecticut over the absorption was at its height, a Guilford man had put himself under Connecticut's legal protection. This enterprising person had induced two Connecticut constables to come down to Guilford "with sundry others" to show their authority, which they did by galloping into the sleepy little village in the dead of night and "shooting off sundry guns," thereby throwing the quiet community into great excitement. Governor Leete, of Guilford, though a Connecticut-party man, had no liking for this sort of thing and sent friends to Branford and New Haven for help. A disorganized rabble of New Haven-party settlers responding, the Hartford gentry discreetly withdrew and Governor Leete requested the Connecticut Colony to suspend further show of authority until the question had been threshed out between the two Colonies.

Yet at its best, the New Haven plan had never been a complete political success. When the town had been originally laid out, "quarters," or sections had been occupied by the various original parties. The idea seems to have been for the Kent, Yorkshire, Herefordshire, and London groups to maintain separate, almost "township" characters. Davenport's views, however, could not have been wholly acceptable to them. The Herefordshire people, under Prudden, removed to Milford almost immediately, and were never in entire sympathy with the Davenport church-state thereafter, though a part of it. The Yorkshire contingent, arriving later than the first planters, remained only after their minister found it impossible to join Davenport's fantastic schemes. The Kent party, under Whitfield, soon settled at Guilford, and were never in close touch. All through the eighteen years of the New Haven Jurisdiction, the evidence is cumulative that John Davenport was having no easy time of it in his effort to create his own kind of a theocracy. This trouble had been increasing as the older leaders fell away and a new and younger group came on.

Branford and Milford, however, had stood with the conservative majority of New Haven during these years. In the former town Abraham Pierson had supported John Davenport with all the energy of one of the most sturdy Puritan pioneers of the four colonies. But this support was not sufficient to ward off the coming end. The New Haven Jurisdiction sent an appeal to the old Confederation, but nothing came of it. They rained appeals and protests upon the Connecticut General Assembly and nothing came of them. They stood their ground manfully in their own General Court. But to no effect. The younger element in the Jurisdiction was going over to Winthrop's Connecticut, Governor Leete had become an advocate of the absorption under the new charter, the long-suffering non-church members of the Colony broke out into a most hostile attitude on the ground that the New Haven Court had no independent legal status under the new English King, as indeed it hadn't. The long-coming tidal wave of discontent over John Davenport's famous theocracy was now thundering in. Several elected magistrates in New Haven refused to serve their terms. There was no money to pay the civil magistrates. The new party was strengthening itself with the passage of each new week. The other towns of the Colony were divided and were slowly turning toward the Connecticut plan. The Court itself was challenged (that court which was to dispense the laws of Moses to the new metropolis of Governor Eaton). There were not enough supporters of the Davenport theocracy left to fill the magistrates' chairs. The end was now in sight of that Utopia that John Davenport had so ardently planned but a little over a quarter-century before. Matters had become desperate indeed.

But John Davenport still held out, sturdy old fighting Calvinist that he was. For three years more, until March, 1665, he continued his fight to keep New Haven out of the new Connecticut, refusing all sops and compromises, even the offer to make New Haven a joint Assembly town with Hartford. Then he had to give in. New Haven voted to send her belated delegates to the Connecticut Assembly, and, with this act, the old New Haven Colony, the Utopian city of the idealistic John Davenport, became by its own acquiescence an integral part of that Connecticut which we have since then known.

But even this was not done without protest. In 1666, twenty-three irreconcilable settlers from Branford, under the unchangeable and adamantine Abraham Pierson, and forty-one from New Haven, Milford, and Guilford, removed to Newark, New Jersey, there to carry on the original New Haven plan of a Puritan church-state for a few remaining years, when, as we shall see, it disappears from American colonial history.

IV

We may picture the venerable founder of this now crumbled church-state, in these last days of his stay at New Haven. A tall and now emaciated figure, he sits, maybe, at his high writing-desk in the old study of his great Elm Street house. From his window he may look down across tilled fields and orchards to the harbor shore, where the three or four trading sloops of his parishioners are now awaiting their first sailings of the new Spring commerce. Through the bare tree-tops he may look at the thatched-roof lines of the scattered homes of his people, whom he had essayed so confidently, twenty odd years before, to lead, as Moses led his people, into the Promised Land. About him are the shelves of his library, loaded with the old uncompromising Calvinistic books that formed one of the great libraries of his day. I think that, feel as we may about the impossibility of the great life plan that he had tried to carry out, it is a pathetic scene that we may now look in upon, and a pathetic figure in the center of it, if still a vigorous one. From under the small black skullcap of the old man's sacred calling, escape the short rolls of his curly and now snow-white hair. Under the high-arched eyebrows that we may see in the portrait left to us of him, the prominent black eyes still hold the holy fire of that youth and young manhood which he had devoted to God's service, as he saw it, on earth. He wears a small level white moustache and a white tuft under his lower lip. His broad, square, white Geneva band fits closely under his chin and flares down on his black silk gown, over his erect if narrow shoulders. He may well feel himself the last of that first great company of devout

English Puritans who had begun life anew, with their
devoted congregations, in the free New World. Theophilus
Eaton, friend of his boyhood in the old walled city of
Coventry, has gone; Thomas Hooker, of Hartford, and
John Cotton, of Boston, have passed on to the immortal
Utopia of their Puritan faith. Winthrop, Bradford,
Brewster, all had left their earthly stage. A new generation
was taking that stage, and were reshaping the old theocracy
of the first generation to meet conditions of the second.
New Haven, which he had built to become an independent
community governed by its own religious voters, was now
a part of that Connecticut, whose more liberal theory of
government he had from the first looked upon as dangerous
and degenerating to the purity of the church. A new King
had come to England, who was stamping out the Puritanism
of the older days with an iron heel. "Christ's interest" in
New Haven, John Davenport may well have said, "was
miserably lost." Even now his people would be able to send
to the new Connecticut Assembly, under the Half-way Covenant which he had so devoutly fought, public representatives
who knew not the pioneer church and over whom, as their
souls' pastor, he would have no control. His life work
seemed over.

And yet, I take it, the fighting spirit of this old Puritan
pioneer was still far from being downed. If he had lost
everything in New Haven, there were other worlds to con-
quer, or at least to help preserve against the encroachments
of the new spirit of the times. Before him, as he sits at
that old study desk from which so many chastenings had
gone forth these many years to his flock, is the letter that
he has received from the old First Church of Boston, whose
aged pastor, Rev. John Wilson, has just died. In it is a
call to him to their pulpit as the single remaining great
champion, with Harvard's president, Charles Chauncey, of

the original church purity of New England. Should he
leave New Haven and go? We may imagine the old New
Haven leader weighing the matter as he looks out upon the
village which no longer is his own, as it has been these
twenty-five full years. In Massachusetts one last stand
against the rising tide of liberalism and secularism may at
least be attempted, side by side with that young Increase
Mather who was now coming to the front as the champion
of the old ways. He decides to go.

In April, 1668, all but thirty years to perhaps a day from
that first promising arrival on the virgin Quinnipiac soil,
John Davenport delivers his farewell sermon in the rough
Meeting-house on the New Haven Market-place, and with
his books and belongings, his "clock and his seven high
chairs," his plate and china, leaves for Boston where, two
years later, he is to die. That great rainstorm which over-
took him as he and his family entered Boston, driving them
to friendly refuge, may well have seemed to him the all but
final extinction of God's friendly protection to one of his
most loyal yet hard-used sons.

T. Hooker

PART II
THE FOUNDING OF THE COLLEGIATE
SCHOOL

Andros
Coat of Arms

CHAPTER I

CONNECTICUT AFTER 1664

I

 HE independent New Haven church-state being thus extinguished in its absorption by Connecticut, there now ensued a period of two decades during which the New Haven college project slumbered, and events of a still larger nature were occurring in New England. Such a broad review of those events as will be necessary to our purpose of recalling the background of Yale's beginnings need be but a brief one.

Two years after Charles II, Romanist-Protestant, had succeeded to the Stuart throne, the first result of the overthrow of Puritanism as a political power in England had shown itself on St. Bartholomew's Day, 1662, when one out of five of all the English rectors and vicars were driven out of their parishes for nonconformity to the established Church. A correlative of this sweeping action was the commencement of Royal toleration for the Catholic and Quaker. And it was in connection with the latter incident that New England came into its first important collision with the new King. Exponents of eccentric theological theories had from the earliest days been treated with severity in Massachusetts. Mrs. Anne Hutchinson's Antinomian heresies had been stamped out, as we have seen, when John Davenport was spending his first year in New England. Roger Williams had been banished for his views. A law "against strangers" had been voted. The quaint and crotchety Gorton, once a London tailor and then "professor of the mysteries of Christ" in Massachusetts, had defended his wife's servant at her trial for smiling in church and been banished from Plymouth, later to be shuffled from Massachusetts to Rhode Island, in which latter colony he died at a great age (his last surviving neighbor informing the inquiring-minded Ezra Stiles in 1771 that he was still writing his books in Heaven). There had been a Presbyterian conspiracy that had gone as far as the preparation of papers asking that Presbyterianism be established by Parliament as the institutional New England Church; this had been squelched by heavy fines and imprisonments of the conspirators. The Baptist persecutions of 1651 had followed, ending in the Colony vote to banish all persons who were disbelievers in infant baptism, and in the final theocratic organization of New England Puritanism under the Cambridge Platform.

But these cases, thus disposed of in turn for the preservation of the purity of the original churches, were unimportant compared with the great struggle against the Quakers which came to its height just before Charles II was restored. The arrival of advance agents of George Fox's teachings had been looked upon by the Boston orthodox Congregationalists as a direct attack upon their most fundamental conception of the Massachusetts church-state. The extraordinary persecutions of these people that at once began (and which were not in the least degree allayed by the somewhat braggart acts of the Quakers themselves) were a forerunner of the later Massachusetts acts against "witches." Not only Massachusetts, but the other three Colonies in the New England Union of the day passed "banishing laws" against the Quakers, New Haven (dubbing them "a cursed sect lately risen up in the world") among them. Governor Endi-

cott of Massachusetts went further, and, with the Rev. John
Norton (Cotton's successor in the Boston church), secured
the passage of a Colony law inflicting the death penalty on
the sect,—a law which was literally put into effect on Boston
Commons in 1659, the wife of Rhode Island's Secretary,
one of the prisoners, being reprieved by her son only at the
last moment.

The first public act of Charles II concerning New England was his order of 1661 suspending any more of these
Quaker trials by Endicott. But this act of the new King
had a more significant side to it than the mere holding back
of New England's hands on its own church enemies. The
Act of Uniformity, indeed, had not crossed the ocean, but
Charles II, now that he had sensed the New England situation in the Quaker incidents, appears to have cast a slant
eye toward the whole political and religious organization
of his far-off subjects. Not only did it appear to him (no
doubt as suggested by the various discontented settlers who
had returned to England to state their grievances) that the
New England people, living the last of that independent
Puritan-church life that he had just ended for their Puritan
contemporaries in England, were much too independent in
that life. He was now assured that the New England Confederacy itself was rather more than a loose protective
organization, and had in it the threatening germs of a military union, the ultimate intention of which was to throw
off, by force, the Royal sovereignty. We have seen how
John Winthrop had easily secured the new Connecticut
charter and included New Haven in it. That Charles permitted this may have been because he looked upon it as an
indirect way of breaking up this confederacy and at the same
time punishing New Haven both for its Quaker laws, its
protection of the two Regicides, and its belated proclamation of his own ascension to the English throne. How

Charles now proceeded to undermine the independence of the other New England Colonies, to reorganize them on his own Royal foundation, and to produce religious and political results of much importance to our chronicles, may now be recalled.

II

The nearly complete independence to this time of primitive Massachusetts from England had very largely been due to its remoteness and to the little communication between the two by sea. This had in part operated to keep Charles I from interfering with its development as an independent commonwealth. But this no longer was to be the case under his son. The Dutch War and home politics had, to be sure, allowed New England affairs to drop from the new King's immediate attention in his first few years on the throne. Besides the matters just mentioned, the Navigation Acts of 1660 and 1663 had been the only large Royal business with New England until 1672. Charles II had been content, until that time, to assure the Massachusetts agents that their charter would not be interfered with, providing the colonists swore allegiance to him, quit persecuting his Quaker protégés, changed their suffrage laws so as to permit non-church members to vote, and permitted Church of England Episcopalians to worship unmolested. But he now went a step farther. The Act of Trade of 1672 required a duty to be paid at the New England ports on goods which were not to be shipped to England. The English view of the New England colonies seems to have been that they were "plantations," like Virginia, and, as such, should properly contribute to the financial good of the mother country rather than to their own. Throughout New England quite the reverse had been true of the colonists' own views on the matter, and we may well imagine that the

New Englanders had paid but little attention to the Acts. By 1675 Charles had found the time to turn again to New England affairs, the "Lords of the Committee of Trade and Plantations" had been formed to overlook them, and the brusque and tactless Edward Randolph sent to Boston to see how the Massachusetts people were obeying the Royal orders.

The arrival at Boston of this notoriously high-and-mighty emissary marks the beginning of a new era for the independent old Puritan church-state of the Bay, as indeed, in its far-reaching results, it was to change the whole complexion of New England social and religious life and to have its marked effect upon Connecticut. It was no wonder that the doughty Governor Leverett kept his hat on while he read the King's message, handed to him with much show of pomp and ceremony by Randolph, and that he deliberately inquired as he returned it who the devil the "Henry Coventry" was who, as the King's chief secretary of state, had signed it. The indignant Randolph reported matters to Charles as being in a bad way in Massachusetts, the result of which was for the King to send a peremptory letter to that Colony, commanding, this time, all of the things which in 1664 he had graciously hoped that the colonists would do.

And thus was fired that famous train of circumstances which was to end, in 1684, in the annulling of the Massachusetts Colony charter, as the town charters of England had been annulled at almost the same time, and in the incoming of a broad stream of English authority in Massachusetts affairs. The succession of James II, a year later, did not better matters; they at once became worse with the arrival of Sir Edmund Andros as the officially appointed overlord, or Governor-General of all New York and New England, Connecticut included. His brief but haughty career ended in 1689. The reassertion by Massachusetts of its rights to a Colony charter from the new King, the Dutch Calvinist, William III, resulted in the new and different charter of 1692, which was secured largely through the good offices of Increase Mather, now minister at Boston and president of Harvard College, and at the time in London. By the terms of this charter an entirely new principle had to be admitted by Massachusetts, if it was to have a charter at all—that of Royal appointment of the Colony officers instead of the previous home elections. Freehold property became, through it, the basis of political rights; appeals from court judgments to England were permitted, and Royal power was admitted to veto Colony bills. Increase Mather, champion of the older and independent order that he was, returning from England as the chief supporter of the new charter, found himself widely spoken of as having "betrayed his country." The troubles of his next ten years, bringing about, as they did, a situation at Harvard which was to have its important effect on public sentiment in Connecticut toward that College, were nearly all traceable to the unlucky day when he accepted the new charter on behalf of his Massachusetts fellow citizens.

III

While these large matters concerning New England's relations with the changing English kings were proceeding abroad, a second and hardly less important complication had been arising at home.

The primitive Puritan conception of a church-state in the New World had been founded on a lofty ideal. In Massa-

A Hartford House in 1660

chusetts, and as we have seen in New Haven, this had taken
the form of such a close relation between church and state
that, to all practical purposes, the two had been indistin-
guishable.   This ideal theory, in these two colonies, had
gone so far as to establish the government of the state upon
the bed rock of church membership.[1]   During the first years
of the Bay Colony this had worked out fairly well.   Religion,—and by that they meant the orthodox Calvinistic
theology of the original settlers,—was the chief passion of
these early founders, and the maintenance of it, in all its

[1] The first John Winthrop was no such democrat as was Thomas Hooker.
He was definitely opposed to universal suffrage. "The best part of a community," he wrote, "is always the least, and of that best part the wiser is
always the lesser." The church-membership franchise of early Massachusetts and New Haven was built on this oligarchical theory, Connecticut
on the universal-suffrage principle.

original purity, their chief political purpose. To maintain this the orthodox leaders had seen to it that the church membership was kept within the circle of the orthodox, and this had very naturally resulted in the ministers, whose authority in that matter was all but supreme, becoming very important factors in the civil government itself. But as the years had passed, and the original stout-hearted pioneers in this ideal church-state society had been succeeded by a second and less-rigidly orthodox generation, public sentiment in Massachusetts regarding the church-membership franchise had changed. By the year 1684 it was said that but one in five of the citizens of that colony were church members and thus voters on public affairs. The "Half-way Covenant" of 1657, though the result of quite different causes, had operated to ameliorate this condition, and Charles II had insisted upon the entire abolition of the old suffrage laws just before he died. While the extension of the suffrage to non-church members was slow, it was fought with tremendous energy by the older party, which recognized in its approaching success the end of the old régime. It had been to wage a final fight against it, as we have seen, that John Davenport had left New Haven, where the battle had been lost, for Boston, where it was still proceeding under President Chauncey of Harvard. Under Andros the new party had had for the moment an ascendancy, but the moment that he had been expelled, the orthodox theocrats, led by Increase Mather, the new Harvard leader, had regained their ground.

But now, in the charter of 1692, the last vestige of the old religious order, in so far as its political side was concerned, had passed away in the Royal command that a property qualification should replace membership in the traditional Massachusetts churches as the basis for the franchise. The disintegration of the New England churches, which had been coming on ever since the days of the struggle over the "Half-way Covenant," now proceeded by rapid strides. Bereft of political power, the churches now found themselves losing ground as a spiritual power. Five years had not passed after the new charter had been secured, before the freethinking element among the Boston folk, led by Thomas Brattle and John Coleman and John Leverett, established in the town that new and liberal church which led Cotton Mather to exclaim in his diary: "I see Satan beginning a terrible shake in the churches of New England. Wherefore I set apart this day again for prayers in my study, to cry mightily unto God." The breakup of the old Massachusetts Puritan theocracy, all but complete with the introduction of the new political conditions of the charter of 1692, was now about to come in earnest. The witchcraft explosion of 1692, in Salem and Boston, was the dying convulsion of the old theocracy. Under such fanatical leaders as Cotton Mather and Stoughton and such temporarily misguided men as Samuel Sewall, the older party's intellectual balance seems to have been lost. The progressive leaders of the new party would have none of the Salem delusion.

What had been going on in Connecticut during this period now calls for attention.

IV

Whatever one may have to say of the comparative conditions in the two commonwealths in later years, it is certainly true that in this first half-century of their history, Connecticut, excluding primitive New Haven, had had a broader and more liberal community and religious life than had Massachusetts. Thomas Hooker built a strong social structure in that crude Connecticut Colony of his at Hartford and Windsor, Wethersfield and Farmington,—a structure which rested on the broadest and soundest principles (viewed from our modern conception of a democratic government) of any of the New England Colonies. "In matters of greater consequence," he had written to Governor Winthrop on his removal to Connecticut, "which concern the common good, a general council, chosen by all, to transact business which concern all, I conceive, under favor, most suitable to rule and most safe for relief of the whole." In his sermons Hooker went even further, and laid down, in his "assertion of the right of the people not only to choose but to limit the power of their rulers [as Johnston, Connecticut's historian, says], an assertion which lies at the foundation of the American system. . . . The birthplace of American democracy is Hartford."

It was because of this difference between the two Colonies that Massachusetts, during these years after 1660, had had an experience more akin to New Haven's early history than to Connecticut's. When the Connecticut absorption of New Haven had come, the dissatisfied old Davenport party, as we have seen in the elder Pierson's case, and again in Davenport's, left to carry on the original theocratic principles in other places. As a result, Connecticut had amalgamated all of its warring public elements, had found itself practically rid of dissenters from its church-and-state policy for the next twenty years, and thus had suffered little of the theological and political internal turmoil that was the lot of Massachusetts, still bent on carrying out the original theocratic theory. So that the suffrage question had never been a serious one either in the old or in the new Connecticut.

Nor had the political complications of the older colony with England had their counterpart in Connecticut. The annulment of the Connecticut charter had not been officially enrolled, as it had happened, when Charles II had summarily canceled the New England charters in 1684. The Colony had adroitly avoided giving up that charter to Andros in the following year at Hartford, and had merely renewed its former home rule under the original charter when William III succeeded his uncle. Connecticut having had no occasion to seek a new charter, as Massachusetts had been obliged to do in 1692, thus escaped the complications that we have recalled in the older colony. With the Winthrop charter of 1662, Connecticut entered upon a long and quiet provincial life, without internal difficulties of any serious sort, enjoying a peacefulness that compares strikingly, as we turn the yellowed pages of the ancient histories, with the uproars and confusions, political and theological, of the contemporary Massachusetts. So careful had the Connecticut people been to avoid notice by and entanglements with the Crown, that they had managed to reinstate their own elected magistrates without attracting attention from London, and even succeeded in securing a legal confirmation from the Royal Secretaries in England of their original charter, with its right to elect their own Colony officers.

While, on the religious side that was so prominent a part of this second period in New England history, Connecticut had seen after 1660 no such irruptions as had exploded in Boston, a very considerable change had taken place in the attitude of the people toward the churches and the place of the churches in the state. The "Half-way Covenant"— permitting the children of non-church members to be baptized—had had small results in Connecticut, so far as any fundamental change in the suffrage was concerned. Thomas Hooker had founded his Colony on that very freedom of the vote which it took the "Half-way Covenant" and

Charles II combined to force upon the older element in Massachusetts. And for the first decade that change had had little or no effect on the broadening of church membership. The real difficulty in Connecticut during this period seems to have lain in the continued feeling of independence of the separate church congregations from legislative, town, or synod control, and the consequent difficulties of settlement of such internal troubles as they had over the choice of ministers and the demand of outsiders to be given the right to vote on church questions in return for their duty of paying taxes in support of the church and minister.

Yet there had been one very great public change. The gradual adoption, after 1664, under legislative urging, of the "Half-way Covenant" had resulted (in the large) in a gradual decline of the church, both as a public institution and as the upholder of the individual religious sentiment with which the founders of the colonies had been so ardently endowed. So that, some twenty years after the reorganization of Connecticut, matters religious had reached the lowest point in the history of the Colony. Divisions in the churches had sprung up broadcast, and the widespread religious declension had resulted in a number of originally strong churches (among them those at New Haven, Branford, and Milford) being without settled ministers for protracted periods. If the educational and commercial and political ambitions of early New Haven and of Connecticut had by 1660 come to the low pass described in previous pages, two decades later the religious plans of the settlers had fallen into as sad repute. It was when a remedy for this situation was looked for as described in the following chapter that these seacoast towns of Connecticut entered upon a renewed agitation of the project for John Davenport's Colony college.

CHAPTER II

NEW HAVEN AND JAMES PIERPONT

I

E left the Hopkins Grammar School starting out in 1668 as a small endowed Latin school on the New Haven Market-place, under the management of a board of trustees chosen from the New Haven church and town and from Connecticut Colony officialdom. For the seventeen years now to elapse, this new Hopkins school led much the same chequered existence as its unlucky predecessors. For the first nine years of this period, Samuel Street, the minister's son and a Harvard graduate, was in charge. Upon his resignation in 1673 the school was practically closed, not having sufficient public support again to afford a teacher. The impecunious George Pardee now reascended the rostrum and for several years, to the few boys who appeared before him, taught English grammar and as much of Cheever's Latin "Accidence" as he himself could comprehend. But this was again but little. The "college" project having long since entirely dropped out of sight, the New Haven grammar school, which John Davenport had propped up so many times without result, again seemed tottering on its last legs.

This New Haven condition, however, had its counterpart throughout the new Connecticut. There had been a general educational decline during this period, in the entire Colony. So serious was this, in its important relations to the continuing of an orthodox ministry for the churches, that, in 1672, the legislature acted on the matter, granting each of the four counties public lands for the upkeep of their grammar schools, and requiring every town of more than one hundred families to maintain one. But New Haven still lagged behind and was publicly complained of for not keeping a grammar school under the Colony law. The upshot was a "loving debate" in a New Haven town meeting, ending in an appropriation of town money and the hiring of another schoolmaster. By 1684 the results of this final action seem to have been fairly successful. The new Hopkins Grammar School on the Market-place was established, and was now admitting the New Haven boys free, and charging outsiders ten shillings, dividing its scholars into "English" and "Latin" groups, teaching the latter what was required by Harvard College at that time, and excluding "all Girls, as Improper & inconsistent with such a Grammar Schoole, as ye law injoines & is ye Designe of this Settlement." The Latin required at this period was sufficient to understand Cicero and to recite Latin prose and verse from memory; in Greek the boys were put through the elements of the grammar only.

I have told of the group of boys who went up to Harvard during Ezekiel Cheever's New Haven days, and of the hiatus that then ensued, owing to the financial disasters of the people. A perusal of the antiquarian records of Harvard College shows how few were the Connecticut matriculations up to 1690. During this period only some thirty New Haven and Connecticut boys were graduated among the nearly three hundred Harvard graduates. Roughly speaking, New Haven had sent up eleven of these, Hartford eight, Milford and the present Clinton (then Killingworth) two each, and Guilford, Branford, Stratford, Middletown, Windsor, and Wethersfield, one each. No New Haven boy went up, after Cheever had left, until Samuel Street, the son of John Davenport's second assistant minister, who received his degree in 1664. John Harriman, to be graduated two years later, was the son of the New Haven innkeeper (a highly honorable calling in those hospitable days), and he, with Abraham Pierson of Branford, was the sole New Haven college product of the canny Jeremiah Peck. Twelve years later two more New Haven youths went to Harvard,—one of them that little Noadiah Russell who was to be one of the founders of the Collegiate School. John Davenport's grandson, later to return to Connecticut and to take a foremost place in these pages, was graduated in 1687, but can hardly be called a New Haven school product, as he matriculated from Boston.

The older Connecticut Colony's slower rise in educational ambitions has been noted in the fact that no Connecticut boys went to Harvard until New Haven's first flush of energy was dying out. The four remaining Hartford youths went up at various intervals later on. Of the men later to be identified with the Collegiate School, but two went to Harvard from their Connecticut homes after 1662: Nathaniel Higginson, the son of the colleague of Rev. Mr. Whitfield, of Guilford, who was graduated in 1670, and Timothy Woodbridge, of Killingworth, graduated in 1675.

Of these thirty or so Connecticut graduates of Harvard before 1690, twenty-three became ministers. Nine of these latter settled about Hartford, and one went to Stratford, one to Stamford, and one to Killingworth. Three taught in the New Haven school for brief periods, and one became a magistrate in New Haven. Taken as a whole, with the purpose in mind of the New Haven and Connecticut Colony founders to provide a second generation of educated public leaders for "church and commonwealth," this short list of Harvard graduates from the two Colonies was but another phase of the general failure of the original plans. Not only had church and school development been checked at home, but there had been a signal decline in the colonists' interest in sending to the only higher educational institution of New England a succession of youths who could be relied upon to return to their communities and carry forward the primitive faith of their fathers.[1] This fact had its distinct bearing upon the situation which was shortly to force upon the Connecticut leaders,—particularly those near New Haven,—a realization of their need of a home institution.

We have recalled the lapse in the ministry in three of the original New Haven Jurisdiction churches, New Haven, Branford, and Milford. In New Haven, the gentle-mannered and mild Rev. Nicholas Street,—Oxford graduate and assistant to John Davenport after Hooke had departed to Cromwell's unstable protection,—had been min-

---

[1] It was merely another indication of the partial failure of New England's idealistic church and educational theory, that measures had to be taken early to keep in New England the young fellows educated at Harvard. When the "College-corn" contributions were falling off, the New Haven people were told that it would not be used for any Harvard scholars who were not to remain in the country. Harvard itself had to take action on the matter later, as the number of young graduates removing to England had become a serious question.

ister for many years. But the Reverend Street was possessed of no special qualifications for public leadership in
the declining times of his ministry, his church had slowly
disintegrated, and he had been succeeded by a series of
temporary preachers. Matters had gone from bad to
worse, and the church people, owing to their division over
the acceptance of the "Half-way Covenant" in their membership, were divided over the call to a new minister. So
low had Davenport's great scheme fallen that the town now
took over the unsteady support of the church to save it from
entire failure. Its independent identity gone in the changed
conditions under Connecticut, its school and church nearly
extinct, its business in a state of general collapse, with no
leaders like the old ones, with such as there were now
resident in adjacent towns, and with the Royal Governor
Andros parading the countryside and ordering the unseating
of the Colony's magistrates in the name of a Romanist
King, New Haven's original dream of a permanent Puritan
commonwealth in the New World had now fallen away
like a house of cards.

It was at this low tide in New Haven's higher fortunes
that a new personality was to come to the disheartened community, and,—exercising that spirit of leadership during
new and better times which John Davenport himself showed
in the primitive days,—bring in a new era, in which we shall
find ourselves much interested.

The three churches at Branford, Milford, and New
Haven, now called to their pulpits three young Harvard
graduates. Branford called the Rev. Samuel Russel; Milford, the Rev. Samuel Andrew; and New Haven, the Rev.
James Pierpont.

II

These three young men were of about the same age and
all were Massachusetts-born. Samuel Andrew, the eldest

of them, had been graduated from Harvard in 1675, and
had been a Fellow there under President Urian Oakes, and
a tutor. At Harvard he had been a classmate of the Rev.
Timothy Woodbridge, who, oddly enough, was ordained to
preach at Hartford on the same day in 1685 that Andrew
began his career at the old Prudden church in Milford.
Samuel Russel was graduated in 1681. He was the son of
that minister at Hadley, Massachusetts, who had had a
large share in diverting to Hadley that part of the original
Hopkins gift which had been given to Connecticut under
the Hopkins will, and who had sheltered the Regicides in
his parsonage. The younger Russel must have known of
the secreting of Colonel Goffe in his father's house at
Hadley, and imbibed strong anti-Royalist sympathies
thereby. He had been teaching in the Hopkins Grammar
School in Hadley when he was called to the elder Pierson's
vacant pulpit in Branford. James Pierpont, the third of
this group, was a classmate of Russel's.[1] He was a Rox-
bury boy, and, since leaving Harvard in 1681, had been
awaiting a call to the ministry.

James Pierpont arrived in New Haven over the old
Post-road from Boston in August, 1684. Heralded by the
church committee who had been sent to look him over, as
"a godly man, a good scholar, a man of good parts," and
"likely to make a good instrument," he had been recommended by the deacon who had chosen him as one who
would "desire peace in the church and town and rejoice to
hear of it, and that there may be no after-troubles." To
this end the New Haven people had assembled in their
homes and Meeting-house for a day of fasting and prayer,

[1] The Harvard Class of 1681 contained four men who were to have
important places in Yale's early history. Besides Samuel Russel and James
Pierpont, a third member of this Harvard Class, Noadiah Russell, was to
be one of the founders of the Collegiate School. The fourth was John
Davie, whose financial aid to the enterprise will later be told.

"wherein to confess their sins before God," and "beg pardon." So that young James Pierpont, now twenty-nine years old, began his life work in John Davenport's historic church with good hopes of a reawakened town giving him more support than it had given his itinerant predecessors in its long-vacant pulpit.

I suppose that this young newcomer to the New Haven Meeting-house was probably not the equal of John Davenport in purely intellectual endowments. He does not rank with his New England contemporaries in this respect, as Davenport did with his. But one sermon of Pierpont's has come down to us, his "Sundry False Hopes of Heaven, discovered and decried," preached at Cotton Mather's North Church in Boston in 1711 and published with a characteristically laudatory preface by Mather. Though this sermon falls short of the originality and intellectual vigor that mark the performances of Davenport, "it proves,"—if we may rely upon Dr. Leonard Bacon's dictum,—"that its author's eminence was not accidental." Yet he was unusually endowed in other ways. He was the possessor of social graces and a force of character that were to make him one of the leaders of his times and to gain him a success in life that had been denied Davenport. Contemporary references sufficiently bear this out. The sprightly diarist, Madam Knight, for instance, journeying through New Haven in 1704, wrote him down as "the holy Mr. Pierpont." He was "greatly distinguished," says Dr. Bacon, "and highly honored in his day." In that preface to his Boston sermon which Cotton Mather wrote, he said that Pierpont "has been a rich blessing to the Church of God," and added: "New Haven values him; all Connecticut honors him. They have cause to do it."

There exists a contemporary painting of James Pierpont, done at Boston in 1711 "by a superior English artist,"

doubtless when Pierpont was preaching of a week-end to
Cotton Mather's conservative Boston folk. It shows a
face of more than usual sweetness and charm. In it is a
certain gentleness, far different from the bold austerity
which we associate with the long-faded lineaments of his
predecessor. It shows James Pierpont with his long curly
hair falling over his shoulders, instead of the usual wig of
his day, and his white square ministerial band on his chest.
His forehead is high and broad, his mouth sensitive, his
large, dark eyes contemplative and even beautiful. This
old painting well conveys the feeling of a spiritual leader
and a well-born gentleman.

And well-born James Pierpont was. His grandfather,
James Pierrepont, was a Puritan refugee, and a nephew
through a younger line of the Sir Henry Pierrepont from
whom sprang the Dukes of Kingston, and of Sir Henry's
sister who married Francis Beaumont the playwright. And
he was interested in this connection. An odd story might be
told[1] of the long effort of the New Haven Pierponts, living
in the crude little Connecticut village, to establish a right
to the succession to the Kingston dukedom in the event of
a lapse in male heirs of the elder branch. This effort was
mildly begun by James Pierpont when writing to Jeremiah
Dummer, the London agent, in 1711, and was energetically
continued by his son. The story tells how that son urged
matters with much enthusiasm, and how he was finally fore-
stalled by a cousin who, not content with merely introducing himself by letter, went over to England in person and,
calmly assuming the New Haven Pierponts' claim, was
received with amusement by His Grace and had a more
fortunate experience with him than Thackeray's Harry
Warrington had with his relatives. At the time that the

[1] Mr. Henry T. Blake has an entertaining account of this in volume VII
of the New Haven Colony Historical Society Papers.

Rev. James Pierpont was making his mild beginnings in this sequence of events, the Earl of Kingston was that Evelyn Pierrepont who had married a cousin of Henry Fielding and whose daughter, Lady Mary Wortley Montagu, was to become famous as the author of one of the most agreeable volumes of tittle-tattle of the times. Lady Mary tells of the scandalous costume of the fair Elizabeth Chudleigh at the King's fancy ball. She is said to have been the prototype of Thackeray's "Beatrice Esmond." When the kindly New Haven minister was unsuccessfully trying to find some way in which his branch of the Pierrepont family might be brought to the attention of Evelyn Pierrepont, Duke of Kingston, that gracious noble, in peruke and sword, was dangling at the embroidered petticoats of Miss Chudleigh, and giving no small amount of piquancy to the gossip of London and the Court thereby.

III

But all of this fashionable world of over the seas was far removed from the provincial life of such a New England minister as James Pierpont. A far more serious business lay before him than this Vanity Fair of William and Mary's Court, as he found himself commencing his career in John Davenport's old pulpit in New Haven. He had work to do.

We may please ourselves with the picture of this young Harvard graduate, as he enters on that long life in New Haven during which he was to prove of such usefulness to his people and to the generations which followed him.

He comes by horseback over the King's Highway, this energetic young Congregational clergyman, accompanied by a man sent over New London way to meet him on his journey. He is doubtless met at the Neck by the sedately-garbed deacons of the church, and brought to town over the

Second Meeting-House
1685

old College Oystershell-fields, to enter the outskirts of the New Haven village of 1684 about where Olive Street now is. The widow of John Davenport's only son was now living in the ancestral Davenport homestead on lower Elm Street, with her daughter Abigail, then twelve years old,— her son John then being in his Sophomore year at Harvard. To this house, so full of memories of the first John Davenport, the youthful James Pierpont is doubtless escorted through the shady lanes of the village, bowed to reverently by the men (and observed as cannily), and peeked at through the casement windows of the village houses by maids and maidens to whom the coming of so noble a bachelor divine was an event of no little romance and importance. Here, in the library looking down over the fields and orchards to the harbor, where old John Davenport had ruled his theocracy for twenty-odd years, the young Pierpont settles down to take his place in a new generation and carry forward the church.

And I fancy that we may properly enough find in this accidental circumstance a double inspiration for the young Harvard minister. Coming from the increasingly liberal Massachusetts of his recent years at Harvard, young Pierpont agreeably found himself in the midst of a New England church life of the primitive type. To many of his congregation, this life was still of the old Davenport pattern, in spite of the Connecticut absorption, and, for his first year, he was to be the guest of a daughter of the elder Pierson and daughter-in-law of old John Davenport. It was this early sympathetic touch with the older New Haven that was largely responsible, I fancy, for the immediate success which James Pierpont had in bridging over the gap to the new generation of which he was now the leader.

During this first year of James Pierpont's life in New Haven, the church people were building a new parsonage

for him, on the Eldred lot on Elm Street. The new minister had come with few personal belongings, so the villagers
furnished the parsonage for him, one man bringing, as his
best gift, two elm saplings which he planted before the
house door. These elms became in time an historic landmark in New Haven. Under their broad canopy, forty-odd
years later, Jonathan Edwards was to woo James Pierpont's
daughter. Under them, in twenty years more, Whitefield
was to stir up the religious emotions of the townspeople in
the Great Awakening. They were to see the little troop of
New Haven militiamen march off with Benedict Arnold
to fight the British at Cambridge, and, come the turn of
life's wheel, see the effigy of that debonair militia captain
hooted through the village streets after his apostasy to the
British. They were to see the British troops in 1779
parade noisily into the quiet town and bivouac on the Green.
One of these trees was said to be standing as late as 1840,
"the tallest and most venerable of all the trees in this city
of elms and ever the first to be tinged with green at the
return of spring."

IV

The Puritan village in which James Pierpont thus began
his career of thirty full years was still more or less in its
original condition. It had been repalisaded against the
threatening troubles of King Philip's War but a decade
before, and a few of the great gates that had then been
erected at the street ends of the outer square were no doubt
still in use, if only to keep in the cattle. The Market-place
was still much as it had been in John Davenport's day,
though there were fewer trees and more tree-stumps. The
causeway that Davenport and Governor Eaton had used to
cross the alder swamp was now gone, and a new and larger
wooden Meeting-house had been built in the middle of the

Market-place, a little southwest of the first one. The watch-house and the stocks still stood on the College Street side, though perhaps less used than formerly. The original log schoolhouse of Ezekiel Cheever and John Bowers was still in use, though now, somewhat enlarged, the Hopkins Colony Grammar School. A few improvements had come in with the absorption with Connecticut, and the town was not, in many ways, as provincial as it had been a few decades before. Yet the people lived under very much the same social conditions as in 1650. The ancient town watch had passed out as a standing police force, as had the town drummer, whose merry business it had been for twoscore years to beat the town drum at sunset and for half an hour before sunrise, and twice on Sabbath days. The long roll of the too-lively Bassett's drum had been superseded in 1681 by the jingling echoes of a church bell that had been purchased after much wagging of heads from a tramp skipper anchored in the harbor. One Joseph Pardee, son of the impecunious schoolmaster, was the bell ringer when Pierpont arrived, and, except for one short period when the bell was sent to England for repairs, was to make its music float out over the village tree-tops on Sabbath days and for curfew at nine o'clock each night while Pierpont was the minister. With all these changes, the Town Crier had become an institution, and, as occasion called, paraded the sandy footpaths along the village streets, calling out lost cattle and strayed children, notices of sales and public meetings, and such great news as might come in by travelers or in letters from abroad.

Nor had the character of the New Haven people, or their manners and affairs, changed much since John Davenport had left them. All of the original commercial promise of the settlement had long since disappeared, and, while there was a little trading by the Sound, especially to Boston, the people had but little to do except to plant the fields, trap for furs, and attend to the manifold handicraft occupations of every small community. Except in their dress, the people of James Pierpont's New Haven had not progressed very far beyond John Davenport's. The great change in this respect that the arrival of the retinues and hangers-on of the Royal Governors had made in New York and Boston, had not at this date permeated to New Haven. So that the magnificent wardrobes of some of the Boston English-i-fied dandies of the day were hardly paralleled here. No such ornamental persons paraded the village streets of New Haven in 1685 as were not infrequent sights in the Boston lanes of the day. These gentry, so the old inventories and diaries tell us, wore such splendid garments as "satin coates" embroidered with gold flowers, and blue breeches, or scarlet coats and breeches, and "damask small clothes." Yet the New Haveners of that day were not too provincially attired. Wigs, of course (those "horrid bushes of vanity"), were now common elsewhere in New England,— even servants and soldiers, and sometimes children, wearing them. Doubtless many New Haven burghers wore them under their now lower if still broad-brimmed black beaver and castor hats. Perhaps some of the better class of men in Pierpont's congregation (like the New London gentry of their acquaintance) wore broadcloth coats with red linings, and white serge coats, cut square after Charles II's Royal dictum. They all still wore the great capes of the early days, though the old Elizabethan doublets had long disappeared for jerkins and coats. Here and there some wealthy citizen might have a bit of lace at his shirt front or wristband. Everybody, however, wore gloves from England, men and women alike wore muffs and rings and riding masks, and the women sun-masks of divers colors. The Town Crier no doubt frequently called articles of this

Governor Andros
in
New Haven

sort up and down the village streets, when some messenger arrived from Boston with the latest fashions in that dress which, in spite of all Puritan qualms and regulations, persisted in being of the keenest interest to all New England provincials.

It may well have been the Town Crier who, two years after James Pierpont had settled in his new house facing the Market-place, gave first notice of the approaching visit of the Royalist Governor, Sir Edmund Andros. This Colonial officer, tradition has it, had arrived in New Haven fresh from his unlucky rebuff before the General Assembly at Hartford, where the Colony charter had been hidden in reply to his Excellency's demand for it. His visit, therefore, was something of a test of the stuff of which the young New Haven clergyman was made, as it also furnished a proof of how far he had come, in his few years out of Harvard, into the independent political attitude of his New Haven congregation. Under the circumstances, it is a fair guess that the Royal officer stopped at John Harriman's tavern instead of at the minister's house. It was of a Sunday, and the spirit of John Davenport that was in James Pierpont rose to the occasion (if the story of that day can be believed, as I hope it may). Andros and his retinue walked across the Market-place to the Meeting-house, where all of the townspeople who could manage it were on hand. But though in Royalist New Jersey or New York the occasion might well have been one of special services, young Pierpont, facing the Royal officer's party over the heads of his stalwart deacons, conducted the services with as little consideration of the rank of his new auditors or to their feelings as John Davenport himself had tendered to that visiting Royalist predecessor who had listened to his belligerent sermon on hiding the Regicides. The young Harvard minister selected for the hymn,—so the story goes,—reading from his high pulpit each line before it was sung, as was the custom in those days, that vigorous hymn of independence of the old Puritan churches, which began

> Why dost thou tyrant boast abroad
> Thy wicked words to praise,

and which ended, undoubtedly to the keen relish of Pierpont's black-cloaked congregation, if to the astonished anger of the scarlet-resplendent Andros in the chief pew below,

> Thou dost delight in fraud and guile
> In mischief, blood and wrong.
> Thy lips have learned the flatt'ring style
> O, false deceitful tongue!

Under a young minister who could be as bold as this in those trying times, the New Haven church again prospered. A dozen years slipped by, quiet years for the minister and his provincial little flock. During them Pierpont wooed and won the fair daughter of the widow Davenport and busily attended to his congregation's souls, until a question arose which was, in the outcome, to be a most important one for the Colony.

James Pierpont's *Chair and Table*

Increase Mather

CHAPTER III

THE NEED OF A COLONY COLLEGE

1

HIS question was the old one of a college for New Haven. As to just when the renewal of this old ambition of John Davenport's was made, or who made it, the old-time records are silent. It is not until about the years 1700-1701 that we find any documents relating to the plan, and it is not until that time that we find any of the Colony leaders becoming publicly active in its behalf. Yet, without doubt, the reëmergence of the old New Haven college project during or just before 1700 was not as sudden as it may seem. It was the logical conclusion of a general situation, largely theological, that had been forming during the years just after 1692.

It would take a theologian to understand all of the complications of that period of Puritan religious decline; yet the general outlines of things are clear enough. I have referred to the efforts to work out a new state-and-church system in the face of a growing town independence in Connecticut in the first few years after the new charter. If we add to this difficulty the further complication that the churches themselves rather generally seem to have held to the original ideal of subservience to no earthly master, and yet were declining in power and being taken over by the towns, we may understand a little of the situation. The Hartford church split, ending in the settlement of Hadley, had been one result of this. There were other similar divisions elsewhere, as at Wethersfield and Windsor, and in 1650 the Assembly had to forbid the formation of new churches without the consent of the Court and of neighboring churches.

And another factor was entering into this church situation. About 1680 it was reported to England, in reply to an official query, that the "people, in this colony, are some of them strict congregational men, others more large congregational men, and some moderate presbyterians. The congregational men of both sorts are the greatest part of the people in the colony." The entrance of this "moderate presbyterian" idea had become a considerable factor in Connecticut ecclesiastical matters by the time James Pierpont arrived in New Haven, as it had in Massachusetts. While the time was not then ripe for the advanced step to be taken at the Saybrook Synod in 1708, and the formation of the modified Presbyterian form of church organization which was then adopted, the period of fifteen years before the year 1700 saw this question widely agitated, and the controversy over it becoming one of the principal public matters of the day. I do not think that we can pore over the old records of church and Colony affairs during this period without coming to the conclusion that this growing demand for some sort of church union to take the place of the complete independence of the early churches, was one of the principal factors in that demand which, in 1700, was to come for a Colony college. The commonwealth had found itself possessed in the Winthrop charter of centralized authority over its independent towns; the churches were now groping toward a "consociation" which would bring about a somewhat similar, though much looser, central or at least common authority over church affairs; as a bulwark of this latter development, there were to be those who favored a college, under the associated-church control, which should furnish the churches with their ministers.

The need of these orthodox religious leaders, as we have seen, had from the first been a serious problem. After the year 1692, when the inhabitants of the Colony had increased very considerably, and when many new towns and churches had been established, this need became acute. As the venerable historian, Trumbull, says: "the calls for a learned ministry, to supply the churches, became more and more urgent," and, in consequence, "a number of the ministers conceived the purpose of founding a college in Connecticut. By this means, they might educate young men, from among themselves, for the sacred ministry, and for various departments in civil life, and diffuse literature and piety more generally among the people."

But another, and, broadly speaking, even more important, situation had been developing. This was Connecticut's relation to Harvard itself, and to Massachusetts. We have seen how President Dunster's Harvard troubles had started a New Haven college agitation in Davenport's day. President Mather's difficulties were now leading to a renewed interest in that situation. This, taken together with the

growing demand for a church organization at home, fur-
nishes us with the main background for the talk that now
began again among the Connecticut ministers for a college
of their own.

A letter written in 1723 by the Rev. Moses Noyes, of
Lyme, one of the founders of the Collegiate School, is to
the effect that "The first movers for a college in Connecticut
alleged this as a reason, because the college at Cambridge
was under the tutorage of latitudinarians." Another letter
of that later time, from two other trustees, has it that "our
fountain" was "hoped to have been and continued the
repository of truth and the reserve of pure and sound principles, doctrine, and education, in case of a change in our
mother Harvard." It is doubtless true that, in a surface
analysis, local conditions, and the demand therefrom resulting for a Connecticut college to uphold the Connecticut
churches, were to be the chief reasons for the founding of
the Collegiate School. There can be no serious question,
however, that these references to the Harvard of the last
years of the 17th Century point to a second and perhaps
even more important factor in that demand. Just what that
situation was, it is therefore necessary to outline.

II

The breakdown of the original Puritan theocracy in
Massachusetts with the charter of 1692, and the rise of a
new political and religious faction under it, as evidenced in
such a case as the formation of the new Brattle church, had
placed the supporters of the old régime in that Colony in
a precarious position. After that year, old Increase
Mather, the spiritual head of the conservative party (which
contained such men as Stoughton, and Judge Sewall, and
Secretary Addington), had found himself rapidly losing his

Harvard College in 1700

former hold on public affairs and on the theological opinions of his people. Shut out from his erstwhile public influence and facing a new church movement, it was therefore with very good reason that Increase Mather began to look, after 1692, upon Harvard College as the last remaining sphere in which he and his fellow conservatives could maintain their former grip on political affairs and preserve the threatened purity of the Calvinistic theology which they and their forefathers had preached.

Yet even here, the new Massachusetts political situation was having its serious results. The annulment of the Massachusetts charter by Charles II had carried with it the loss of the Harvard charter, originally given to it by the Colony Court. So it had to have a new one, and that new one had to be brought into line with the new public conditions in Massachusetts and accepted by the English Crown. The new relation to England had brought about the first steps in what was to prove a radical change in the character and manners and church interests of the Boston people. A miniature Royal court had been set up in Puritan Boston by the English Governors, the imported riffraff of which brought over English ideas and customs and extravagance of dress. Massachusetts was becoming Londonized in its scale of living, and losing its old austerity and religious seriousness. Nor was this all. New theological views came over with the Royal Governors and Church of England communicants. A new Congregationalism, much more liberal and far less open to hypocrisies for political ends than the old, was developing in Boston as an offshoot of the Latitudinarian movement in London. Its adherents both in and out of the College circles desired a share in the government of Harvard and proposed to get it. To President Mather and his son Cotton, this situation was the signal for a determined effort to preserve this last stronghold of the old faith and manners, if not their last chance to regain something of their own fast-dwindling prestige.

And so we see a battle royal,—the last stand of the old Puritan guard against the incoming new times,—beginning by 1692 in that Harvard from which the Connecticut ministers were still hoping to receive their new generations of preachers of the older church. The chronicles of this seven-year war are lighted up by highly entertaining episodes for us of today, serious enough as they were to the participants in them. Old Increase Mather, intent on fortifying this last refuge for himself and the traditional church, made five separate onslaughts on the General Court to secure a new Harvard charter which should give him what he wanted. His complete failure spelled the last stand of the old party. For, from his first effort for such a charter to his last, the old Puritan fighter was meeting increasingly heavy odds. And he must have seen the handwriting on the wall from the first Harvard charter which he drew up and somehow or other passed through the General Court and put into effect before it had been received for acceptance by the English Crown. In that charter he had named a perpetual body of Harvard trustees from among his friends, including his son, and this corporation had immediately given him the honorary degree of Doctor of Divinity, the first to be granted in this country. President Mather, however, had proceeded without waiting for the signing of this new charter by the King, so that the sudden arrival of William's veto of it must have been extremely embarrassing to him, as well as a source of keen amusement to that large body of Boston citizens who, under the new charter, were against him. Other attempts at a new charter failing, President Mather, in 1697, rose to his last effort. In this he inserted a religious-qualification clause, which harked back, of course, to the Mather Congregationalism and the Cambridge Plat-

form for its theology.   Passed by the General Court, it was
as promptly vetoed by the newly-arrived English Governor, Bellamont, and the end was in sight of the Mather
effort to keep the broadening Harvard in the traditional
Puritan church fold.

III

By the year 1699, therefore, we can see that Harvard
College was fast slipping into the control of the reform
party in the church and Colony, a party that proposed to
have the suffrage broadened so as to include all members
of the churches, and to admit Church of England members
to it as well, and that, theologically, proposed to reform
New England religious thinking along new and, for the
time, advanced and even heretical lines.   The Mathers,
and such members of their circle as were still in public life,
were now all but defeated.   A new generation was coming
upon the scene in Massachusetts that was more inclined to be
at peace with the Crown than the sturdy old original
settlers ever had been willing to be.   And, so far as President Mather's relations to Harvard were concerned, there,
also, he was losing ground.   An important factor, personal
with President Mather, had contributed to this later situation.   In spite of repeated urgings and indeed several orders
by the General Court, the elder Mather had peremptorily
declined to resign his Boston church and remove to Cambridge and there be in residence as the College head.   In his
long absences across the river in Boston, the College affairs
had been in the hands of two young tutors,—John Leverett,
later to become President of Harvard, and William Brattle,
classmates at Harvard in 1680, and one year senior there to
James Pierpont and Samuel Russel.   Both, as it happened,
were recruits to the new church that was starting in Boston,
and both were hostile to all of the ceremonials of the

traditional theology and church government. Brattle had become the local minister in Cambridge during this period, and was there introducing. the new Congregationalism. Both he and Leverett were excluded from the College in the proposed charter of 1697, and both left it at that time, to throw themselves into the new theological movement and to help start Coleman's new Boston church.

We may well surmise, therefore, that by the year 1699, not only were political conditions in the old Massachusetts Colony such as to cause fear that, unless the tide were stemmed, the days of the traditional Puritan church in New England were numbered, but the religious-reform movement threatened to sap the traditional orthodoxy of Harvard itself and result in sending a new sort of minister into the churches, tinctured with the Latitudinarianism of the new religious faction. There can hardly be doubt that this condition, coming to a serious climax in President Mather's final failure to force Harvard into his own mould, was a cause for very great interest and solicitude in far-away Connecticut, and that some of the Connecticut leaders were now giving it prolonged and prayerful thought. Increase Mather's resignation in October, 1700, and his enforced withdrawal about a year later, were but the after-events of a situation that, by 1698 or 1699, must have brought the proposed Connecticut college project to the forefront of public discussion in the younger colony.

So, while we now have no means of knowing the precise time when this project actively came up, I imagine that we shall be well within the truth if we consider it to have been somewhere between the years 1697 and 1700. Kingsley, in his "Yale College," suggests that it could not have been long after James Pierpont arrived in New Haven in 1685, and that its postponement at that time may have resulted from the upset public conditions that followed, in New

England, upon the long war between England and France which closed with the Peace of Ryswick in 1697. However that may be (and it is interesting to recall it) there could hardly have been much public support for such a new and, at the least, expensive enterprise as the establishment of a Connecticut college during these ruinous years. Connecticut, to be sure, was protected from French and Indian attacks from the north by her situation below Massachusetts; but her military and financial help was possible and was called upon. Captain Bull had been sent from Hartford with soldiers into New York. Throughout the French and Indian War, Connecticut contributed troops and money to the English Colonies' joint cause, spending upwards of £12,000 to this purpose, and even then got into such difficulties with a scheming New York Royal Governor that an agent had to be sent to England, at still further expense, to secure protection. But with the end of the war between William III and Louis XIV of France, there was a short lull until Queen Anne's War broke out in 1702, and the same struggle of Connecticut to keep from being annexed to New York began over again. It was no doubt during this brief respite from public relations with the neighboring Colony, and when Connecticut's church-organization question and Harvard's internal affairs were reaching the points described above, that the Connecticut college scheme was again seriously broached.

IV

The exact sequence in the events that now occurred, as well as the precise nature of some of those events, we do not now know. Contemporaneous records of the founding of Yale are extremely meager; nor was much added later,— by actors in this first scene in Yale history, or by historians of the next generation,—which can be said to make every feature of the episode wholly understandable. The question is still an open one, when and where the Collegiate School was actually "founded"; it is not precisely known what the relation to the project was, at its start, of a number of Colony leaders who afterwards became closely identified with it. I have attempted, in the following pages, however, to piece together what we do know about these rather interesting matters, and to present the facts so that we may at least have a realization of such of them as we may accept.

We have President Thomas Clap's authority[1] for the statement that "The Design of founding a College in the Colony of Connecticut was first concerted by the Ministers; among which the Rev. Mr. Pierpont of New Haven, Mr. Andrew of Milford, and Mr. Russel of Branford, were the most forward and active."

Of these three young men, James Pierpont has been given the leadership by all the chroniclers of Yale's beginnings, and with good reason. We have seen the kind of a man he was, and the influence that he wielded among his fellow ministers. He had become the owner of the books that John Davenport had been accumulating for a New Haven "college" library, and had thus become heir, in a sense, to the long-forgotten educational enterprise. And Pierpont had formed, early in his life at New Haven, still another connection with Davenport. During those first years, as we have seen, he had been a sentimental traveler down the shaded Elm Street footpath to the widow Davenport's house, where his famous predecessor had lived his long New Haven life, and there had been married to the youthful Abigail (granddaughter of John Davenport and the elder Abraham Pierson), whose death came three months later

[1] "The Annals or History of Yale-College," published at New Haven in 1766.

from exposure during a storm.[1]   So that John Davenport entered into James Pierpont's life in more ways than
one, and the connection bridges for us the gap between the
first efforts for a Colony college and its later establishment.

Under the frowning Calvinistic labels of the old Davenport books in Pierpont's parsonage library in New Haven,
and over the barrels of green wine, and the tobacco and
pipes, and rum, which he laid in from the thrifty Captain
Browne's voyages to Boston, there now must have begun
that long series of talks between him and his neighboring
ministers, Andrew, Russel, and Abraham Pierson, which

[1] James Pierpont married Sarah Haynes, granddaughter of Governor
Haynes of Connecticut, in 1694, and, on her early death, married Mary
Hooker, granddaughter of Thomas Hooker, in 1698. Sarah, daughter of
this third marriage, became the wife of Jonathan Edwards.

Increase Mather's house, Boston

were to do with the condition of the Colony, the serious affairs at Harvard, and the need of a college of their own.

In Connecticut, as we may well imagine Pierpont outlining the conditions that faced these ambitious young ministers, matters church-wise were going from bad to worse. But a few years before, the half-dozen New Haven County ministers had joined in instituting "lecture-days" to stem the rising tide of general indifference to spiritual matters. Even that effort had had to be supported by town-meeting vote, so that the town constables should be urged to "prevent all disorders" on lecture-days, "and particularly that there be no horse-racings, it being a great disorder." And it had been found necessary to have the town officers instruct the heads of families that on such days "none of their children or servants be allowed to frequent the ordinaries, or any private houses for tippling, neither with strangers or others," the "strangers" undoubtedly being such boozing sailors as had from the early times led New Haven youth into bibulous temptations.

To such a pass had come that Puritan religious fervor which the New Haven church had been established to make endure. Nor were the churches themselves much better off. The traditional independence of the several congregations had led to intolerable conditions, in that many young men— mostly Harvard graduates—who were hardly known to the settled ministers of other churches, and whose theological tendencies were, to say the least, under suspicion, were being informally introduced to vacant pulpits and settled there without the sanction of the older ministers. Matters were in such a state, Pierpont would have said, that, unless something definite were done, it would be but a short time before uninvited teachers of the new theology of the Brattles and John Leverett would be spreading from Boston through the Connecticut pulpits.

And even Harvard itself was in a dangerously unstable state, in relation to this impending trouble in the Connecticut churches. "Degrees at college" (Pierpont might, in 1699, have said, as wrote Trumbull a century later) "were esteemed no sufficient evidence of men's piety, knowledge of theology, or ministerial gifts and qualifications." So that the Harvard situation under Increase Mather, which we have noticed in previous pages, was likewise undoubtedly taking its place in these serious New Haven conferences. We have no absolute knowledge of James Pierpont's attitude toward the Harvard troubles of these few years before 1700. But, if we group together his later correspondence with both the Mathers; his friendly relations to the younger one, and his own position of compromise on the Connecticut Presbyterian movement in the days of the Saybrook Synod, we are probably safe in assuming that, between 1697 and 1700, James Pierpont was in active sympathy with the elder Mather's Harvard troubles and that these very largely came to form a part of his own thinking on the need of a college at home.

Quarterly ministers' meetings now began to be held in New Haven County, and to these meetings came the other ministers of the county. If we may rely upon tradition, the college project was undoubtedly now laid before these ministers, and, after it had been canvassed and the situation set forth pretty much as described above, before a still wider circle of Connecticut leaders, including "the principal gentlemen and ministers" of all four counties.

The Branford House Doors

CHAPTER IV

THE "FOUNDING" BY THE MINISTERS

I

 HILE the original leaders of the Colony had now passed off the stage, this wider circle of Connecticut "ministers and gentlemen" contained some of the strongest men in Connecticut colonial history. Robert Treat, of Milford, had just declined the Governorship after serving fifteen years, and, now an old man and famous for his military campaigns against the Indians at Springfield and Hadley and for his loyalty to the charter when Andros arrived at Hartford to take it away, was now Deputy Governor. He had been succeeded as Governor by Fitz-John Winthrop of New Lon-

don, son of that John Winthrop who had secured the Colony charter. It is among the ministers of the four counties, however, that we still find, by 1700, the leaders in public affairs. Their acquaintance, inasmuch as they will come to the front in the ensuing chapters, will be worth making.

In Hartford County the aged Gershom Bulkeley of Wethersfield, for many years unable to attend to church affairs, was one of the best known of these ministers. Three young Harvard men were in pulpits at Windsor, Glastonbury, and Simsbury. The county had, however, three Harvard graduates not far past forty years of age, who were among the active leaders in the Colony. These were Timothy Woodbridge of Hartford, Samuel Mather of the first church in Windsor, and Noadiah Russell of Middletown.

Of these, Samuel Mather was "little & feeble," as he said of himself, and was not in good health at this time; yet he had had "judgment, and consummate tact," as had been shown in his settlement of the long-standing Windsor church difficulties. "A solid & Orthodox Divine is also got to Heaven," wrote his classmate Sewall at his death many years later. He was a son-in-law of Deputy Governor Robert Treat. Noadiah Russell of Middletown, "little of stature, pious and holy" and a classmate of Pierpont and Samuel Russel, was in excellent standing among the Hartford ministers. He had been born in New Haven and gone to Harvard from the Hopkins Grammar School. He had made a catalogue of "ye double books" in the Harvard Library, had become the Ipswich schoolmaster, and there had compiled his famous almanacs which we shall refer to later on, and had then come to Middletown. He had early grown up under John Davenport's keen eye, and, as Middletown's minister, "well performed his work, and effectually

molded the character and formed the habits of the people"
there. There is an extant memorial of him where we read:

> His head with learning, prudence, holy art;
> Firm faith and love, humility his heart,
> Peaceful and meek, but yet with courage stout,
> Engaged the fiend and did him sorely rout.

Timothy Woodbridge, of Hartford, however, was the
leading Hartford County minister. A distinguished Colony
leader and a considerable figure in the early annals of Yale,
this Harvard graduate of 1675 was an able successor to
the responsibilities of Hooker and Haynes. He had been
born in the parish of Barford St. Martin's, Wiltshire,
England, the son of a clergyman and the grandson of
Governor Thomas Dudley of Massachusetts, and was at
this time forty-four years old. He appears to have been of
much importance in the Colony affairs of the day. He had
drafted the Colony Address to King William, and he was
a writer of more than the usual number of works,—all
sermons,—that came out of a Connecticut parsonage study
in his lifetime. In the fulsome obituary notices of the day
he was given a more than customary list of accomplishments. He was, it was said, "a star of the first Magnitude.
He had also an happy Evenness of Temper, and was
adorned with all social Virtues, whereby his Conversation
became sweet and amiable." Jonathan Edwards was to
say of him at his death that he had a "Comley Majestic
Aspect (being much Taller than the common Size)," and
that he had "Great Courtesy & Affability." As we shall see,
he was the leader of the opposition to James Pierpont in
the coming organization of the Collegiate School, though in
later years to become one of its strongest friends and supporters. Woodbridge seems to have been one of the leaders
in the Connecticut church-synod party.

In Fairfield County there were at that time four ministers: Israel Chauncy, then fifty-six years old, of Stratford;
Joseph Webb of Fairfield, and John Davenport of Stamford, both just past thirty; and the young Stephen Buckingham of Norwalk. They were an interesting and very
active group of public men. Israel Chauncy had been
graduated from Harvard in 1661, the third son of President Chauncey of Harvard to be in that class. Beginning
his career as the Stratford schoolmaster, he had been chosen
by the people there for their minister five years later, and
was the hero of the contemporaneously famous story which
had it that at his ordination by the laymen of his church the
good elder had forgotten to remove his gloves (it being a
cold December day) and, in the imposition of hands on
the new minister's head, had done his part in a leather
mitten. This affair of the "leather mitten" was made much
of by ridiculing Episcopalians of the time, and, later on, by
Presbyterians. Chauncy got into several heated theological
controversies at Stratford, and seems to have been a staunch
independent of the old school. He was chaplain of Colonel
Robert Treat's Indian expedition, and "chirugian," in which
latter post he used the considerable, though crude, medical
knowledge that he had picked up when at Harvard. Israel
Chauncy had in his day "a high reputation for scholarship."
He was, an old lady long afterwards said, "one of the
most benevolent, hospitable gentlemen" she ever knew.
He wrote the parts of the "New England Almanac" for
1663 dealing with the "Theory of Planetary Orbs" and
eclipses. Joseph Webb was prepared for Harvard under
our old acquaintance, Ezekiel Cheever, at Boston, was
"thence translated to the College at Cambridge and de-
servedly wore the Honours of it," was graduated in the
Class of 1684, and was now thirty-four years of age and
minister at Fairfield. While a Sophomore at Harvard

young Webb had come under the Corporation's discipline
for hazing Freshman, refusing to obey College rules, and
staying away when President Rogers sent for him. He
was expelled, and, having asked for his Bible with his name
on the fly leaf, was given it by Increase Mather, then a
Fellow, who handed it to him after tearing out the leaf.
But the young culprit, even after this harsh treatment,
publicly apologized and was reinstated. He had now been
at Fairfield for six years, and, with his neighbor Chauncy,
was one of the staunchest of "the Congregational men"
whom we have heard about. A picture of him by a contemporary is an attractive one: "He was hospitable in his
House (says this acquaintance), free and facetious in
common Conversation, and most tenderly affected towards
his relatives." He was a firm Calvinist in principles.
Three years his junior, John Davenport, grandson of New
Haven's founder, was the Stamford minister at this time.
He had for a short period after 1687 been the Hopkins
Grammar schoolmaster at New Haven, and had now been
in Stamford six years. While I am not sure that we can
think of him as quite so attractive a man as was Joseph
Webb ("he was not over-careful of pleasing Men, but ever
fearful of displeasing God"), we have many evidences that
he had inherited with that characteristic the mental vigor of
his famous grandfather. "Eagle-eyed to discern the
Approaches of Sin," and a great temperance preacher, he
was said to have been as familiar with Hebrew, Greek, and
Latin "as with his Mother Tongue." With Increase
Mather holding the fort against the encroachments of the
new doctrines in Massachusetts, young John Davenport,
Calvinist and orthodox Puritan theologian, may well have
been looked upon, "seated" as he was "so near the Western
Limits of New England, as a Bulwark against any Irruptions of corrupt Doctrines and manners" from that godless

quarter. Stephen Buckingham, of Norwalk, then but twenty-seven years old, with Davenport, does not appear in Yale chronicles until some years later.

In the New London corner of the Colony there were nine settled ministers at this time, all but one of them Harvard graduates, and nearly all of them to become closely identified with Yale's beginnings. In 1700 the two oldest of these were the brothers James and Moses Noyes, both now around sixty years of age, and settled over the churches at Stonington and Lyme, respectively. They had been graduated together from Harvard in the Class of 1659, with Samuel Willard (later to be Vice-President of Harvard), and Samuel, son of Ezekiel Cheever. James Noyes, the elder of these "Noyces Ambo" (as the Harvard Steward's books of their college days dub them), was, like Israel Chauncy of Stratford, a doctor as well as a minister. He "gave away [so it was said] more in Medicines, than his Annual Salary as Minister amounted to." Very likely he was a good upholder of the traditional independence of the various Connecticut churches, it being said of him that he "was a great friend to Liberties both Civil & religious, and no man more Vigorous to stand up when any unjust Encroachments were made upon Either." As a man "he was extraordinarily Hospitable to all Strangers," and "like a Father" to his flock. In his church relations he was "mighty in Prayer" and "knew the art of Wrestling with God." When he was attempting to reclaim some backsliding member of his congregation he had the generous habit of "laying himself under Voluntary bonds of Self-denial" to encourage his parishioner in his. Among people, it was said, "his Presence was grave and Venerable, such as struck an awe into the boldest Offenders, they being afraid or ashamed to Discover their follies in his sight." As he came into old age, he was widely accepted as a leader in church affairs and as a presiding officer at conventions. One of his chief contributions on such occasions, it was said of him, was his "true spirit of the Peacemaker." His slightly younger brother, Moses Noyes, now minister at Lyme, was one of the last of the Connecticut ministers to go over to the principles of the "Half-way Covenant." So set in his ways was he, and so "truly Calvinistic," that he was one of the most energetic critics of the declining ministry of the times. So stoutly opposed was he to the "Errors which he feared were creeping in among us, particularly in the Schools and young Candidates for the Ministry," that it was not until the Collegiate School had been going for seventeen years and he had become assured of its orthodoxy, that he would accept a graduate of it as an assistant in his pulpit. Thomas Buckingham, minister of the Saybrook church, and Abraham Pierson of Killingworth were next oldest of these New London ministers,—both being fifty-five at this time. Of Abraham Pierson, his particular place in Yale history calls for the more extended account of him and his life which I give later on in these pages. Concerning Thomas Buckingham, taking hardly a less important place, we know but little. He was the only New London County minister not a college graduate. He was of a pioneer Milford family and received what education he had at the Hopkins Grammar School in New Haven.[1] As events will show, he was not only an able man, but a stout believer in his own views. At this time he was looked upon as one of the most capable men in the southern part of the Colony.

[1] I am indebted to Miss M. C. Holman of Saybrook for the further information about Buckingham that he was the son of Thomas and Hannah Buckingham, who came over in the "Hector" with Eaton and Davenport. He studied for the ministry with the Rev. John Whiting of Hartford and preached for a short time in Wethersfield before taking the Saybrook Meeting-house. His parish included the present towns of Essex, Chester, Westbrook, and a part of Lyme.

Gurdon Saltonstall, minister at New London (and at this time just coming into public notice), was the fourth of the important New London County ministers. Time was to bring this really remarkable man into the forefront of the builders of Yale. He was the pastor of Governor Fitz-John Winthrop, and was to become his successor as the Colony's chief magistrate, leaving the ministry for that public service. But Gurdon Saltonstall, seven years before that time, in 1700, and when he was but thirty-four years of age, was beginning to show his exceptional talents for public duties. I presume that, of all the Colony ministers of his day, Saltonstall was, by natural endowments, the most conspicuous and capable. He was the son of the Nathaniel Saltonstall who was the classmate of his neighboring ministers, the now elderly Noyces Ambo. At the early age of eighteen, when he himself received his Harvard degree, he had been renowned for his "vast proficiency in all the parts of Useful Learning & giving Early Hopes of that future great man which he afterwards proved." He had been ordained at New London when he was twenty-one years of age, and immediately came to the front as a young man of exceptional knowledge of affairs and promise. Before he was out of college six years, he was being consulted at his New London parsonage by magistrates and clergymen from all parts of the Colony. Three years later he was chosen for an important public commission. Though home rule under the Colony charter had not been taken away, it had been suspended under Andros from 1687 to 1689, and now had been resumed under Governor Treat. The appointment of the Governor of New York to command the Connecticut militia, however, had renewed the charter question, and Fitz-John Winthrop of New London was sent to England to look into it. Winthrop asked his young minister, Saltonstall, to accompany him. The upshot of their visit in London was emphatically for the continued legality of the original Winthrop charter, the Royal Attorney General deciding the case as presented by Winthrop and Saltonstall. When Fitz-John Winthrop became Governor under this confirmed charter in 1698, his pastor, Gurdon Saltonstall, naturally came into still broader relations to Colony affairs, and was appointed chief judge of the county court.

We have already made the acquaintance of James Pierpont, and of his two neighbors, Samuel Russel and Samuel Andrew. The Guilford minister at this time was young Thomas Ruggles, ten years out of Harvard. In Wallingford Samuel Street was still the minister, and in Derby was the youthful Joseph Moss, just graduated from Harvard.

All but two or three of these thirty-odd Connecticut ministers of 1700 were Harvard graduates. They were all settled over Congregational churches, and, in their quarterly meetings and in occasional chance conversations, as the college leaders went about their counties on horseback, attending to the sick and backsliding, were being consulted as to the proposed school.

II

Placed before at least a number of these ministers who lived along the Long Island coast, the first stumbling-block which appears to have been encountered was the turn the project took, among a number of prominent "ministers and Gentlemen," in connection with the increasing demand for some better form of church government. Both in Massachusetts and in Connecticut a movement was now under way so to organize the traditional New England churches that they could meet the oncoming change in theology and morals with a common front. This was meeting with difficulties in the changing Massachusetts of that day. In

Connecticut it was taking the form of a demand for a church synod which should organize the various independent congregations in a Colony church of a loose presbyterian mould.

Just how the Connecticut ministers divided on this question we do not know. There were, doubtless, the usual two extremes; the strong Presbyterians and the rigid adherents of the traditional independence. And there were the middle-way men, who were prepared for some church organization and yet unwilling to see an ecclesiastical central government fastened upon the churches. This latter party was undoubtedly led by the New Haven promoters of the college. For, if any one fact stands out from the hazy outlines of the years 1700-1701, it is that this group,—consisting of such seacoast-town ministers as Pierpont, Andrew, Buckingham, Chauncy, James Noyes, and Pierson,—declined to have their college come under church control, however much they were in favor of such an ecclesiastical organization for the Colony. Rev. Gurdon Saltonstall and Rev. Timothy Woodbridge appear to have been of the church-synod party.

That this was a crisis in these preliminary negotiations between the Connecticut ministers, needs no argument. The character of the coming Yale College was in the balance. Had the synod party won their point, the Collegiate School would not have been established for several years, if at all, and when established would have been the victim of the long-drawn-out controversies and troubles that came to the Colony churches when the Saybrook Platform was finally adopted. Looked at from this point of view, we may well accept James Pierpont's services at this time, as of the utmost importance to the future Yale.

And so, if, as the historian Trumbull tells us, the college scheme was publicly broached by Pierpont some time after 1698, it is probable that the next two years saw its general discussion along the lines just mentioned, and, for the reasons stated, nothing done about it. But in 1700-1701 the project rather suddenly came to be a public question.

There are two accounts of the progress of the college affair during these two years.

Both of these come down to us from President Clap. His "Annals of Yale-College," printed in 1766 at New Haven, gives the date 1700 for "the first Founding thereof." In this narrative President Clap proceeds to tell how in that year "ten of the principal Ministers in the Colony were nominated and agreed upon by a general Consent both of the Ministers and people, to stand as Trustees or Undertakers to found, erect, and govern a College,"—adding the ministers named in the legislative document of 1701 as these trustees. He proceeds to say that these ministers "met at New Haven and formed themselves into a Body or Society, to consist of eleven Ministers, including a Rector, and agreed to Found a College in the Colony of Connecticut; which they did at their next Meeting at Branford." He then gives the story which has become traditional, that "Each Member brought [to Branford in 1700] a Number of Books and presented them to the Body; and laying them on a Table, said these words, or to this effect; 'I give these books for the founding a College in this Colony.'" President Clap then says that these Founders "afterwards began to doubt whether they were fully vested with a legal Capacity to hold Lands, and whether private Donations and contributions would yield a Sufficiency to carry on so great a Design; it was therefore proposed to make Application to the Hon. the General Assembly of the Colony for some Assistance, and to ask for a charter." Meetings were held on this question, says Clap, and the advice asked of "some of the ablest lawyers both in, and out of the Government." It being decided to do this, goes this tradition of Yale's beginnings, the trustees of the already-founded school wrote to Judge Sewall and Secretary Addington of Boston for the draft of a charter. This was presented to the Assembly in 1701, with a public petition, and the charter was granted.

This understanding of the facts of the "founding" passed current for generations after President Clap's "Annals" were published in 1766. The first President Dwight accepted the date 1700. The one hundred and fiftieth anniversary was celebrated in 1850. It was so accepted by every authority on Yale's founding until a reëxamination of the contemporary documents in Yale's possession, and of President Clap's own manuscripts, threw doubt upon its accuracy.[1] That the year 1700 was commonly accepted during the early 18th Century might appear from the fact that, at the College Commencement in 1750, there were suddenly given a much larger number of honorary degrees than had been given before that date,—eight as against not over two previously, and to distinguished non-graduates rather than to young Harvard men and occasional donors.

Another date,—1701,—however, is likewise given by President Clap. Written in 1747, one manuscript of the "Annals" gives this second year as that of Yale's founding. President Clap likewise gives this year in a pamphlet published in 1754. In this second though earlier published account, Clap narrates a much simpler story of the charter granting than in his account published in 1766, and, the facts appear to warrant the assertion, a much more likely one. So far as the date goes, it is quite probable, as Professor Dexter believes, that there was a reason for this

---

[1] The reader is referred to Professor Dexter's study of this question in the published papers of the New Haven Historical Society, and to Professor Charles H. Smith's exhaustive restudy of it, also published in that series some years later.

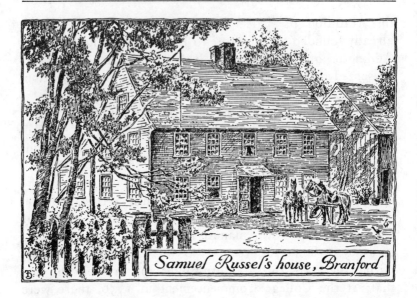

Samuel Russel's house, Branford

change by Clap.   In the year 1766 Clap was engaged in the
most important struggle of his administration.   He was
then defending the College's priority of right to manage its
own affairs against the right to interfere that the Assembly
was demanding.   Priority of the actual "founding" thus was
necessary, and so, say the students of this question, the year
1700 was belatedly and inaccurately advanced instead of
1701.

However that may be,—and I do not need to go into
the pros and cons of what is perhaps a purely academic
question at the most,—the whole matter has been one of
much confusion and, even today, acknowledged uncertainty.[1]
There is much to be said for both narratives.   The point

---

[1] The Bicentennial Celebration of the University was held in October,
1901, the University thus accepting the second date as a result of Professor
Dexter's researches.   In the historical table in the University Catalogue,
however, both 1700 and 1701 are given as the dates of the "Meeting of the
Ministers at Branford, for founding a College."

turns, I take it, upon the use of the term "founding." There can hardly be any question that meetings, perhaps frequent, were held in the year 1700 and possibly before that time (as Clap's "Annals" asserts in its marginal dates), at which the college project was discussed. Branford being midway between the extreme towns of the seacoast ministers, it is quite possible that several meetings were held there, and that the traditional "founding" meeting of 1700 did occur in Samuel Russel's parsonage parlor, as the story has it. But, judging from the evidence of dated letters in the early fall of 1701, it may be said that, if these meetings were held, they could not have been as formal, or have come to such precise ends as tradition has held that they did. If it was generally considered that there were to be eight trustees, as appears from at least one letter of September, 1701, Clap's story that the final ten had been chosen in 1699 and had "founded" the School in 1700 hardly holds water. I imagine that we need not entirely discredit the engaging Branford "founding" story of 1700, if we at the same time believe that nothing so formal as that procedure occurred until a year later.

III

Which brings us to the year 1701, famous in Yale annals.

In the summer and early fall of this year the long-discussed and postponed matter of establishing a Connecticut college was rather suddenly brought to a climax by the leaders in it.

That this was the result of the unexpected decision of the General Assembly to meet in New Haven in October of that year, for the first time since the absorption of the old New Haven Colony by Connecticut, would seem to be the fact. When the hard struggle of Davenport's people against absorption by Winthrop's Connecticut had been at its hottest, the latter Colony had proposed, as a sop to the dissatisfied New Haveners, that New Haven should be made a coördinate capital of the new commonwealth with Hartford. Davenport had abruptly refused this offer (as he had refused all compromises on the question of New Haven's independence), and it had not been renewed after the consolidation. The annual meetings of the General Assembly, therefore, had been held at Hartford ever since 1664, to the increasing discontent of the second generation of New Haven voters. But in 1698 an important reorganization had been enacted of the Colony legislature. Fitz-John Winthrop, of New London, had been elected Governor as a reward for his successful securing of a confirmation of the charter. The Assembly, which previously had consisted of but one house (the magistrates sitting as an independent court) was now reformed with two houses,—the Governor and Magistrates to form the Upper, and the Deputies from the various towns the Lower with power to choose their own speaker. The consent of both Houses was ordered for the passage of any act.

What was the particular cause of the vote to hold the October meeting of that year and thereafter, in New Haven, and thus bring the two old sections of the Colony into harmony, does not appear. But the knowledge of this decision was public property early in May, 1701, and, if the personal relations of the college promoters to the leaders of the coming October session were of any promise, it may be considered that Pierpont and his friends saw their opportunity to proceed at once upon their plans. We have seen that Governor Winthrop was the close friend and parishioner of Gurdon Saltonstall of New London. Deputy Governor Treat, of Milford, was the father-in-law of Samuel Andrew. Speaker Peter Burr was in Andrew's church. Many of the best men in the two Houses were parishioners of the ministers interested in the scheme. In the light of these fortunate circumstances, the occasion that thus presented itself was the first that promised results since the college project had been broached.

I suppose that further and energetic meetings now began among the small group of ministers along the Long Island shore who had fathered the college plan, and that the situation created by this sudden meeting of the Assembly in New Haven was thoroughly discussed by them. The General Assembly was to be asked for a charter. As President Clap says, no doubt this decision had been the occasion of some debate and misgivings. It had been held in Harvard's case that her charter had expired with the annulment of Massachusett's, and that a new one must have the agreement of the Crown. Connecticut had not lost her charter, and had had it confirmed. Yet the relations between that Colony and England were still on such a slender thread that there might be serious danger were the Connecticut Assembly to proceed, in the light of the Massachusetts experience over Harvard's charter, to grant to the proposed founders of a Connecticut college one of their own. There were other questions also involved, regarding rights of the Colony over the proposed school and the legality of gifts received if a possibly illegal charter were granted and the Royal officers in England annulled it.

Matters being in this hazy state, and the sessions of the General Assembly for the first time in New Haven but three months away, the more energetic of the college promoters seem to have now taken their first definite public step. They now sent out, either together or singly, a number of letters, asking for advice, not only on the educational side, but on the highly important matter of the legality of a Connecticut-Colony-granted charter, and, if that were to be legal, what it should contain. Letters were sent, therefore, to Cotton

Mather and to Increase Mather, representing Harvard; to Judge Sewall and Secretary Addington of the Massachusetts Province, representing the Royal government in New England; and to at least three Connecticut gentlemen, old Gershom Bulkeley of Wethersfield; the Colony Secretary, Eleazar Kimberly, and John Eliot, a young Windsor lawyer who was to be a member of the coming Assembly.

The four Massachusetts men thus resorted to were recognized leaders of the conservative party there. All four were out of sympathy with the new times and hostile to the new Harvard régime. That they were asked for their opinions, amply appears from their replies.[1] These came very much to the same conclusions, and are so worded that it is obvious that they were in response to requests for them and probably written at about the same time. Cotton Mather's letter was probably the first to be received.[2] This was a very carefully-drawn up "Scheme for a College" (or "Instructions for a Collegiate School," as James Pierpont endorsed it). But it was not at all what Pierpont and his friends had wanted. It was a modified Presbyterian proposal, calling for a synod of the Connecticut churches which should establish "an University, that shall be the school of the churches." The Synod should choose the first President (wrote Mather) and his successor should be appointed by the "Inspectors (or Pastors of such twelve churches as the Synod shall pitch

[1] President Quincy, in his massive "History of Harvard," turns this about and makes it appear that the impetus in the founding of Yale came from these dissatisfied and defeated Massachusetts conservative leaders, among whom these four were the most prominent. But his view of the case is not supported by the facts. The invitation to help the Connecticut project came from the Connecticut Colony.

[2] President Clap dates this 1700, but it was more probably a year later.

upon)" whose choice should be laid before the churches by letter for acceptance. A number of rules were suggested, leading to the maintenance of the traditional New England theology. There should be no attempt made to build a "college house," though one room would be needed for meetings. The churches should, at least at first, guarantee the salary of the President and "two tutors." And there should be a confession of Faith, "relating to the purity of religion," which the college officers should subscribe to. The "Inspectors" should visit the school at least twice a year.

In general, this "scheme" by Cotton Mather incorporated most of the important things that his father had been unable to secure for Harvard. The reply of old Increase Mather, dated September 15, 1701, a week after he had been removed from Harvard's presidency, was also received by Mr. Pierpont. In briefer form it was a repetition of the main points in his son's letter. He touched, however, upon the charter question, as Cotton Mather had not. "If the Connecticut government [he wrote], before their charter is taken from them [in this he chose the prevalent public worry of the times], shall settle a revenue for the maintenance of such a school, 'tis probable that property will not be taken from you, though government should."

The letter to Judge Sewall had been sent on August 7, 1701. It had been a round-robin letter, signed by five of the seacoast-town ministers,—Israel Chauncy of Stratford, Thomas Buckingham of Saybrook, Abraham Pierson of Killingworth, James Pierpont of New Haven, and Gurdon Saltonstall of New London. This was an important letter, —perhaps the most important that the trustees sent,—and we should not overlook the significance of these signatures or the obvious contents of the letter itself, as reflected in Judge Sewall's answer of September 17. The ministers of the upper-Colony towns had not come into the affair when this letter was written. The college project, up to the first week in August, 1701, had remained in the hands of the original leaders, to whom had been added several others of the Long Island Sound villages, who were of their way of thinking.

And the reply of these two Crown officers fits in, also, with the situation as I have presented it. Said Sewall: "I have been thinking that considering the present distress [no doubt referring to political difficulties with England], it may be best to do as little by the government as is possible with attaining the end. And therefore should not be eager in building a college [by which he meant a house] or settling revenues by a law." The letter proceeds to suggest that "the act only contain authority for such a person [the President] by himself and Tutors under him to instruct youth in academical learning, and give them degrees. And let the act oblige the president to pray and expound the Scriptures in the hall," and so on. The significance of this reply is clearly twofold: that there had been no formal "founding" of the college up to that time,—August, 1701, —but that the project was still in a hazy state; and that the signers of the letter were proposing to go before the coming Assembly for some "action" regarding the scheme. Sewall adds the interesting remark, regarding this latter plan, that he hopes "within these few days to send something more mature and in form either by the post or some other good hand." And he drops the matter there with the voluntary promise to send them his "small essay towards opening the eighteenth century; and a sheet to discourage our trading to Africa for men."[1]

[1] This was the first anti-slavery document to be published in New England, though its point must have been considerably dulled by Captain Sewall's public purchase of a Negro slave a short time afterwards.

We may take it, therefore,—in concluding our chronicles of this admittedly hazy year,—that in August, 1701, the college plan had not proceeded beyond the point where the original promoters of it, and a few of their friends and neighbors along the shore of their own way of thinking, had, with the approach of the Assembly, written to Judge Sewall asking for an outline of a college charter which they could lay before the friendly Colony legislature which was in October to meet for the first time in New Haven.

IV

The summer of 1701 now passed while the reply of Secretary Addington was awaited. "Instructions" for a charter,—probably by Pierpont,—had been enclosed for Secretary Addington in the letter to Sewall, and had been handed to him by the latter. Until these arrived, and with the near approach of the Assembly which was set for the first week in October, I think we may safely say that the consultations of James Pierpont's friends must have been as frequent as the means of travel allowed, and were rapidly coming to a climax. The synod proposal for the college control was doubtless still in the air by September, 1701, and the two Mather letters had been on that side. These had been side-tracked by the Pierpont party, now in active charge of the undertaking. But the large question still remained, whether the Colony legislature had the legal right under the Colony charter to "give a liberty" to such a college, and whether they would do so.

V

Lacking the precise facts, we have to depend upon conjecture only when we say that Pierpont and Andrew and Pierson, and the others of their party, now proposed to take

time by the forelock and, by "founding" the college themselves, forestall the very probable opposition that might
crop out in the coming Assembly against the legality of the
proposed charter. This is probably a safe conjecture.
Adopting it, we shall at least be sure that there was some
gathering at Samuel Russel's house in Branford immediately after the first of October, 1701. This is proved by
the superscription on the letter of John Eliot, a Windsor
lawyer, who, replying under that date to questions asked
him, sends his letter to Abraham Pierson "at Branford."
For it may be said that the contents of all of the extant
letters of the Fall of 1701 to the college promoters certainly
go to show that, up to October, 1701, there had been no
"founding" by anyone. President Clap's single authority
to the contrary is met by the significant fact that, where he
says from hearsay long afterwards that ten ministers had
been chosen previous to this time, Eliot's letter of October 1,
1701, refers to the "said eight Elders and said Master,"
(as if each county were to have two) and that the final
number, eleven, was not arrived at until after the Assembly
had met, and Pierpont had inserted it himself in the draft
of a charter.

The Branford of the elder Pierson's day had expanded
by 1700 into a scattering hamlet running north from Branford Point to the present village Green, the latter a rough
open space of hollows and hills, studded with huge boulders.
"Sabbath-day" houses stood about this Green, the square
wooden Meeting-house in its center. "Whipping-post Hill,"
so named from its use for the town stocks of previous days,
sloped away from this central square. Just south of the
present burying ground was the parsonage of the Rev.
Samuel Russel. This was a large and even handsome house
in its day, of the gaunt and quite unlovely "lean-to" variety
that had come into style a little earlier throughout the

Colony.[1] One of the four large first-floor rooms of this house, the "south parlor" as it was called, was traditionally the place for the first formal gathering of the sponsors for the proposed Colony school that we know anything definite about.

All of the evidence in the matter goes to show that the single purpose of this meeting in Branford about the first of October, 1701, was, by "founding" the college, there to establish a priority if the Assembly declined to accept the responsibility.[2] This was probably done, as tradition says, by promising to give to the School a number of books. In all probability no actual books were there given, President Clap to the contrary. A letter from Rev. James Noyes, expressing his regrets that he could not attend the Saybrook organization meeting in the following month, seems to settle this point. He speaks of some very recent journey, likely enough to this Branford meeting, and says that he had authorized his brother to "give out of my books at his house my full proportion, and in nothing would I be behindhand in so public a good." If any books were actually given at Branford, they were too few in number to be of any consequence.

Abraham Pierson brought two letters to this Branford meeting bearing on this all-important necessity for a prior "founding."

Old Gershom Bulkeley, under date of September 27, had sent to Mr. Pierson his reply to the request for his opinion on the legality of a Colony charter. The old gentleman

[1] The old Samuel Russel house was pulled down about 1836, but the doors were saved and today may be seen set into the walls of the Librarian's office in the University Library. (See page 148.)

[2] Professor Dexter guardedly suggests this in his paper referred to, and Professor Smith, in his study, remarks that "This view has the merit of making the donation [of books at Branford] intelligible." Against it is President Clap's statement that it occurred a year previous.

thought that the Assembly would not enact one, and that it would prove a boomerang to both the college and the Colony if it did. He strongly advised that the agitators drop the plan for Colony assistance and humbly ask the King and Parliament for a charter. Pierson's second letter, which he laid before his friends at Branford, was from Eleazar Kimberly, the Secretary of State of the Colony. The Secretary believed that such a charter as was proposed by them would be legal. Awaiting Mr. Pierson at Branford was the third letter, that of young John Eliot, which has been mentioned. It had just arrived by messenger over the rough back-country bridle-path from Windsor. It was a comprehensive and scholarly lawyer's document for that day, replying to several questions asked him by Mr. Pierson, and concluding that the Colony government had every right to grant the proposed charter. On less vital matters he averred that the school property "for the present" should be in the hands of a third party, to be distributed by the trustees, and that, to avoid notice abroad and jealousies at home, the school should not attempt to give degrees.

In the face of these conflicting opinions, the weight of which, however, was on the side of proceeding with the plan, I take it that the college party saw every reason for immediate passage of the charter by the Assembly. The indications are all to the effect that this Branford meeting of October 2 or 3, 1701, was a hurried final meeting of the promoters, and that there, by a common agreement to give books, the coast-town ministers hoped to establish an organization and property rights that would give the coming Assembly some precedent to confirm, rather than a new enterprise to establish on its own responsibility. If we are going too far to assert such astuteness on the part of the college party, the event undoubtedly showed that this action had been well taken. While the actual founding of the Collegiate School, under the permission given by the charter to do so, came a month later, this Branford meeting unquestionably established a prior act of some kind that was necessary. The whole question of the independence of Yale College from the State, that came up for settlement a generation later, depended upon the historic certainty of this previous action by the ministers.

Cotton = Mather

CHAPTER V

THE GENERAL ASSEMBLY CHARTER

I

OUBTLESS it was a red-letter day for James Pierpont's good people when the General Assembly gathered for its first session in New Haven on October 9, 1701.

For the arrival of the honorable members of the two Houses, the Governor and Deputy Governor, and the usual number of curious and interested outsiders, brought a novel and exciting week and taxed the town's accommodations to the utmost. Probably the hospitable New Haven folk opened their houses for the official visitors and guests and entertained them in the generously hospitable manner of the day. Scattered farmhouses at that time dotted the broad village lanes on all of the eight outer squares, the greater number being on the southern side, where there was easy access to the harbor and that "little wharf" that jutted out southeast of the present State Street. The town gaol and courthouse of John Davenport's Mosaic common-wealth were still standing on the upper Market-place, and on that open public square were the Meeting-house, the Hopkins Grammar School, and the village cemetery. The original creek up which John Davenport's colonists had sailed to the old corner of College and George Streets was still in use. Much of the traveling then was done by small sloops and a convenient way to come to New Haven was up this narrow creek to the town landing-place at College Street. But a short distance north of this dock, up College Street, about where the present Taft Hotel stands at the Chapel Street corner, was Captain Miles' Tavern. This was the famous old "mansion" of Deputy Governor Goodyear of Davenport's days, which had been offered to the "college" in 1658 as the "president's house."[1] It still

---

[1] I am indebted to General George H. Ford of New Haven both for the loan of a painting in his possession of Miles' Tavern (upon which Mr. Diedricksen has based his drawing on page 175), and for some interesting historical notes concerning it. This land originally had been allotted to one William Hawkins of London; he did not emigrate and the lot was bought by Deputy Governor Goodyear, whose first New Haven house was next east on Chapel Street. Goodyear built this house,—known as "the Mansion house,"—on the Hawkins lot, and offered it, as we have seen, to the New Haven Colony for a "president's house" for its college. After his death John Harriman, innkeeper, bought the place, and managed it as an "ordinary," his son succeeding him. John Miles, Dragoon Captain and a New Haven Deputy to the Assembly, probably kept the tavern shortly after 1690, and bought it in 1703. It became the "Beers' Tavern" around 1750, and, with an added low covered porch on both street sides, was the town's chief hostelry until the year 1850, when it was torn down for the first "New Haven House." John Adams was a guest here in 1774 on his way to the first Continental Congress; General Washington and staff stopped here overnight on his way to take command of the Continental Army at Cambridge in 1775; Mrs. Washington and Mrs. General Gates were

stood in its six acres of pleasant meadow and orchard that ran south along College Street perhaps to Crown, and easterly down Chapel nearly to Temple. Joseph Brown's quaint old map of 1724 shows this house, and none other, on the present Chapel Street side of the modern Green down to the corner of Chapel and Church Streets, where the now abandoned Gregson homestead stood. Miles' Tavern must have been the chief rendezvous of the Assembly during this first session at New Haven. During the next Assembly he was voted £5 "to pay for the Colony expenses in his house." The townspeople, however, had prepared for the week's stay of the honorable body by extending permission to five other residents to "Sell Rum only while the Court sits." As there was then no other large public building than the Meeting-house, the Deputies seem to have met there, the Council no doubt sitting in one of Captain Miles' upper rooms, where they could discuss the public business in retirement with the Governor, and whence they would proceed down across the public square to join the Deputies in the Meeting-house when occasion demanded.

II

Since the final Branford meeting, the week previous, the Pierpont group of coast-town ministers had been anxiously awaiting the arrival of that draft of a charter which they had asked of Judge Sewall and Secretary Addington of

entertained here that same year, and Mrs. Washington again on her return journey from Boston; Baron Von Steuben was here in 1779, and the British officers had a look in on its pantry and wine cellar in their invasion of the town that year. In 1783 Mr. Beers opened a bookshop in one of the first-floor rooms, and rented rooms to Yale students in the upper part. It later became a private residence. The first "New Haven House" was built there by Mr. Augustus R. Street, of the Class of 1812, and, on his death, the property was left by him for the support of the Yale Art School. The College sold the land in 1867, applying the proceeds to the Art School cost and other endowments given by Mr. Street.

Miles' Tavern
in 1700

Boston. This had not come when the Assembly had begun its sessions on October 9, and we may imagine the college promoters, who would naturally have come to New Haven to see their charter passed, in a great to-do over the delay, until it arrived by post from New London the next day. The Boston packet was addressed to the Reverend Buckingham, and it was now gone over by the ministers at Mr. Pierpont's house and the petition which was to accompany it written.

This final discussion of the charter seems to have taken four or five days. For the form in which it had come from the Massachusetts framers was not, in some essential points, to the New Haven ministers' liking. The "Instructions" that had been sent to the Boston lawyers had been a layman's general ideas of what was wanted. The Boston reply was not only a lawyer's codification of these ideas, but, in a few main matters, to quite a different purpose than the original New Haven design. While perhaps a small matter in itself, this difference has more significance than has usually been assigned to it. For the two points of view which had been at loggerheads over the college appear to be rather clearly shown thereby. The New Haven ministers' preliminary draft (no copy of which is now in existence) had undoubtedly been quite in line with the traditional and independent Congregationalism of Pierpont's circle. The Boston reply very emphatically hints of the increasing sentiment in the Massachusetts of that period for a stronger church association. The Pierpont scheme had been less, probably, for a Congregational-church school than for a public academy that would bolster up the Congregational churches and yet not be controlled by them. It was possibly because he did not have these original papers before him, that President Clap did not make this clear in his "Annals." From that circumstance arose the flat statements by President Quincy of Harvard that the

Massachusetts church leaders not only began the Collegiate School project, but furnished its charter for it, and, therefore, should be considered its founders. The result of this has been some misapprehension of the facts involved, in spite of exhaustive proofs of the real situation by such critics of President Quincy's "History of Harvard" as the late Professor Kingsley[1] of Yale and Professor Dexter.

Not only was the Massachusetts church-control theory shown in this charter of Addington's; I surmise that the hand of an influential Connecticut faction may likewise be discerned in it. Judge Sewall's diary records the fact that the Rev. Timothy Woodbridge, the Hartford minister, was at this time in Boston; says Sewall: "Mr. Timothy Woodbridge remains here lame by reason of a humor fallen into his right leg." This was written under date of October 29, 1701. Now the records of the First Church of Hartford show[2] that Woodbridge was absent from Hartford for most of the year 1701 and for all of the year 1702, "apparently ill, in Boston." Repeated efforts were made to secure his return to his Hartford congregation, which did not succeed until February, 1703. During most if not all of this long absence, Woodbridge appears to have been ill, suffering from some "sorrowful circumstances which the providence of God hath laid him under" (say the Hartford records). Captain Sewall writes in his diary of dining with him and Increase Mather in October, 1702. In January, 1703, Woodbridge "Prayed at the opening of the

---

[1] Professor Kingsley's criticism of Quincy will be found in The American Biblical Repository for 1841. While successfully demolishing the Massachusetts faction's establishment of Yale, Professor Kingsley undoubtedly went too far to the other extreme, and denies the very evident influence of the Massachusetts theological uproar of 1698-1701 on the Connecticut establishment.

[2] This is stated by the historian of the Hartford church, George L. Walker.

Court at Charlestown," etc. Inasmuch as he was a resident of Boston during 1701-1703, and hence at hand during the period when Sewall and Addington were drawing up their draft of the Collegiate School charter, it is entirely probable that he was consulted in it, and thereby added his own theories as to the course Connecticut should take to those of the Massachusetts lawyers, with whom, as with Mather, he appears to have been in very friendly relations. If we could be certain of this (and the fact has not been suggested before, to my knowledge), we have the interesting situation that, where James Pierpont had been careful to "found" the Collegiate School before the Assembly convened, Timothy Woodbridge was party to the Boston legal suggestion that the Assembly "found" it, instead, and to the theory of governmental visitation and church-synod control advised by the Mathers.

The letter from the two Boston lawyers, accompanying their charter draft, is still extant. In it they "crave pardon" for the long delay, but excuse themselves, both on the ground of many other duties, and because of "not knowing what to do for fear of overdoing." And they had stumbled over one thing especially. This was that "there is no mention made [in the 'Instructions'] of any visitation, which is exceedingly proper and beneficial; all humane societies standing in need of a check upon them." This was exactly what Pierpont and his friends had not wanted. The Boston men proceeded: "We know not how to call or qualify it, but that in a little time it might probably prove subversive of your design." Regarding the School they said: "We on purpose gave your academy as low a name as we could, that it might the better stand in wind and weather, not daring to incorporate it, lest it should be liable to be served with a writ of *quo warranto.*" They "should have traveled further in it [they added], if your instructions or our invention had dictated to us, not knowing well what scheme to project, because we could not tell how far your government will encourage the design." Sewall and Addington, good legal conservatives that they were, hoped that matters, however, would turn out well, as "We should be very glad to hear of flourishing schools and a College at Connecticut, and it would be some relief to us against the sorrow we have conceived for the decay of them in this province." And they added, as a special urging for the theological provision in their charter, that "as the end of all learning is to fit men to search the Scriptures," the "Rector should expound the Scriptures diligently morning and evening."

The New Haven group of ministers, however, were far from being as fearful of the illegality of the act they were to ask for, and of its consequences, as were the Boston lawyers. They knew their Connecticut better than that. They had taken the bull by the horns, if the Branford "founding" tradition may be believed, so far as any danger of asking the Assembly to act on its own responsibility was concerned. Nor were they in sympathy with the idea of making their school as much of a theological seminary as the two elderly Boston Puritan leaders proposed. Their plans for their Connecticut college were much broader than to make it a "school of the churches" or a theological seminary.

I need not go into the very many changes which Pierpont now made in the Sewall and Addington draft.[1] But the main

1 Judge Sewall was informed of the passage of the Collegiate School Act in letters from the Trustees which he refers to as dated the "15th and 16th" of October, 1701,—references which give us the latest dates for the

alterations and additions need to be noted, as they clearly show what was in James Pierpont's mind. The Boston draft was "An Act for Founding a Collegiate School." Pierpont's significant alteration is to "An Act for Liberty to erect a Collegiate School" (already, we may thus surmise, "founded"). The term "Collegiate School" had occurred in several letters of the earlier fall, and doubtless had been accepted, partly because the enterprise had not yet risen to the dignity of a "university," or even to that of a "college" in the contemporary use of the term, and partly because it seemed that caution should be used in not making too noticeable a beginning. A further important element in the Boston draft was omitted, wherein the Westminster Confession, as expounded in Dr. Ames' "Medulla Theologiae" (the famous Calvinistic doctrinal book of the earlier Puritan days), was ordered "diligently read in the Latin tongue, and well studied by all scholars educated in the said school." While Dr. Ames' book became one of the text-books of the Collegiate School in good season, the Pierpont founders evidently did not think it best to so order it in the charter. In the concluding paragraph, the Boston draft empowered

passage of that act. On October 29 he writes that he would like to see the charter, "as an ample Reward for any thing we have done for you." He also wants to know "the Place where the College is to be, as soon as you have Appointed it." This was very likely a matter for curiosity to Timothy Woodbridge, near Sewall, if not in his house, at the time, and the question may have been suggested by him. The Boston judge remained a good friend of the Connecticut academy in later years. He sent "five Volumes of Pole's Synopsis Criticorum," to the School in 1707, though he seems to have had difficulty in getting the books delivered. "They have been Transported from Boston to Woodbury; and back again," he writes to the Trustees. "If it please God they get well to Saybrook, I would have them rest there, and move no more." The last word that we hear from him about the School which he helped establish is in this friendly letter. He wishes to be remembered as "a Wellwisher to the Prosperity of your College; tho possibly, it may import the less increase of our own, I hope the Interests of Christ's Kingdom in general, will be promoted; wch is that we should aim at."

the trustees to receive gifts "as from time to time shall be
freely given," for "the founding, erecting and endowing of
the same." In the amended draft, Pierpont inserted after
the reference to the gifts the phrase "as have heretofore
already been granted," for the "founding," and so on.
Here again is a change which very logically points toward
some preliminary organization and the giving of property
to it.

One other important alteration in the Boston draft remains to be noted. Sewall and Addington had left the site
for the school blank, and had arranged for certain "Ministers and Gentlemen," unnamed and their number left blank,
to become the "trustees." At the meetings at Pierpont's
house, the references to a site were struck out, the word
"Gentlemen" was omitted, and the blank left for the number of trustees filled by inserting the names of ten ministers:
"The Rev. Mr. James Noyes, of Stonington, Mr. Israel
Chauncy, of Stratford, Mr. Thomas Buckingham, of Say-
brook, Mr. Abraham Pierson, of Killingworth, Mr.
Samuel Mather, of Windsor, Mr. Samuel Andrew, of
Milford, Mr. Timothy Woodbridge, of Hartford, Mr.
James Pierpont, of New Haven, Mr. Noadiah Russell, of
Middletown, and Mr. Joseph Webb, of Fairfield."

Just what had happened to produce this particular list of
trustees we do not know. Evidently the "Instructions" of
August 7 had contained no specific number of founders.
We have seen how the enterprise up to that time (and, so
far as contemporary documents go to show, up to October
9) had been entirely in the hands of the group of ministers
along the Sound. To John Eliot on September 17 it had
been written that "eight elders" and a Master were to be
the number, evidently two for each of the four counties. It
had now been decided to increase the number of trustees to
ten. Gurdon Saltonstall, of the original movers, and

Samuel Russel, were not included among those selected, and three new names—Timothy Woodbridge, old Samuel Mather, and Noadiah Russell—had been added.

I fancy that one conjecture as to this selection is as good as another. Yet we are probably somewhere within the facts if (with our recent acquaintance with the bigwigs of the Colony in mind) we consider that as matters concerning the founding of the Collegiate School had approached this critical pass, and as the news of the proposed founding was noised abroad, the traditional jealousy between the old Connecticut and New Haven Colonies had again broken out, and that the Hartford ministers had come into the situation, if belatedly, with some precipitation and for purposes of their own. Events were to show an underlying hostility to the Pierpont party, on the part of Timothy Woodbridge, whose residence in Boston at that moment, close to Sewall and Addington, must have been well known. That Hartford County received three trustees at this time, was likely enough for "reasons of state." In that event, both Woodbridge and Russell were natural choices. But Samuel Mather was an invalid, and never attended a Collegiate School trustee meeting. His choice, in the face of this well-known expectation, could hardly have been but for his prominence in his county, his relation as son-in-law to the Deputy Governor and brother-in-law to the Rev. Samuel Andrew of Milford, and because, by adding him, such opposition as was forming around Hartford to the Pierpont leadership might be curbed by taking in all of the chief objectors. That New London County should have three was probably because the Pierpont party had it in mind to choose Abraham Pierson for the first Rector, and that his place on the board of ten would then be taken by another from another county, as was the case.

But why the important selection of a site, which naturally would have been incorporated in the charter under ordinary conditions, was left out, is not so clear. Undoubtedly, however, the omission points to this same collision between Hartford and New Haven interests. It can hardly be believed that James Pierpont, following out in his mind, as he must have done, the earlier efforts of his famous predecessor for a New Haven college, did not hope, if not expect, to settle the Collegiate School at New Haven. And it is just as well established that the Hartford party wanted it there. So there appears to have been a deadlock on this question from the start. As the charter was drawn up, it would appear that this trouble caused both the omission of a site for the school, and the concession to the Hartford party of an extra trustee.

In the meantime, the Council and the Lower House had been going about the regular Colony's business. The presentation of the tax list had been attended to, Hartford and New Haven leading and Waterbury, Derby, and Killingworth ending the list. The annual rates are imposed, two and a half penny a pound, to be paid in wheat, pork, etc. The salaries for the year are fixed, the Governor being voted £120, though he has to pay for his own "waiting men and horses." Each of the four counties is ordered to maintain "a sufficient gaol or prison house." It is decided to print fifteen hundred copies of the Colony laws. A committee, of which the Rev. James Noyes of the College founders and young John Eliot of the house are members, is named to treat again with Rhode Island about the long-disputed boundary line. The Colony College project then comes up. The charter, accepted by the Governor and his Council in agreeable conference at Captain Miles' Tavern, is now to go to the Lower House. Here its reception may have been considered problematical.

III

We may fancy ourselves present at the scene in the rough wooden Meeting-house on the New Haven Market-place on that Friday morning, October 16, 1701, when we may take it that the final act in the long succession of efforts which we have been reviewing, for a Connecticut Colony college, was played by the Deputies. John Davenport's persevering spirit, in its glistening robes of that realistic Heaven to which he had devoutly believed that he would go, may well have hovered over that audience of the sons of his troubled earthly generation. The Meeting-house bell reverberates through the fresh autumn morning air. Toward the four-square clapboarded building, with its squat belfry and weather vane surmounting its four-sloped shingled roof, proceed the actors in this final drama of New Haven's long College dream. From Captain Miles' Tavern, under the great oaks and buttonwoods of the public square, comes old Governor Fitz-John Winthrop, a famous dandy of his day, in periwig and gold-laced cocked hat, scarlet-lined coat, lavishly-embroidered waistcoat, blue silk stockings and silver-buckled shoes. With him walks the aged Robert Treat, now Deputy Governor, in the sedate white band and somber garb of the older days. The ten Assistants come out over the ancient sandy square from the several streets, —in their white or scarlet square-cut coats, broad skirted with large cuffs, gold and silver buttoned, in ruffles,—no doubt discussing with the ministers, who have come to town to see the college charter passed, the possibility of the Lower House concurring in their own favorable action. The Deputies from the towns of the Colony saunter over, doubtless with their New Haven hosts, the country delegates in their crude imitations of the now somewhat gaudy attire of the bigwigs. James Pierpont, in his black-crêpe ministerial robes that he has recently ordered from Boston,

The Upper House Granting the Charter

and the charter under his arm, comes out of his parsonage with Gurdon Saltonstall and Abraham Pierson and Thomas Buckingham, and crosses the Market-place to mingle with the audience of the day's discussion. The magnificently-garbed Governor goes up into the high pulpit which had been moved back into the addition built the year before to the Meeting-house. The Deputies take their places; the Council scatter about,—dignified spectators of the day's affairs;—the townsfolk and visitors, with here and there a bevy of great ladies of the Colony, in those wigs and hooped petticoats that had just become the rage, overflow into the rear and side benches, while the less-important populace climbs up into the two narrow galleries. A minister, possibly James Pierpont by right of his local authority, opens the session with prayer and the business of the day begins.[1]

The records of the Assembly's discussions on this occasion are lost, and we shall have to depend upon conjecture for our view of what occurred. But I think that we know enough about the situation to venturè it. The clerk calls for the Act concerning the proposed Collegiate School, as

[1] Attending this first New Haven session of the General Assembly were the following: Governor Fitz-John Winthrop and Deputy Governor Treat of Milford; Magistrates Leet, Fitch, Mason, Wetherell, Stanley, Mansfield, Pitkin, Curtis, Chester, and Rossiter; and the following Deputies: Hartford—Hooker and Cook; New Haven—Osborn and Alling; Windsor—Wolcott and Eliot; Fairfield—Wakeman and Speaker Burr; New London—Smith and Hough; Stratford—Judson and Coe; Wethersfield—Treat and Wells; Guilford—Bradley and Fowler; Milford—Clark and Peck; Windham—Ripley and Crane; Branford—Malbie and Clerk Stent; Wallingford—Hall and Merriman; Woodbury—Sherman; Derby—Johnson and Riggs; Stamford—Waterbury and Holly; Haddam—Chapman and Brainerd; Middletown—White and Sumner; Waterbury—Judd and Bronson; Glastonbury—Smith and Hale; Saybrook—Nathaniel Lynde and Chapman; Norwich—Tracy; Lyme—Ely and Peck; Stonington—Mason and Saxton; Simsbury—Higlee and Wilcockson; Killingworth—Crane and Lane; Farmington—Hooker and Bull; Norwalk—Messenger and Keeler.

passed by the Assistants. And he reads the vigorous preamble, or petition,[1] introducing it, which Pierpont and his
friends had during the past week been busy upon and securing signatures to. Then the Act itself "for Liberty to erect
a Collegiate School" is droningly read. The famous
meeting is open.

Judging from all the attending circumstances, I do not
suppose that a very serious effort is made to side-track the
charter. The Pierpont party has had full opportunity from
Tuesday until Friday to acquaint the leaders in the House
with the latest developments in the plan of which they must
already have had full knowledge, and the phrasing of the
charter no doubt has been submitted to them. Yet there
is opposition. Gershom Bulkeley's timorous idea that the
Assembly would only get itself into trouble with the Royal
authority by granting a Connecticut college charter undoubtedly has its adherents, and we may believe that this
is the first point raised and argued. It has, however, been
thoroughly canvassed before this, and the Assistants have
expressed their minds on it, in passing the Act. It may well
have been left to Deputy John Eliot to explain this common
sentiment, as he had done in his letter to the Branford
meeting. The Colony had every right (says Eliot, standing

[1] This preamble, based on the petition already in circulation, was as
follows:

"Whereas several well disposed, and Publick spirited Persons of their
sincere regard to & Zeal for upholding & Propagating of the Christian
Protestant Religion by a succession of Learned & Orthodox men have expressed by Petition their earnest desires that full Liberty and Priveledge
be granted unto certain Undertakers for the founding, suitably endowing
& ordering a Collegiate School within his Maj[ties] Colony of Connecticot
wherin Youth may be instructed in the Arts & Sciences who thorough the
blessing of Almighty God may be fitted for Publick employment both in
Church & Civil State. To the intent therefore that all due incouragement
be Given to such Pious Resolutions and that so necessary & Religious an
undertakeing may be sett forward, supported and well managed:—BE IT
ENACTED by the Govern[r] & Company," etc. etc.

up in his flowing cloak) to charter such a school, and such a charter could not be "overthrown by law regularly executed," though, of course, it could be by force from England,—a contingency that Connecticut wit will continue to avoid. He cites a number of cases where the various Colonial General Courts have created and incorporated societies. He would admit the possibility of trouble, both for the school and Colony, as had been advanced by previous fearful speakers, if the projected academy was, in the first place, to be incorporated outright at this session, or, in the second place, if it were planned on any grand lines that might attract undue attention abroad. As to the first difficulty, we may fancy the young Windsor lawyer saying, it had been very properly avoided by the fact that the school was already "founded" and already held property, at least in the promises of books from its promoters. Concerning the latter, it was doubtless observed by the honorable gentlemen of the Assembly that the ministers who had brought this matter up had been most careful not to overstep the bounds of caution. They had asked merely for a charter for a school which should have no high-sounding name, and which should be presided over by a Rector or Master and Tutors and Ushers instead of by officers going under the more magnificent titles at Harvard and abroad. And the petition for it was signed by many of the great men of the Colony.

No doubt some arguments are made against proceeding even under these promising conditions, on the ground that it were a rash act that gave complete control over so important an enterprise as a Colony college to any self-perpetuating body of men, even if they were such men as the distinguished ministers named. Where was its visitorial power to be located? And what influence would the churches have over it? Mr. Woodbridge's party may have raised this question. I fancy that, if they did, they were as easily met. The Act deliberately forsook the traditional form of university government, to be sure. It differed from Harvard in that no resident body of Fellows or Overseers was named, and in that it gave the Assembly no right of visitation. But conditions were different in Connecticut from what they were in Massachusetts. The educated men of this Colony were scattered about among the towns, where in Massachusetts they were to a very considerable degree gathered in Boston. And the intention was to have the master of the school not necessarily a trustee, and certainly under the control of the remaining ten ministers, who therefore assumed, for the public at large, the right of visitation.[1] And if the church-synod organization question comes up, I imagine that it is as easily overthrown, if it needs any arguments before an Assembly the leaders of which are largely in sympathy with the desire of Pierpont and his friends to rid the enterprise of such an entanglement and who were not yet prepared for the Saybrook Platform. The plan of the founders had been a refrain of Davenport's ill-fated earlier college plan, to establish a Colony school for the education of the youth in "the arts and sciences," and for "public service to both church and commonwealth." It was not alone, or, perhaps especially, to be a theological seminary for the churches.

So, when the question is finally put to the Assembly, maybe John Eliot arises again to draw together the threads of the statement for the college promoters, or Speaker Burr of Samuel Andrew's church—speaking from the chair—clearly assures the Deputies that they are within their rights

[1] The Rector did not become necessarily a trustee until the charter of 1723 was passed.

to act, and are establishing a promising educational institution for their descendants.

The Act is passed, just before the Assembly rises, promptly to be signed by the much belaced Governor at Captain Miles' hospitable tavern across the Market-place later in the day. However important the passage of this Act was to the future Yale College, I suppose that it did not make much stir at the time. A group of the leading ministers of the Colony had established a school. This was a desirable business, and it was to be hoped that there would come some good from it. But the train-band captains and lieutenants and village gentry who made up the Lower House, were probably much more interested in other and more practical things. George Pardee of New Haven had complained that he wasn't paid sufficiently for his services as ferryman across the Quinnipiac at New Haven, and the House takes up the question and fixes the rates he may charge. A little squabble between two of the towns over a division line comes up, and the Assembly settles it. A number of people are voted the right to take up former grants of town lands, others are given patents for purchases of land, the trouble between two men over the distribution of an estate is laid over to the next Assembly, Israel Chauncy and others are voted the authority to sell some land as executors "for the procuring of money to defray the charge of curing Thomas Sherwood who is lame," a widow is permitted to sell some land, a committee report comes in on the division and boundaries of land left to two brothers between Killingworth and Saybrook. I suppose that there was more interest in the Assembly in these small matters than there was in giving the ministers the right to start a school. It was only when the Assembly later awoke to the possibilities of the Collegiate School that it began to take a paternal interest in it.

During the morning, and to encourage the new School at its start, Major John Fitch, of Plainfield, one of the Upper House, gave to the Trustees created that day, October 16, 1701, 637 acres of land in the remote town of Killingly (where Timothy Woodbridge had his farm), and a promise of glass and nails to build a college house.

Secretary *Addington*

CHAPTER VI

THE SAYBROOK ORGANIZATION

I

BOUT three weeks later, the organization meeting of the Trustees named in this charter of the Collegiate School was held at Saybrook.

This old Connecticut town is today a very different place from what it was in 1701. There were but few houses in the wooded tract which is now Saybrook to the hurried traveler along the shore, the village then being far down on what is now Old Saybrook Point. One walks today through the broad, elm-lined main street of the newer and upper part of the town, between rows of substantial old mansions built during or just after Revolutionary times, and then crosses a long, sandy stretch that dips down to tide-level marshes, to rise gradually again to the Old Saybrook of Thomas Buckingham's time. This old part of the town is historic soil, where much had happened previous to 1701. Six years before Plymouth was settled, tradition has it that Dutch skippers discovered the strategic advantages of this neck of land commanding the approach to the broad Connecticut River and the fertile farming lands far up its banks where Hartford now is. It was a Dutch Amsterdam trading post with the Indians until 1632, and was claimed a purchase by them. Just before that year, Viscount Say and Seal, and Lord Brook, dissatisfied with the Puritan party prospects under Charles I, had secured the transfer from Warwick of the Plymouth claim to the Connecticut River, and had offered to young John Winthrop, son of the Massachusetts Governor (and later to be Connecticut's most famous Governor), the Governorship of a new English Puritan colony to be settled there. Winthrop took charge of affairs with his customary energy. He built a fort and manned it with twenty fighting men and guns, just in time to head off a Dutch invasion belligerently intent upon the same business. A surveyor arrived in 1636, and the town (named "Say-Brook" after its two noble patentees) was laid out, much on the lines on which John Brockett three years later was to survey New Haven. And the Winthrop ambition was very much like Theophilus Eaton's. Say-Brook was to be a great commercial center. And it was to be more than that, if all traditions are not astray. It was to be a New England Puritan colony transcending in political importance any of its neighbors. For tradition (possibly apocryphal) has it that there was good expectation that a group of the great English Puritans of that day, led by Pym and Hampden, and including Cromwell and Milton, was to leave old England and establish a second commonwealth there.

It was in view of these possibilities, so it is said, that surveyor John Gardiner laid out Old Saybrook with two great central squares, on which the Meeting-house and public buildings were to be built in good time, and about which were to rise the great houses of these important settlers. A wooden fort was built on the riverside,—later to be replaced by stone battlements facing the Sound itself,—

and a strong palisade was erected across the low neck of land connecting the Point with the mainland to the north. Here, no doubt, Eaton dropped anchor on his way to look for a site for his New Haven Colony in 1637. Here, two years later, Colonel George Fenwick, one of the lesser patentees, with his charming lady, arrived overland from New Haven, driving before him that herd of Devonshire cattle the descendants of which do the major service on southern Connecticut farms today.

The Winthrop scheme failed completely, however. The great Puritan statesmen never arrived. The great marketplace dwindled to a village green. Saybrook was sold to the Connecticut Colony some five years later, to begin that quiet and uneventful farming life which lasted without anything of interest happening, except a very independent reception of Andros in 1675 when Thomas Buckingham galloped forth for aid, until this meeting of the Collegiate School Trustees in 1701. The great houses of the English Puritan leaders had never been built. The shallow harbor had never received any great laden English ships. By 1701 the village was barely one of the first dozen towns of the twenty-two in the Colony in tax-paying ranking, and, in spite of its contemporary importance as the strategic defense of the Connecticut River towns, gained perhaps all of its standing in the Colony because of the character and energy of Thomas Buckingham, its Congregational minister. His parsonage faced the village green of Gardiner's original layout, and was not far from the fort and training-grounds which were still in order against a foreign invader. Perhaps not over thirty farmhouses were scattered about the Meeting-house, among their elms and gardens and orchards, when the Trustees of the new Collegiate School rode into town on that November morning in 1701 to organize the Colony Collegiate School.

The First Meeting of the Trustees

II

This meeting was held beginning Tuesday, November 11, a little under a month after the successful passage of the charter.

Six of the ten Trustees named in that Act joined Thomas Buckingham at his Saybrook parsonage at this time. Israel Chauncy of Stratford, with young Joseph Webb of Fairfield, riding over on horseback, doubtless pick up Samuel Andrew at Milford and James Pierpont at New Haven, and the elderly Abraham Pierson when they canter, followed on horseback by their men-servants or slaves, into old Killingworth Street. Little Noadiah Russell rides briskly down the picturesque Connecticut Valley bridle-path from Middletown. Timothy Woodbridge did not come to this meeting (as he had not to the previous two sessions), being still detained by the "humor in his right leg" at Boston. The third Hartford County Trustee, old Samuel Mather of Windsor, sent his regrets (the first of a long series, by the way), as did James Noyes of Stonington. The latter wrote that he was not able to do much for the School, and plaintively suggested that Gurdon Saltonstall undertake for him the necessary drumming up of scholars in New London County that might fall to his lot to secure. His brother, Moses, of Old Lyme across the river, might be with the Trustees in his place, writes James Noyes, but we do not know that he was. This meeting, at which the legal "founding" of the Collegiate School was to be the business in hand, thus appears again to have been attended (with the exception of one newcomer,—Noadiah Russell) by none except the original leaders of the Long Island coast villages, though Samuel Russel of Branford apparently did not appear.

Three days were given by the Trustees present at this meeting to a thorough effort to establish their School, the three important actions in which were to be the choice of a site and of a Rector and the setting up of rules of government for the scholars.

We may permit ourselves a glimpse at the little group of periwigged and black-gowned ministers who now gathered about the great table before Mr. Buckingham's hearth-fire, which no doubt was blazing to keep out the penetrating cold of the first of the wintry gales from the Sound. At the head of the table no doubt sits Buckingham himself, his white hair framing a strong face under his ministerial black cap. About the table are the other founders: Israel Chauncy, now close to sixty, pleasant-faced and kindly; Joseph Webb, with ever-ready pleasantries if the need comes, but strong for authority to be vested in the board; Samuel Andrew, cultivated gentleman, perhaps not too energetic, yet keen of eye and full of enthusiasm for the college project; the little Middletown minister, peering up from his great chair and very much alive to any action which might not meet with the approval of the absent Woodbridge and Mather; James Pierpont, the scribe of the meeting, handsome and charming-mannered, his brown curly hair falling over his shoulders, the papers having to do with the business in hand before him; and the broad-shouldered Abraham Pierson (they commonly called it "Person" in those days), probably the largest man, physically, of the group, slow of manner and quiet, but keenly interested, owing to the developments which he anticipated, in every act of the meeting.

The first business is to hear James Pierpont read the charter which the General Assembly had passed, granting in the language of the founders themselves "a Liberty, and privilege, for the founding, suitably endowing and ordering a Collegiate School, within his Majesty's Colony of Connecticut, wherein youth may be instructed in the arts and sciences, who through the blessing of Almighty God may be

fitted for public employment both in church and civil state."
The seven ministers, most of whom had informally
"founded" the school at Branford before the Assembly
convened, now formally made themselves legal Trustees
under the Colony's charter by accepting the service and
giving books to a library, which books no doubt were now
laid actually upon the table.[1]   Thus organized, the board
proceeded to the three main problems before it.

[1] The resolutions adopted by the Trustees at this opening meeting
referred to their project of establishing a Connecticut Colony school, as
follows: "Whereas it was the glorious publick Design of our now blessed
Fathers, in their Remove from *Europe* into these Parts of *America,* both to
plant, and (under the Divine Blessing) to propagate in this Wilderness
the blessed reformed Protestant Religion, in the Purity of its Order and
Worship; not only to their Posterity, but also to the barbarous Natives: In
which great Enterprize they wanted not the Royal Commands and Favour
of his Majesty King Charles the Second, to authorize and invigorate them.

"We their unworthy Posterity, lamenting our past Neglects of this
grand Errand, and sensible of the equal Obligations, better to prosecute the
same End, are desirous in our Generation to be serviceable thereunto.

"Whereunto the religious and liberal Education of suitable Youth is,
under the Blessing of God, a chief and most probable Expedient.   Therefore,
that we might not be wanting in cherishing the present observable and pious
Disposition of many well-minded People, to dedicate their Children and
Substance unto God in such a good Service: And being ourselves, with
sundry other Reverend Elders, not only desired by our Godly People,
to undertake as Trustees, for erecting, forming, ordering and regulating a Collegiate School, for the Advancement of such an Education: But
having also obtained of our present religious Government, both full Liberty
and Assistance, by their Donations to such an Use: Tokens likewise that
particular Persons will not be wanting in their Beneficence: Do, in Duty
to God, and the Weal of our Country, undertake in the aforesaid Design.
And now being met, according to the Liberties and Aids granted to us for
the Use aforesaid; do order and appoint, that there shall be, and hereby is
erected and formed a Collegiate School, wherein shall be taught the liberal
Arts and Languages, in such Place or Places in Connecticut, as the said
Trustees with their Associates and Successors, do or shall, from Time to
Time, see Cause to order."

After which salutation, the "Rules" of the School are decided upon,
"according to the laudable Order and Usage of *Harvard College,*" etc.

The question of a site and the choice of the Rector were of such closely connected significance that I presume they were discussed together and agreed upon perhaps only at the end of the session. During this three-days discussion other and comparatively minor matters were doubtless passed upon first. It was decided, for one thing, that the Rector (who was not necessarily to be one of the Board) and Tutors should remain in office only under good behavior. No scholar was to be expelled except by a quorum of the Trustees acting with the Rector (we may suppose that Joseph Webb, still smarting a bit under his Sophomore Harvard experience, had a good deal to say about this). In the matter of admission requirements, the Trustees immediately decided that they themselves should not be bothered with such matters. Entrance to the Collegiate School was to depend wholly upon a reading knowledge of the classics. The Rector, with the help of any conveniently-reached neighboring minister, was therefore empowered to examine candidates as they offered themselves at odd times during the year, "and, finding them duly prepared and expert in Latin and Greek authors, both poetic and oratorical, as also making good Latin," should let them in. As to the regular educational business of the school, the Rector was now instructed to teach theological divinity, but in no other system than the Trustees permitted; the Assembly's Latin Catechism was to be recited weekly and expounded by the Rector as was Dr. Ames' "Theological Theses,"—the Trustees thereby following the Boston suggestion which they had not cared to incorporate in the charter itself; the Scriptures were ordered read daily, both at morning and evening prayers, and by the scholars "as at Harvard," and on Sabbath days the Rector was to expound practical divinity or have the students repeat sermons. The contemporary Harvard curriculum was ordered followed, so

Black Horse Tavern, Saybrook

far as the needs of the infant school permitted; the first, or
Arts degree, was set at the end of four years' resident study,
and the second, or Master's, three years afterwards; the
tuition charge was made thirty shillings a year for under-
graduates and ten shillings for graduate students. For the
time being, and until the Trustees could be assured of no
interference with the School from England, there were to be
no public "Commencements," and during that time the
School term might be shortened to three years.

III

The all-important matter of a site and choice of Rector
now came to a decision.

It would appear that these two matters had been
thoroughly canvassed before this organization meeting, as

they naturally would have been almost from the very beginning of the College discussion. And from what happened at this meeting, I should think that the result had been pretty thoroughly understood in advance. There were, as I have shown, two factions among the Trustees who had been named in the charter. The Hartford members,—taken into the scheme as it came to a conclusion,—with the possible addition of Moses Noyes and Thomas Buckingham, were probably opposed to the very natural desire of Pierpont's New Haven group that the college should be begun in the latter village.[1] Nor would the seacoast-town ministers agree on Hartford. The agitation for a permanent settlement at Hartford, which began almost immediately after this meeting, would go to show that little Noadiah Russell, the only representative of that county at the Saybrook meeting, undoubtedly pressed it as his county's claim (which was based on Hartford's known preëminence in population and wealth over the remaining towns). Against New Haven, and doubtless for Saybrook as a compromise, were Noyes and Buckingham, at this time probably supported from the outside by Saltonstall and Governor Winthrop. I judge that the Trustees from the western seacoast towns were for New Haven, as they certainly were steadily opposed throughout the later agitation to Hartford.

As the settlement of this question was bound up in the selection of a Rector, we may take it that the decision was again postponed until that choice was made.

[1] Samuel Mather had written to his fellow Trustees, on October 27, 1701, that he had been ill, but that he was much interested in the School. As to the site, he was then for New Haven, as he says: "My mind is fully fixt in that New-haven Town Plat is ye best place for such a Schole. I have not been able as yet to discourse ye neighbouring ministers concerning yt matter." This was the last we hear of the Windsor Trustee's preference for New Haven. After Timothy Woodbridge had "discoursed" him, we find him enrolled by Woodbridge on the Hartford side.

As this question came to the front, James Pierpont's leadership now again asserted itself. In a memorandum in his handwriting concerning this meeting, we have not only a list of things to be done (all of which were carried out and to the effect above narrated) but we have the significant entry, "to provide if Mr. Pierson refuse." This memorandum clearly shows that James Pierpont had had Abraham Pierson in mind for the Rectorship, and likewise suggests that Mr. Pierson had been approached on the matter and had not fully decided about it.

The election of Yale's first Rector began, however, with a complimentary vote for Israel Chauncy, the son of President Chauncey of Harvard and a well-known scholar himself. This was as gracefully declined by that now aged minister, and Pierson's name seems to have at once been introduced.

In the succeeding chapter I shall gather together what we know of this Killingworth minister. As we have seen, he had been among the earliest promoters of the College plan and had taken the lead in securing Connecticut opinions on the validity of the charter for the Branford meeting earlier in the fall. While others of the Trustees, especially those from Hartford County, had been chosen for their town and sectional representation as much as for anything else, Mr. Pierson's little farming community (it was far down on the Colony tax-list, and a mere village) brought him no such distinction, and he had been made a Trustee wholly on his own account. Yet he undoubtedly had demurred when the proposition had been made to him by Pierpont, because he did not wish to leave his people. Reserving his full acceptance of the first Rectorship of the Collegiate School until a second meeting of the Trustees, to be held at New Haven the following April, Abraham Pierson settled the question temporarily by at least not refusing it. The Saybrook

meeting now adjourned to April in New Haven, and, when
that meeting was held,—very likely at James Pierpont's
house,—Pierson formally accepted, saying that he "durst not
refuse such a service for God and his generation, but submitted himself to take the charge and work of Rector upon
him."

The expectation that he would do this, and that he would
agree to remove to Saybrook, had led the Trustees to vote
to settle the Collegiate School at that town, and to name as
Treasurer one of its leading citizens, Nathaniel Lynde.
But he had either declined or had immediately resigned, and
Richard Rosewell, a newly-settled West India merchant in
James Pierpont's distant New Haven congregation, had
taken his place. Upon Rosewell's death shortly afterwards,
Judge John Alling, another New Haven merchant, was
elected. Judge Alling, whose blacksmith shop probably
stood on the west side of the present Church Street, just
south of Crown, had been Town Recorder for twenty years,
a Deputy in the Assembly from New Haven, a Councilor,
Judge of Probate and of the County Court, and was for the
next fifteen years to be the Collegiate School's financial
manager. One further election ended the legal proceedings
of the Saybrook meeting. Upon the election of Abraham
Pierson as Rector, the Trustees chose Samuel Russel as a
trustee, and thus all three of the original movers for the
Collegiate School began service together as its trustees.

After the Saybrook meeting Thomas Buckingham sent a
letter to Governor Fitz-John Winthrop at New London,
whose interest in the enterprise had been a prime factor in
its success up to this time. The Saybrook minister is evidently elated. Says he, "A very comfortable, unanimous
meeting was had, very well agreeing upon the person, who
under the name of Rector might preside in and take charge
of sd school (viz. the Rev^rnd Mr. Pierson). We^e also had

no great difficultie about the place (viz.) Say-Brook (in case no considerations come in to alter our thoughts), that appearing to be the place for the best accommodation of the Colonies in generall, and adjacent places." And he then reports the final action of the Trustees, in having left a letter "with mee to the people of Killingworth," which he has delivered, and the reply to which he has had, "the summe of which is that they do not see it their duty to consent to the parting with Mr. Pierson." In that ambiguous state the question of Abraham Pierson's residence at the headquarters of the Collegiate School was to be left, until, as we shall see, unexpected circumstances were to solve it, as the Trustees themselves and Rector Pierson never were.

What kind of a man this first Rector of Yale was, and what his life-surroundings had been until this time, I may now digress a bit to chronicle.

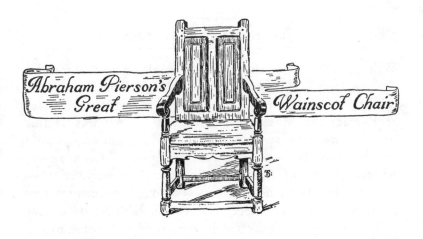

Abraham Pierson's
Great Wainscot Chair

CHAPTER VII

ABRAHAM PIERSON

I

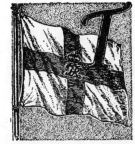

HE Pierson, or Pearson, family, of which the Collegiate School's first Rector was a member, was of an ancient yeomanry stock in Yorkshire, England. The father, Abraham Pierson, Senior, was an early 17th Century Cambridge University man, and had taken Church of England orders at about the time that John Davenport had fled to Holland. By 1639, he, with other advanced Puritans, had found Archbishop Laud hostile to his continuance in the Church. An intensely religious man, he had at that time been forced into that extreme group of Separatists which Davenport had joined. He had emigrated to Boston, where for a time he was an assistant in the primitive Meeting-house of John

Wilson, and supplied the pulpits of neighboring churches, including Lynn. The exiled John Wheelwright, brother-in-law of the famous Mrs. Anne Hutchinson, was then minister at Exeter; the Massachusetts Puritan church was at this time, as we have seen, beginning its long effort to stamp out heresies, both political and religious. As a result, several groups of people were leaving its jurisdiction,— Thomas Hooker among them,—to found more attractive Puritan colonies elsewhere. Pierson, finding his own ideas as to church government much more rigid than those of the Boston leaders, left Lynn with his bride in 1641 for Southampton, L. I., taking sixteen people with him as a congregation of his own, and there establishing a primitive settlement about his own Meeting-house. Three years later this district was annexed to Thomas Hooker's new Connecticut Colony, and Pierson, unable to agree with Hooker's broad political ideas, again moved, this time to Branford, where, several years later, he brought his congregation into John Davenport's newly organized New Haven Jurisdiction and thus found himself finally in a Puritan colony with the theological views and civil government of which he was in full and even violent sympathy. To these views the elder Pierson was to give a lifelong attachment and to be the last to uphold them on New World soil.

II

It was either in the last year at Southampton, or in the first at Branford, that Abraham Pierson the younger was born.[1] It was a crude enough wilderness in which to bring

[1] Abraham Pierson's birthplace is unknown. The antiquarian Savage fixes it in 1641 at Lynn. His gravestone in the modern Clinton, then Killingworth, would indicate that he was born in 1646, at which time his father had moved to Branford.

up a family of children.[1] Fertile meadows swept down from the village center to the narrow harbor, but on all other sides the settlement was hedged in by forests and low hills, in which were the poverty-stricken villages of the Indians. A five-mile fence, or palisade, had originally enclosed the settlement, for the usual Colonial purpose of keeping out wolves and Indians, and young Abraham Pierson must have grown up as a youngster under its great posts and high palings. Tradition has it that the first Meeting-house was built of logs and surrounded by high cedar stakes. This and the planters' homes were built nearer the waterside than the present Branford center, and on what is now known as Branford Point. If so, the rugged shores of the present Indian Neck and the sand beaches at the Point must have been the playground of the Pierson children. Much of this territory was bought directly by the church from the Indians; Indian Neck, so called, and other shore land to the east, is still owned by the Branford Congregational Church, and rented under century-long leases to the large summer colony that now occupies this most picturesque part of the Connecticut coast line.

The London corporate society for the conversion of these unfortunate "Amerinds" was then becoming active, and the elder Pierson, working under this society and the New Haven confederation, undertook to bring the Branford Indians into the Calvinistic fold. No doubt the young Abraham Pierson sat behind his father's chair many times when the natives trooped speechlessly in,—as they had a habit of doing throughout New England,—to squat on the

[1] Two younger brothers, Thomas and John, and a sister, Abigail, were brought over from Southampton with the family. Abigail,—"my choice and precious daughter," wrote the old father later in his life,—was to marry John Davenport's son and become the mother of the Rev. James Pierpont's first wife.

minister's oak-slab floor or stone hearth, and listen to his unintelligible exhortations. The elder Pierson drew up a catechism for these natives, which came to the attention of the London Commissioners in 1656 and which was printed.

Young Abraham Pierson probably received his early education in English and Latin from his father in the family circle[1] and then, so tradition has it, at John Davenport's stern hands, in New Haven, where he may very well have been one of the few outside scholars in John Bowers' log schoolhouse on the public square, as he was finally prepared for Harvard by Jeremiah Peck. When he was about fourteen, young Pierson,—with his Latin books and broad-brimmed rabbit's-fur cap, homespun clothes and leather breeches,—went to Harvard, where he became one of a class of five boys under the mild yet rigidly-conservative President Chauncey. There he spent four years imbibing the traditional Calvinistic theology of the Harvard of that time and a crude scientific education.[2] Among his classmates in 1668 at Harvard was young John Prudden, the son of that Rev. Peter Prudden who had been the first minister at Milford, and very likely a boyhood friend of Pierson's at the New Haven School. Upon their graduation from Harvard, the two chums returned to Milford together,— the Pierson home in Branford having been moved to

[1] Another son, Theophilus, and four daughters were born into the Pierson family during the Branford days. Rebecca, the youngest of these girls, was later to marry Joseph Johnson, son of the tavern keeper at Newark, from whose uncle was to descend the famous Doctor Samuel Johnson, tutor in Yale College at New Haven and later Episcopalian minister and first president of King's College, New York, which was afterwards to become Columbia University.

[2] Physics seems to have been a favorite study of the younger Abraham Pierson. A Latin notebook, taken down in his classes at Harvard, in his handwriting, is now in the Yale Library, and he composed a crude text-book on the subject which, the story is, was used in manuscript for many years in early Yale.

Newark,—and here for about a year they studied theology together under the tutorship of the village minister, Rev. Roger Newton, as was the custom of the day. Young Pierson, however serious-minded he must have been, immediately tumbled head over heels in love with one of the village girls[1] and was married to her in 1673.

It had been, curiously enough, in the same year that old John Davenport, a disappointed man, was leaving his shattered New Haven theocracy for Boston, defeated in his untiring efforts to found a theocratic republic and a Puritan college in the New Haven Colony, that young Abraham Pierson, fresh from the old man's teaching and from Harvard, was coming back to the same scene where, three decades later, he was to be one of the founders and the first Rector of that college which Davenport had done so much to pave the way for, and which he was never to see. But in 1668 this may well have seemed an improbable enough outcome. Independent New Haven had been coerced into joining the more liberal Connecticut Colony at Hartford, the old New Haven Jurisdiction had been swept away, and the supporters of the defeated Davenport scheme in Branford and Milford and New Haven were moving their homes to Newark, where the elder Pierson was to rebuild the pillars of the fallen church and establish another theocracy on the old New Haven lines. Young Pierson for the moment fell in with this new Puritan enterprise, as the year 1670 sees him the assistant to his father in the Newark church, and

[1] This was the vivacious Abigail Clark, daughter of George Clark, one of Milford's first settlers. Her sister, Sarah, became the mother of that future Governor Law of the Connecticut Colony who in 1745 came to President Clap's support and secured the passage of the first great charter of Yale College. The two Clark girls were leaders in Milford youthful society, and, so the story goes, used to sing a topical song of the day while spinning in a room in the Treat house in Milford that hugely amused the Regicides, Whalley and Goffe, who were hidden underneath in the cellar.

three years later bringing Abigail Clark of Milford there as
his bride.

For the next twenty-two years, Abraham Pierson the
younger was to be occupied in carrying on the primitive
church work of this second Davenport theocracy until the
time came when he, too, found himself less and less in sympathy with the New Haven scheme and in turn abandoned
it. The Newark life of those days, and a little of Abraham
Pierson's part in it, emerge from the records that have
come down to us.[1] It is a primitive enough life, as we may
trace it through these early documents. On his settling
there, young Pierson takes a small cabin in the northwest
section of the village, fronting a little stream that runs
parallel to the Passaic and a few rods from it through the
rough-built settlement. His salary, as his father's assistant,
is at first £30, to be increased to £40 two years later, with
lands given him on condition that he remain there "a considerable time." He now moves into more commodious
quarters, taking the widow Ward's "dwelling-house, well,
yard, barn, garden, and orchard, with one acre and three
rods of land." By this transaction he also becomes the
possessor of some of the furniture of the widow Ward's
house, "one great wainscot chair, one chest, two hogsheads,
one kneading and two joint stools, formerly belonging to
Lawrence Ward (of New Haven) deceased."[2] For seven

---

[1] A good deal of light is thrown upon these years of Rector Pierson's
life by the Newark Town Records, published by the New Jersey Historical
Society. There is more or less about him in the Rev. Mr. Stearns' very
lucid lectures on the history of the First Church of Newark,—a book that
visualizes early Newark days in quite the same way that the Rev. Dr.
Leonard Bacon's "Historical Discourses" illustrates the early New Haven
church times.

[2] Deacon Lawrence Ward, whose effects thus came into Rector Pierson's
hands, was an old man when he followed the elder Pierson from Branford,
where he had been an officer of the church. His name appears among the

years father and son were minister and teacher of the Newark congregation, at an annual cost to the town of £120, except for one year, when hard times resulted in their accepting twenty pounds less. The elder Pierson, as part of his share of £80, received annually one pound of butter "for every milch cow in the town."

In 1678, ten years after his old colleague, Davenport, had gone to Boston, Abraham Pierson, Senior, died in Newark, leaving behind him a pious memory, the considerable estate for the times of £822, that included a large collection of books, and a reputation that has come down to us of one of the sturdiest and strongest-minded leaders of that first independent Puritan pilgrimage to the New World. He belonged to the most extreme wing of the English religious immigration; his career, from Lynn, through the Southampton experiment, to Branford, and thence to Newark is the story of a second John Davenport, who was unable to fit himself into the more liberal political conditions that were growing up in Massachusetts and the Connecticut Colony. He was a learned man, though he left nothing beyond his Indian Catechism in print. His library, consisting of four hundred and forty volumes, largely theological, was one of the most extensive in the colonies, and was

original settlers of the New Haven Colony. Among the possessions of Rector Pierson at his death in 1707 was a great paneled chair, which later came into the University's hands, and which was used as late as 1870 as "the President's Chair" at Yale Commencements. It is now in the President's office, among other ancient Yale relics. It is within the possibilities, though nothing certain may be said regarding it, that this old Jacobite chair now owned by Yale is the Deacon Ward "wainscot" chair that Abraham Pierson purchased in 1672 in Newark and later took to Killingworth. If so, this famous chair no doubt stood in Deacon Ward's first New Haven house, which faced the harbor about where Olive Street meets Water Street today, and may more than once have framed the slight form of John Davenport in it.

The First Newark Meeting-house

bequeathed to his eldest son,[1] except for one or two English books which in his will he directed his widow to train up his younger sons in.

Abraham Pierson, the younger, was now elected minister of the Newark church, with a salary of £80, his annual supply of firewood piled in his kitchen yard by town decree, and exemption from town taxes, or rates, granted to him. A strapping young fellow, with a great aptitude for the pulpit, where he probably gave extemporaneous sermons as was the custom until a little later date, and endowed with a warm heart toward the needy of his congregation, the future Rector of the Collegiate School may well have thought himself settled for life over a Puritan church to his

[1] Abraham Pierson the younger brought these books with him to Killingworth in 1694. As he was one of the founders of the Collegiate School at the Saybrook meeting in 1701, and there doubtless gave books to the new school, there is some possibility that his gift to Yale was from among these ancient theological tomes. Nineteen of these volumes were presented to the College Library in 1707 by Pierson's sons.

liking. That he was popular with his people appears from the contemporaneous statement that "great harmony and affection" existed between him and them. One Obediah Bruen, magistrate, writing to his children at the elder Pierson's death, no doubt voiced the town's views when he said that God "hath not left us destitute of spiritual enjoyments, but hath given us a faithful dispenser of the Word of God— a young Timothy—a man after God's own heart, well rooted and grounded in the faith, one with whom we can comfortably walk in the doctrines of the faith." The Newark period in Abraham Pierson's life began with every indication of agreement on these highly important matters of the faith between minister and congregation.

III

And these days must have been busy ones for the future Rector Pierson, marked as they are in the town records by the usual business and political disturbances of the times. It is a transplanted Connecticut village, walking "in the Congregational way," that we now see Pierson preaching to in English-governed New Jersey. Indian scares are, of course, not infrequent,—for these were the terrible days of King Philip's War, and Massachusetts and Connecticut were in a state of terror. Pierson's people protected themselves, as many other villages were doing. "Flankers" or palisade screens, are set by town orders at two corners of the Meeting-house, behind which armed sentries watch for Indian movements in the woods while the minister preaches within the square cabin of a church. "It is agreed," go the records, "that the Drum being begun to be beaten at Joseph Rigg's Gate, and so all the Way up the Street as far as Sam'l Harrison's Gate, and at the Ceasing of the beating of the Drum three Guns being distinctly fired

off—it shall be sufficient Warning for all as are in the
Military List, forthwith to meet at the Meeting-House in
their Arms." The woodland about the village clearing is
regularly burned, partly for safety against Indian attack,
no doubt, and partly for pasturing. Burning these woods is
a serious matter to the village safety, also, while it is going
on; there is an annual committee in charge, and every man
over sixteen has to do his share, both to burn the bushes and
to keep the sparks from setting the thatch-roofed houses
afire. No doubt this annual business is also a protection
against prowling wild animals, as during Pierson's early
days in Newark the records show that generous bounties are
voted for the heads of wolves and for bear pelts. Against
these several enemies, "a Watch" is ordered to be "kept
in the Town, Three in a Night, at some House appointed by
the Sarjeants," who are to call the Town Drummer from
his bed as need arises.

The minister's share in this daily round is very likely
limited to his two long services of Sabbath days, his weekly
"lectures," and his attendance upon the sick and dying,
wherein he is assisted by the elder of the church, and, we
may believe, by his helpful wife. Two settlers of each of
the town-quarters are appointed "to look after the carrying
in Mr. Pierson's Wood for the year." This becoming
difficult to manage, a certain day is set upon which the minister's wood supply is to be cut and dragged in by ox-teams,
and the business of seeing that this is done is divided among
the quarters of the settlement in annual rotation. The
Meeting-house needs repairs "to keep out the Wett and
Cold for the present," the seats are rebuilt, and a new
shingle roof put on. The youth of the village,—and I take
it that the Puritan youngsters were no different in natural
spirits from their descendants,—call forth numerous rulings
of the nonplussed town meetings. The boys are misbehaving

"both in the Meeting House and without by the House Sides" on Sabbath days, and Mr. Pierson's younger brother or nephew, Thomas, is ordered to look after them. He has not succeeded in doing this, come a few years, and the town meeting names another man,—in fact, a long succession of citizens is called upon to keep an eye on the disorderly youth and snap their ears with the pole kept for the purpose in the Meeting-house. Nor do the youths of the village limit their pranks to the long, dull Sabbaths. Safety valves seem to burst out of their restricted lives in various directions. It has to be voted by town meeting assembled that all entertainments in the village houses shall end at nine o'clock of the evening,—"to prevent disorderly Meeting of Young People at unseasonable Times," indignantly scratches the dignified town clerk on the record book.

But the town life of the little Puritan settlement goes on, quietly, throughout all of these difficulties with human nature. The town gravedigger is voted "3s. for a Man's Grave, 2s. for a Middle Person, and 1s. 6d. for a Child." The seating order in the Meeting-house is not satisfactory, "and it is agreed that Persons should be placed according to Office, Age, Estate, Infirmity and Desent or Parentage" (so oligarchical has the second Davenport theocratic democracy become in its transplanting). A shoemaker,—one Whitehead,—is invited to settle by a special town vote, "provided he will supply the Town with Shoes." An experienced boatman is likewise honored, on the understanding that he will ferry citizens back and forth across the narrow river from Boatman's Neck. The fences about the private house-lots make continual trouble, and many town votes are recorded about them. The matter is decided by ordering each householder to set up stakes, inscribed with his initials, at either end of his fence and to make that fence four feet four inches high,—very like the palisades that shut out the New Haven settlers from the roadway before their home-lots.

Throughout this quarter of a century, Abraham Pierson was no doubt contented with his lot. But, by 1692, a change came. Some misunderstanding or other arose,—what we do not know. But it is reflected in his church relations. In 1687 an original levy on the rate-payers for the minister's salary had been changed by town vote "to pay the Minister by Contributions." There being some difficulty even about this, it had been decided to have fifty of the villagers guarantee the original £80 by voluntary taxation, with firewood extra. But this plan lapsed, and the result was that Pierson went without salary for two years.

The long-continued harmony between Pierson and his Newark church was now breaking up. Several things had their part in this change of relations. The money trouble seems not to have been a chief cause (Pierson's old college chum, John Prudden, who succeeded him in the Newark church, had the same trouble over collecting his salary), but rather a symptom of a more fundamental difficulty. The whole period of Pierson's last ten years in Newark, we may recall, was one of wide political and financial disturbance throughout the province. The Dutch had been driven from New Amsterdam and Sir Edmund Andros had become Governor of New Jersey, New York, and New England. A new King had come to England and Andros had been seized and removed from office at Boston. As a result, all public and private affairs were in a serious state. In Newark the town meeting had to take steps to protect its citizens' property rights. So the Newark financial support to the church languished. Yet the trouble between Pierson and his congregation lay elsewhere,—in a gradually widening difference of opinion between them over matters concerning the church itself. Jonathan Dickinson, later president of

Princeton College, was to be one of Pierson's scholars at the Killingworth School and must have known what there was to know about this difficulty. Writing about it many years later, he criticises the Newark people as being "culpable for managing a controversy with their worthy minister upon these points" (Presbyterianism and Congregationalism). Pierson, says Dickinson, "removed from their abuses to New England, where he was received with great kindness, and died in the highest honor and esteem among them, notwithstanding his Presbyterian principles." The affair is quite unimportant except as it throws light on the little-known character of Abraham Pierson, and on his theological views. A long-current interpretation of it, out of which Pierson comes in rather sad disrepute, has been to the effect that he "had imbibed moderate Presbyterianism from his father, and when at Cambridge College, he had received strong prejudices against Plymouthean independency; and after his father's death he was for introducing more rigid Presbyterianism into Newark." His church matters had been peaceable during his father's time, goes this legend, but the congregation did not take kindly to his "pride of directing . . . far beyond anything that the congregation had been accustomed to witness." He had "distinguished talents and accomplishments, but had neither the meekness, patience, nor prudence of his father." As this tradition started a century after the episode itself, I imagine that we may rely more precisely upon the contemporaneous Dickinson story of it. This puts Pierson in rather a more favorable light, to be sure, but which would seem to be more likely than the later and doubtless warped story.

The question of Presbyterianism, however, was shortly to become a large matter in Newark, as throughout New Jersey, and in fact New England. Originally founded as a New Haven Congregational church, the Newark settlement had come into touch with the Scotch Presbyterians who had begun, by 1682, to settle throughout the province. Pierson could hardly have remained unacquainted with the more aggressive leaders among these newcomers,—neighbors as they became,—and from their arrival no doubt found himself more and more inclined toward his early leanings to their form of church organization. He was a "Scotch Presbyterian," his grandson many years later told President Stiles. There was, of course, practically no difference between the theology of the New England Puritan-Congregationalists, and the various Presbyterian elements that from the earliest days came into New England church life, and which now, in some numbers, had come directly from Scotland into New Jersey. Many of the foremost Massachusetts Congregational church founders were "Presbyterians." The only serious difference between the two groups had to do with matters of church organization, with the duties and powers given the elders and the synods,— that "consociational government" which the historian Trumbull speaks of.

Abraham Pierson's Newark people, by 1690-1692, were not as ready as was Pierson himself to join this new movement, and his dismissal resulted.

It is curious to see how matters turned out as the years came around, both for the Presbyterian Pierson and for the Congregational Newark church that dismissed him. The next three ministers of that church were undoubtedly Congregationalists of the New England order: Pierson's college chum, John Prudden; Jabez Wakeman, Harvard 1697; and Samuel Whittlesey, who later studied with Pierson at Killingworth and who was graduated from the Collegiate School in 1705. Then the Scotch Presbyterian movement seems to have gained headway. Joseph Webb, a Yale graduate of 1715, the son of the Rev. Joseph Webb of

Fairfield who had been one of the Collegiate School founders
with Pierson, was introduced to the Newark people by
Rector Samuel Andrew of Yale College as their pastor.
Presbyterianism had now absorbed Congregationalism generally throughout New Jersey, and Joseph Webb easily
carried his Newark people into that church organization
with him. Abraham Pierson's son, John, a Collegiate
School graduate of 1711, became the minister of a
neighboring town and associated himself with this movement over his long career of fifty-three years. Pierson,
however, returning to Congregational Connecticut as a
moderate Scotch Presbyterian, passed the remainder of his
life in the older church,—the dominant independent-church
sentiment of Connecticut having absorbed the Presbyterian
movement, compromising with it only halfway in the famous
Saybrook Platform of 1708.

Abraham Pierson left Newark in 1692, made a brief stay
in Greenwich, Connecticut, and in 1694 was called to Killingworth, where he took the long-vacant pulpit of John
Woodbridge. Welcoming him to the Colony, the General
Assembly in 1695 grant him "two hundred acres of land
for a farme," and exempt him from "paiment of rates for
his stock and land." Six years later he becomes the first
Rector of the Collegiate School.

Abraham Pierson's Statue on the College Campus

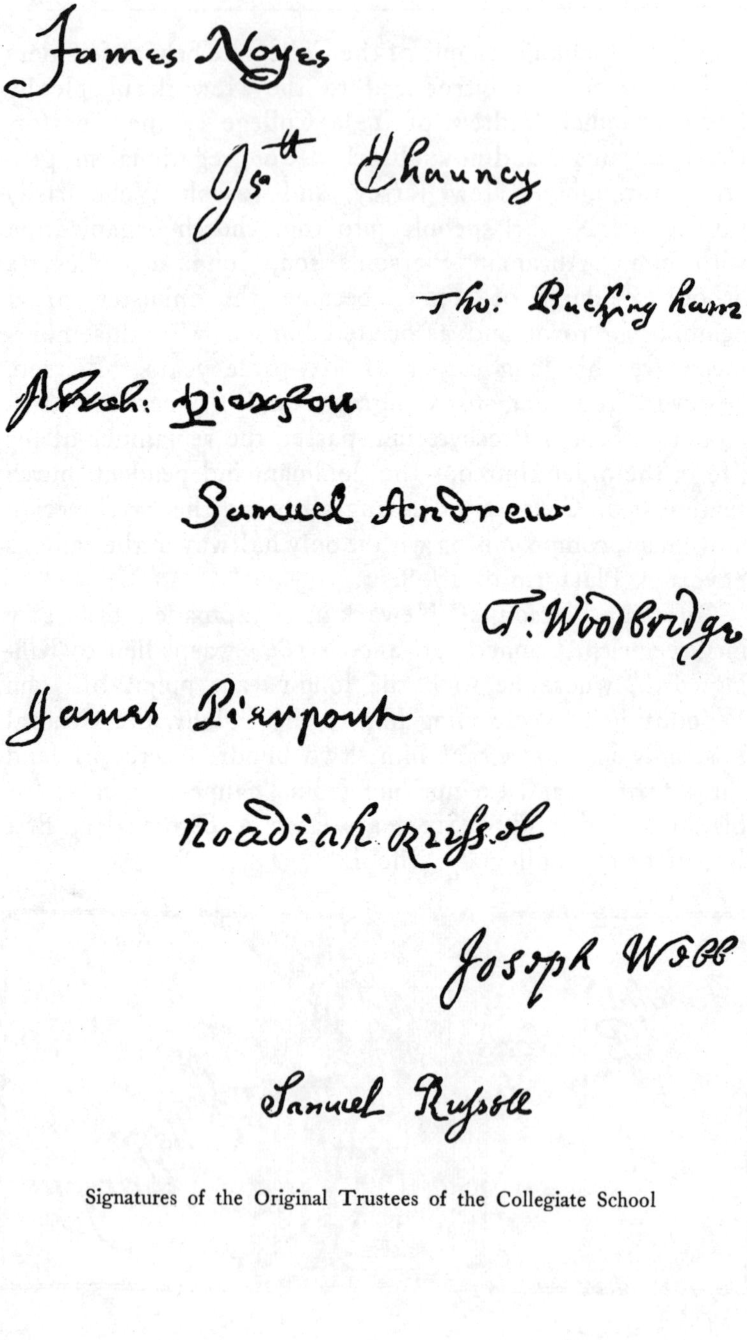

James Noyes

Js^tt Chauncy

Tho: Buckingham

Abrah: Pierson

Samuel Andrew

T: Woodbridge

James Pierpont

Noadiah Russel

Joseph Webb

Samuel Russel

Signatures of the Original Trustees of the Collegiate School

PART III

THE COLLEGIATE SCHOOL AND YALE COLLEGE

The Yale Arms
and Crest

The Franklin Mile-Stone

25 NH

CHAPTER I

THE KILLINGWORTH BEGINNINGS

I

YOUR modern traveler, gliding on his comfortable way along the Connecticut shore of Long Island Sound, finds himself in a pleasant land, the open country and thriving towns of which reveal to him, with each passing mile, a smiling corner of a prosperous modern New England.

Yet such a traveler, in his fleeting glimpses of ancient white churches and weather-beaten houses, prim old-fashioned gardens and broad New England village streets under their elms, might well fancy himself, here and there, two centuries back of his own generation, and journeying in Colonial times. For he is on historic ground. From Stamford on the west, through Milford and New Haven and Branford, to New London on the east, this was the ancient highway that bound together the first Puritan settlements of the Connecticut coast. Over it, when it was no more than the Pequot Trail, had passed the Puritan soldiers in the Pequot wars; over it, when it had become the King's Highway, had gone the good folk of the old New Haven Jurisdiction,—steeple-hatted ministers in their cloaks and black doublets, scarlet-coated emissaries of the English Kings, country folk and the great men of the four colonies. Within sight of it Theophilus Eaton had sailed to Quinnipiac. Upon it the gracious Lady Fenwick and her lord had journeyed from New Haven to Saybrook Fort. A rough bridle-path by 1650, it had seen the New Haven Colony ministers travel to Boston for the Bay synods of their times, and, a few years later, John Davenport ride over it in his exile to Boston from his foundered New Haven ship of state. The Boston Post-road by 1673, mail carriers had then begun those irregular monthly journeys on horseback over it that had first brought provincial Connecticut into touch with cosmopolitan Boston. As such, the young Harvard graduate, James Pierpont, had ridden over it on his entrance upon that New Haven career one result of which had been the Collegiate School. This ancient path, a beaten if rough roadway by 1700, had given Madam Knight, the sprightly Boston school-ma'am, plenty of peril and amusement on that famous horseback ride of hers from Boston to New York, all of which she has set down in her diary. Ebenezer Hurd, most renowned of the postboys who galloped on the public's business over this ancient highway in still later Colonial times, was to journey upon it for forty-eight years until 1775, when he was to make his last and most famous ride, bringing the news of the Battle of Lexington to Connecticut colonists already prepared for independence by the sturdy Puritanism of those pioneer days. And Benjamin Franklin, Postmaster General, was to drive over this highway in more settled times, in his cushioned chaise, with gangs of men behind him in carts filled with stones, which they dropped as each mile was registered on the quaint cyclometer that their inventive chief had attached to his chaise wheels.

One of these stones, marked "25 N. H.," may still be seen on the south side of the Clinton main street, just east of the village Green.

II

It is directly across the main street in Clinton from Benjamin Franklin's ancient marker that one may step out of the bustle of the modern highway onto ground historic in Yale annals. For it was here that Yale began its existence. A monument, properly inscribed in Latin and English and surmounted by sculptured books, stands on the old Meeting-house Hill, and informs the wayfarer that a few rods east is the site of Rector Abraham Pierson's Killingworth parsonage, in which the Collegiate School of Connecticut was first kept.[1] Traces of the Killingworth of those early days are not hard to find, and a drowsy summer afternoon's search for them will be found worth making.

[1] The Stanton House, built in 1789, when Rector Pierson's house was torn down, stands at the street end of the lot on which the Collegiate School stood. Parts of the old Pierson homestead were built into this successor to it. The sills of Yale's first home, for instance, may now be seen in the Stanton House cellar, laid across great stone piers and thus supporting the two immense stone chimneys. There is good reason to think that some of the odd-shaped attic windows of the Stanton House may have been in Rector Pierson's. In the Stanton garden the old Pierson well was recently uncovered and marked,—the well at which the first Yale students drew their water supply. An ancient iron key was dug up when this well was found in 1913; from its location it undoubtedly was a door key to the Pierson parsonage, though whether it dates back to 1701 may not be determinable.

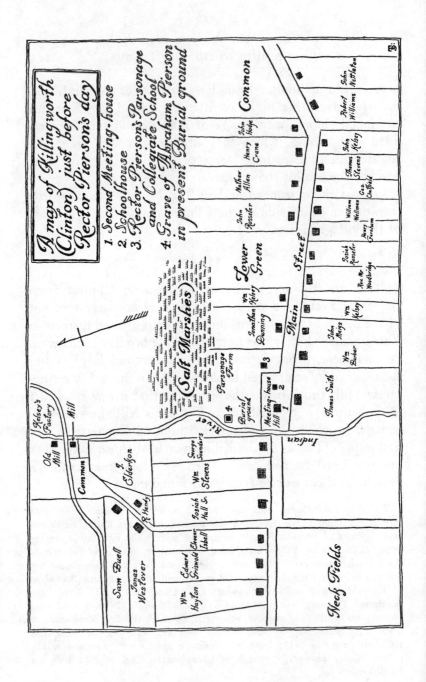

A map of Killingworth
(Clinton) just before
Rector Pierson's day

1. Second Meeting-house
2. Schoolhouse
3. Rector Pierson's Parsonage
   and Collegiate School
4. Grave of Abraham Pierson
   in present Burial ground

(Salt Marshes)

Lower Kelsey Green

Wm Kelsey

Jonathan Deming

Parsonage Farm

River

Indian

Kelsey's Factory

Old Mill

Mill

Common

J. Elderson

George Saunders

Wm Stevens

R. Handy

Josiah Hull Sr.

Edward Griswold

Elnear Isbell

Sam Buell

Jonas Westover

Wm Hayton

Neck Fields

Burial ground

Meeting-house Hill

Thomas Smith

Wm Barber

John Meigs

Henry Kelsey

Rev. Mr. Woodbridge

Josiah Rosseter

William Wellman

Geo. Chatfield

Mary Grenham

John Rosseter

Nathan Allen

Henry Crane

John Hodge

Josiah Rosseter

Thomas Stevens

John Kelsey

Robert Williams

John Nettleton

Common

Main Street

All of this section of the Sound coast was bought in 1641 from Uncas, the Mohegan sachem, by George Fenwick of Saybrook. Killingworth village was settled in 1663 by a few families from East Guilford,—now Madison,—who gave it their old Warwickshire town name of Kenilworth,— a name that by later usage of careless town clerks became Killingworth, and later still was changed to the present Clinton by the legislature. When Abraham Pierson settled here in 1694, the village was a straggling double row of unpainted, roomy farmhouses that stood at irregular intervals facing the Boston Post-road from their roughly-cleared and cultivated farm plots. Indian River crossed this highway, as now, a little east of the village center, and travelers had to go north when they came to it, to a ford above the present burying ground, where there was easy passage to the opposite shore. Overlooking the river stood the Meetinghouse, on its small rise of ground, with its cemetery behind it. A map, reconstructed from the list of original land allotments of 1665, was recently made by the Killingworth town clerk, and has been redrawn, with notes added of the town as it was in 1701, to accompany this chapter. There were then no houses on the now settled south side of the main street west of Indian River, and there was a broad Common at the east end of the village, where the Trainband perhaps had its maneuvers. Traveling at this early time was difficult. The Boston Post-road entered Killingworth from Guilford from the north, where the "Farm Bridge" crossed the Hammonasset River at an old fording place, the present main highway through the village to the west being a later addition. Until just before 1700, when a rough wooden bridge was built, the only way to cross the Menunketesuc River, east of Clinton, was over a "ridingway" at low tide near the mouth of that river. The common route for pedestrians between Saybrook and Guilford,—so impassable were the woods and so numerous and unfordable the rivers,—was by the beach. North of the Killingworth home-lots, during Abraham Pierson's period, were thick virgin woods, stretching unbroken,—except by Indian trails which had by then become bridle-paths,—from Middletown to Wallingford. These woods came down to the village, close to the burying ground.[1]

Rector Pierson, surrounded by his family (his own tombstone overshadowed by a more pretentious memorial to his less famous son), lies on the northwest slope of this burying ground, a few rods away from the New Haven railroad, over which the iron successors of Ebenezer Hurd now roar through the old Pierson farm a score of times a day.

III

When the first scholars rode over the old Boston Postroad to the opening of Abraham Pierson's primitive Collegiate School, the center of the Killingworth town life was about the old Meeting-house Green. Here, when Pierson arrived to be the minister, had stood one of the typical New England meeting-houses of the day,—the usual square, rough-clapboarded, turreted building that was the practically invariable style of the first period of New England Congregational-church building. No representation exists of this ancient Killingworth church, fort alike against prowling Indians and an ever-watchful Satan, but it was doubtless like the first New Haven Meeting-house, and others of that early day, a very good picture of which one may see on an early map of Newark, where Pierson preached for years. But one of the first results of Abraham Pierson's coming to Killingworth was the erection of a

[1] I am indebted to Mr. John A. Hull, of Clinton, for a number of these facts regarding ancient Killingworth.

The Killingworth
Meeting-house
in 1701

second Meeting-house on the hill, and a picture of this has
come down to us on an ancient panel owned in the village.[1]
It must have been a hopelessly inartistic edifice, if this old
panel painting tells a true story, as no doubt it does. It was
square, as had been its predecessor,—thirty-five feet each
way,—clapboarded, with a central door between rough
windows on the east and west sides, a small window high in
the south end, three windows on the second story on either
side, and a small square turret, surmounted by a miniature
spire, on the south. What its interior was, when Abraham
Pierson preached there, we now have no means of knowing.
It had an advantage over its predecessor, however, in that
a bell instead of a drum called the Killingworth church

---

[1] This panel belongs to the descendants of the Rev. Jared Eliot in
Clinton. It was painted in 1710 by an itinerant "Boston artist." This
second Killingworth Meeting-house was built in 1700.

people to the Sabbath-day meetings.[1] No doubt there was the usual high wooden pulpit within, with the great sounding-board above it, and no doubt it was furnished with the usual heavy oak-slab seats of that early day (this was before the later era of family pews came in). As in all other New England colonial churches, there was no stove,—a habit which the New England Puritans brought over with them from England, and which many English country churches carried on for generations after. A well-sweep appears in the panel of this ecclesiastical stronghold, and a small building just east of the church, which may be taken to be either the end of the parsonage beyond, or the village schoolhouse that Mr. Pierson managed to get his congregation to build in 1703.[2]

It was ten rods east of this spot (so President Stiles has it in his "Literary Diary," and modern investigation proves it to be correct) that Rector Pierson lived in his parsonage, facing the village Green.[3]

President Stiles describes this building as a large, two-story house, likely enough similar in appearance to the usual great-roofed, two-story (or "double") homesteads of the

[1] A new drum was bought in 1698. In 1703 the Town accepted the gift of a bell from some of the church people.

[2] This schoolhouse was barn-like, with a stone chimney at one end, and stood between Mr. Pierson's parsonage and the new Meeting-house. Parts of the framework of the original Meeting-house were used in this building. The first schoolmaster had been an old parishioner of Mr. Pierson, an uneducated countryman named Brown, who, at Mr. Pierson's suggestion to the town, had been hired "to keep skoul for one quarter of a year, and for his pains" to have £9. When this new schoolhouse was built, seven years later, Captain "Henery" Crane of the "Train-band" was "voated" the position.

[3] Rev. W. E. Brooks, in his historical address at the bicentennial of the Clinton Congregational Church in 1867, said: "The College building was established here in what was then Killingworth, near the edge of the Green, and a little south and east from the barn which stands on the Stanton place."

day, of which several survivors have come down to us. It
faced west, looking up a slight rise under the trees, past the
newly erected schoolhouse, to the Meeting-house. On its
east side was the usual kitchen ell and its recently-unearthed
garden well under some apple trees. We may properly
imagine the Pierson lot as narrow on the south, or modern
Clinton main street end, and running deep to the north along
the village Green to the church-society farm of some ten
acres (now the newer and eastern part of the present
Clinton cemetery). Where the Stanton house now stands
on the main street were Mr. Pierson's garden and perhaps
small tobacco field.

Pierson's parsonage had been the "town house," and in
1675 had been fortified against the Indians. It was presented to Pierson in 1695, shortly after he had settled with
his large family in it. In the Killingworth town records is
this reference to the gift: "The town being met together to
consider of something to be done for the encouragement of
Mr. Abraham Pierson. . Do give the said Mr. Pierson the
Town House and Orchard . . upon condition that the said
Mr. Pierson shall plant an orchard of an hundred apple
trees upon the parsonage land, where the town shall judge
most convenient, and the said trees to manure and secure."
There comes out, now and then (as in this instance) in our
acquaintance with the good Rector Pierson, a very delightful
practicality of mind in the midst of his more idealistic labors.
And we may smile a bit, too, in observing the way in which
his suggestion of financial discouragement was met by an
equally canny congregation; for he was to grow the apples
for his own cider, and thus relieve the congregation of a
responsibility for the parson's table that was undertaken by
most of the colonial villages of that date. There must have
been a thriving apple orchard on the Pierson farm when
his first scholars arrived in 1702. He possessed cider

barrels, so the inventory of his estate shows, and kept them in his cellar. And from that same official document we learn that he cultivated his own tobacco on the parsonage land. Like the Rev. James Pierpont over in New Haven, Rector Pierson enjoyed his hearth-fire pipe, and, when visitors came, got out his "canes" of home-grown tobacco, his tongs and tobacco box and cider mugs for an evening's sociability.

IV

Four months after the organization at Saybrook, Rector Pierson took in his first scholar, the nineteen-year-old Jacob Heminway of East Haven, whose pastor, James Pierpont, likely enough, advised the step.

This was in March, 1702. There were no other boys who were ready to come, and so, from then around to September of the Collegiate School's first year, this youth (as he afterward, when an old man, stated to President Stiles) "*solus* was all the College the first half-year." Rector Pierson carried on this young man's extensive classical study and no doubt instructed him in divinity. The young Heminway finally prepared for the pulpit. Mr. Pierson rode over to Saybrook on September 16, 1702, and there, in Rev. Thomas Buckingham's house on the Saybrook village Green, held the first Commencement in Yale history.

The Trustees had, as we have seen, explicitly ordered that there be no public show at these annual graduation ceremonies, so the affair was quiet and, very likely, attended only by the Trustees, and with as little ceremony as possible. The Buckinghams, so tradition has it, prepared a great dinner for this occasion. The Trustees and scholars and young ministers who were there for their M.A. degrees, sat down to a table laden with oysters and other shellfish, venison, succotash, and boiled Indian pudding. At this meeting the Trustees voted to allow "the Gentlemen of our Government," other ministers, "Benefactors to the School" and "all other persons of Liberal Education," in addition to the male parents and guardians of the scholars, to become "auditors" at later Commencements.

Five young men,—two of them Congregational ministers of the Colony and one a preacher,—were given their second degrees of Master of Arts at this first Saybrook Commencement, all of them obviously introduced by the Trustees or friends of the new School, so that it might give a good account of itself to the Connecticut people at its beginnings. Rev. Stephen Buckingham, son of the Saybrook Trustee, and at this time minister at the small settlement of Norwalk, was the best known of these young candidates. He was later to become a Trustee, himself. The four others were Rev. Samuel Treat, eight years out of Harvard and now minister at the little hamlet of Preston on the Thames River, near the home of old James Noyes at Stonington, by whom he was doubtless sent over; Joseph Coit, the preacher at Plainfield, where lived the Collegiate School's first patron, Major James Fitch; Joseph Moss, who had been for three years the Rector of the Hopkins Grammar School in New Haven, and thus close to James Pierpont, and who was later on to help teach the scholars; and Nathaniel Chauncy, who had been privately educated in the family of his uncle, the Rev. Israel Chauncy of Stratford, one of the Trustees, in return for the life-use of the young man's father's library.[1]

[1] The Chauncey family tradition has it that Nathaniel Chauncy joined Jacob Heminway at Pierson's house for a short time before Commencement as a candidate for a B.A., but that, when the Trustees examined him at Saybrook, they found him so far advanced that they gave him his M.A. instead. This may well have been, and it would not necessarily conflict with Heminway's statement that he was the only scholar, or, as he states it, the whole college, for the first half-year.

Immediately after this first quiet Commencement three boys arrived at Rector Pierson's parsonage. Young John Hart, of whom we shall hear more directly, rode down from Cambridge, where he had just finished his Sophomore year at Harvard. He was the son of the Farmington train-band captain and former Speaker of the Connecticut Lower House, and was evidently recalled from Harvard by his father to encourage the Connecticut experiment, if not for other reasons. Samuel Russel of Branford and Samuel Andrew of Milford sent two more youths, the former his son John, and the latter one Phineas Fiske (the son of the Milford town doctor), who was to become a tower of strength to the School before many years had passed.

With these four boys, and Heminway, Rector Pierson seems to have started in in earnest at his rather large undertaking for a busy village minister, and the wheels of Yale's educational history may be said to have begun formally to revolve. During the next two years more scholars arrived from time to time, until, by the middle of the third year, there were probably some fifteen to twenty youths studying at the Killingworth minister's house. A half-dozen of these boys were sons or near relatives of the Trustees or of influential friends of the School, or were influenced by them to come to it. The two Hartford Trustees, Samuel Mather and Timothy Woodbridge, sent their sons, as did Nathaniel Lynde of Saybrook, whose interest in the School was well known. Samuel Russel of Branford sent his nephew. James Pierpont sent over one other New Haven boy besides Heminway. Thomas Buckingham had his hand in introducing two Saybrook youths, one of them Samuel Whittlesey, who was later to be the Hopkins Grammar School Rector. Crotchety old Gershom Bulkeley of Wethersfield, now that the illegal founding had been so rashly accomplished, fearsomely let three of his neighbors' sons run

the risk of English parliamentary disapproval by going
down through the wilderness to Killingworth.   Abraham
Pierson himself brought in two boys from the neighboring
town of Guilford,—Samuel Cooke and Jared Eliot, both to
become in later life Trustees of the School, and the latter
one of the most learned men of his day.   And Rev. Gurdon
Saltonstall sent one youth from his New London congregation.   The great expectations, however, of numerous
scholars coming to the Collegiate School from towns east
of the Connecticut border did not materialize.   One came,
indeed, in these first years from as far away as Marthas
Vineyard, and two from Northampton—the latter being
relations of the learned Nathaniel Chauncy and parishioners of old Rev. Solomon Stoddard, whose friendly relations with the Mathers and Samuel Sewall doubtless led him
to interest himself to this extent in the orthodox experiment
at Killingworth.   But the outsiders were few.   The Colony
at large had not as yet come to the support of the School,
and if the Trustees had not secured students themselves, the
enterprise would very likely have died in its birth.

All of these young fellows, nearly all of them from leading Connecticut families, were, so far as we know, boarders
at one time or another in the Pierson household, and certainly they all were instructed in the Rector's house.   Though
probably not more than a dozen or so were under instruction
at the same time, the good wife of Rector Pierson must have
had her hands full with this group of active and hearty
youngsters, scholars that they were.   Her own family was
large (the Piersons seem to have had three sons and six
daughters then living[1]) so that during this period the Killingworth parsonage must have been a lively household and,

---

1 John, the youngest son, was at this time twelve years old.   In addition,
the Killingworth church records of the time show that three other members
of the family were church members,—Abraham, Jr., Sarah, and Mary.

Tutor John Hart's Chair

when the Trustees' laws were not too rigidly enforced, merry enough. How the good Mrs. Pierson managed to look out for the moral and physical well-being of this large establishment is not on record, but she managed it, and graciously avoided the domestic pitfalls that had been the undoing of Mrs. Nathaniel Eaton during the similarly small beginnings of Harvard.

Making one more in the Pierson family, but doubtless helping to manage it, the Trustees had allowed an assistant to the Rector. Young Daniel Hooker, of the Farmington Hookers, a youthful brother-in-law of James Pierpont and a Harvard graduate of 1700, had come to the Killingworth parsonage in this capacity in 1702, but had resigned at the first Commencement. His place was then taken by John Hart, the former Harvard Sophomore and single graduate of the Collegiate School in 1703, who became Tutor to the two lower classes and, by virtue of his office, "Sir Hart" to the scholars and Killingworth townspeople. While this young Tutor was preparing for his own degree of B.A. in 1702-1703, he received no pay for his services. He could, however, collect fines for disobediences to the Trustees' regulations, and I surmise that it was in some measure due to this fact that the records for that year show that there were "discontents in some of the students for the time being, in relation to the present tutor." This uprising,—the first Yale student rebellion,—was promptly squelched by the Trustees, who upheld Sir Hart and tendered him their thanks for his "hitherto service" and £50 in country pay for such work in the School as he should thereafter do.[1] He left in 1705 to enter the ministry in East Guilford, and Phineas Fiske succeeded him. This third assistant had been one of the three graduates of 1704 and had finished a postgraduate course in theology with Mr. Pierson the year after that.

V

Though we have to depend largely upon what we know of the Saybrook days that followed, we may picture in some degree the daily round at Rector Pierson's double establishment as the future Yale College now slowly got under way. And it is a pleasant picture that we may thus visualize for ourselves.

As the sun rises over the level Killingworth salt meadows from Saybrook way, Rector Pierson's household assembles in the great living "hall" for morning prayers, when the Scriptures are read by the minister and expounded, accord-

---

[1] This squelching of the scholars was done at a discreet distance, at a Trustees' meeting at Branford. Rev. Mr. Pierpont drew up a "Memorial" to the students at this meeting. The Colony, he said, had promoted "a Collegiate Society," and had given the ministers in charge authority to manage it. He reminded the scholars at Killingworth of "the hitherto success & hopeful appearance of ye enterprise," and then warned them "agst such spirits & methods, as have a tendency to discourage so great & happy an undertaking." The responsibility of choosing the Rector and Tutors of the School had not been left to the scholars, hints Mr. Pierpont, but to the Trustees, "as those accounted capable to judg who are most fitt for such stations." It behooved the students, therefore, to "pay those regards wc are proper" to their instructors. The Memorial closed with the Trustees' assurance of "support in his trust" to Sir Hart, and that was the last that was heard of the uprising.

Rector Pierson's
Parsonage
in Killingworth

ing to the Trustees' laws, in the ancient tongue. Classroom work immediately begins, perhaps as early as half-past six o'clock, the Pierson children romping off to "Henery" Crane's schoolhouse through the garden gate at the same early hour. A half-hour comes for breakfast; and, this over, the young Piersons scamper back to school. Mistress Pierson begins her household rounds, jingling "equipage" at her girdle, and the Collegiate School reassembles for its serious work of educating Connecticut's church and public servants.

Pleasant it would be to look on the Pierson household, as it thus starts its day. And we may from our reading of the old college records. Tutor Fiske takes the two lower classes of a half-dozen boys each into one of the great rooms downstairs, while Rector Pierson calls the Senior classes into his study, where are his father's four hundred-odd, old-time theological books that he had brought from Newark. The morning is given up to a solid drill for the Freshmen in Greek and Latin grammar and composition, in translating Tully and Vergil, and in elementary Hebrew,—the three studies that are to become such necessary accomplishments in a later life of public service to an orthodox Calvinistic commonwealth. The Sophomores proceed further in the three languages, under Sir Fiske, using the Psalms for their Hebrew reading and the New Testament for their Greek. And Sir Fiske gives them a taste of logic from the Leyden Latin manual of Burgersdicius so soon as their command of the language makes it possible. The Seniors are at the same time reading Latin treatises on metaphysics and studying the rudiments of mathematics and physics. No doubt Rector Pierson, seated at the end of his library table in his wig and black crêpe gown, his square-cut broadcloth waistcoat and smallclothes, examines his own manuscript treatise on the latter subject as he lectures. This treatise, we are told, remained the College text-book on "Physics" for many years, and has since been lost, with all its copies in the note-books of the scholars. What sort of science it taught, we shall see in a later chapter of these rambling chronicles.

And so the Collegiate School fell into its daily routine. Twice a week the Seniors "dispute syllogistically" in Latin, and on Saturdays Dr. Ames' "Medulla" is recited in the same tongue, and his "cases of Conscience sometimes." Rector Pierson exercises all of his students in rhetoric and lectures on theology to them. It is the rule of the School, as it has been for decades at Harvard, that all the oral work is to be in Latin, as well, I believe, as the conversation out of classroom hours among the scholars and between them and their Rector and Sir Fiske. The leather-smocked-and-coated village bumpkins, gaping in at the open door of the Killingworth parsonage in these days, must have conceived a lofty opinion of the intellectual heights which were being scaled within, as time was to show that they had little patience with them.

This rigorous morning work, we may suppose, lets up for the substantial boiled meat and vegetable dinner of midday, with its cider and beer in quantity, and then comes an hour and a half of recreation, doubtless spent under the tutor's eye in the orchard or on the banks of the near-by Indian River, where was good fishing in season and much dexterous crabbing in the summer time. And then begins the after-noon drill, ending in early evening prayers, when the Scrip-tures again are read and expounded. Then the day's work is over except for those who desire to study in the evening until the good country hour of nine o'clock, when everyone has to be in bed, with "lights out" for the night except for Rector Pierson's own postponed sermon writing and study, which ends at eleven. Twice each Sunday, in order to make orthodox Connecticut church members out of the scholars

under Rector Pierson's charge, the Collegiate School boys
troop out through the parsonage-garden gate and up across
the village Green to the Meeting-house, there to sit for
more long hours and hear their Rector's preaching (he was
a very able preacher, it is said) and survey the assembled
village congregation. It was bitter cold for the congregation in the depth of winter on these occasions, and more
than once, no doubt, as Judge Sewall's diary reports
happening in Boston, even the broken bread froze on the
communion plates. But the villagers were all there, and
their fair daughters, and no doubt warm hearts beat under
the caped greatcoats of the Pierson scholars. Under such
circumstances, the upperclassmen frequently must have had
some difficulty in paying enough attention to the sermon to
repeat it to Rector Pierson, as they were supposed to do,
immediately afterwards.

Indian River,
Killingworth
1707

Outside of these weekly Meeting-house occasions, there was doubtless little enough in the village life to distract the attention of the Collegiate School scholars. Killingworth had a "Train-band," to be sure, and the military exercises of this small company on the Common were gala affairs. The great men of the village seem to have been Deacon John Griswold and Henry Crane, the schoolmaster. The latter was captain of the "Train-band" in 1704, with John Kelsey for his Lieutenant, and Jonathan Hull for Ensign. The sergeants were John Shether, one Sam Stevens and young John Crane. Killingworth received a patent, with other Colony towns, in 1703, the Proprietors' Committee being Captain Crane, Sam Buell, William Stephens, and John Kelsey. The deputies to the Lower House of the Colony Assembly during these years of the Collegiate School's stay at Killingworth were Deacon Griswold (a more or less perennial election, it would appear), Sam Buell, Robert Lane, and Captain Crane the schoolmaster. All of these gentry had farms along the Boston Post-road on either side of the village Green, and possibly some of them boarded a few of their pastor's scholars when the number of youths at the school became too great for Mrs. Pierson's management. The Killingworth folk, however, were a poor community. From the settlement, they had had all that they could do to support themselves. There would seem to have been no storekeepers until a later period, when a Dr. Aaron Eliot kept a store at the west end of the village street, and Josiah Buell began his horseback journeys to Boston to bring back dry goods. By 1702 the villagers were still sowing their own flax and threshing, spinning, and weaving it into shirts; keeping sheep, and carding and weaving the wool into cloth for coats, catching oysters and carrying them to Hartford in exchange for rye for bread. Shellfish and shad, the latter caught in the river mouths by nets, formed a large part of the Collegiate School students' menus; very likely the scholars themselves helped to furnish Mrs. Pierson's table by using Rector Pierson's fish-net.

With varying annual attendances during these first six years,—eighteen youths in all were graduated with their first degrees at the Killingworth School,—matters proceeded quietly and with no particularly important events, so far as the School life itself was concerned, until the sudden death of Rector Pierson, on March 5, 1707.

The Collegiate School's first Rector left no will, but the inventory of his belongings was filed by his sons at the New London probate office. It came to a round £1,200, a sizable small fortune for the day. From it we may gather a little of the personal surroundings in which Abraham Pierson lived at Killingworth. He had woolen suits and a set of those fashionable linen clothes for hot weather, concerning which young John Winthrop of Boston had written in 1706 to his uncle, Governor Winthrop of Connecticut, that "it is a great fashion here to wear West India linnens. They make pretty light cool Wastcotes and britches." He had the usual bedsteads and beds, woolen bedding, coverlets and curtains, of the day. A small quantity of "armes and amunition" is listed,—doubtless to use against the wolves and wildcats that still prowled in the near-by forests. He had "cubbards, Tabels, and carpits [heavy table coverings], chests, boxes, chaiers and formes and cushing"; pewter and brass household utensils; table and bed linen, fire-irons, a razor, sickles, shears, combs and knives [no forks are mentioned]; shoe-buckles, buttons [great attention was paid to buttons in these days, and much ingenuity given to their design,—even drawings were made of the required patterns by some dandies and dispatched to London for manufacture]; tobacco-box, tongs, chains, and money; glass bottles, money scales, leather, "comed woosted, linen yarns, black stuff, hollan and bags"; three barrels of cider, "tubbs, spining wheals and other lumber." And he left "neats cattle, horses, swine, and a part mantle," farmyard tools and tobacco-raising implements, and yarn for "blankits and fishnet." His Killingworth house was put down at £358, and he had £100 worth of land at Milford (probably his wife's, who was a Milford girl), £80 worth of land at "Cauging-chauge," wherever that was, and the Saybrook house and barn, and lands and meadow, for which he had paid £200 and had never been permitted to occupy.

Mr Pierson's Cider-Cup

The
Pierson
grave-stone

HERE LIETH THE
BODY OF Yᵉ REU-ᴰ
Mʳ ABRAᴴ PIERSON
THE FIRST RECTOR
OF Yᵉ COLLEDGE
IN CONECTICUT
WHO DECEASED
MARCH Yᵉ 5ᵗʰ 1705
AGED 61 YEARS

CHAPTER II

SAYBROOK DAYS

I

IN spite of the quiet progress of events at Rector Pierson's parsonage in Killingworth, the enterprise of the Colony college had by no means been the success up to this time that its founders had expected for it. Financially, it had been hard sledding. Harvard during these years had graduated eighty-three scholars, and, in the year in which Pierson's death occurred, was to graduate as many as the Collegiate School had received in its whole six years to that time. The predicted enthusiastic support of the School had not materialized from without the Colony, and from Connecticut itself very few boys had presented themselves without being drummed up by the Trustees.

But another and more difficult question than this had been troubling the Trustees during Rector Pierson's administration.

We have seen how the selection of a permanent site had carefully been side-tracked at the organization meeting in 1701. To settle this matter appears to have been the Trustees' chief business throughout Rector Pierson's régime. Thus far the Trustees had compromised on Saybrook, which was therefore the official location of the School. But its settlement there had depended upon Rector Pierson's removal from Killingworth, and this his people, exercising the congregational right of the day to dismiss, would not permit. Moreover, the Trustees were by no means agreed upon Saybrook as the permanent School site. Meeting New London County opposition, they had agreed to a compromise vote, in 1702, that the college should not be placed further east than Saybrook, nor west than New Haven. During Pierson's Rectorship, the site question had been left in this unsettled state. Yet during these four years we can follow the course of an active agitation of the subject, and this, no doubt, made many of the Trustees' meetings lively affairs. The later Hartford action to secure the School for some up-river site was not to become noticeable for a decade and more, so that we may suppose that the Hartford Trustees joined with those from New London during this early period in the controversy, to remain at Saybrook. Though James Pierpont's original college party seem to have acquiesced in the Saybrook arrangement, signs are not wanting during this period of preparation for a stand on the question when it should definitely arise. We have seen how first one and then another New Haven merchant had been elected Treasurer after Nathaniel Lynde of Saybrook had declined the place. Samuel Russel of Branford had been elected a Trustee, and, while the next two vacancies had been filled with New London and Fairfield ministers, for the following two New Haven site supporters were selected. In the meantime Pierpont acquiesced in such efforts as were being made to settle Rector Pierson permanently at Saybrook.

And these had been numerous, though to no purpose. The evidence is that Rector Pierson had been ready to remove to Saybrook, so far as his personal wishes went, but that the leaders in his Killingworth church had succeeded in blocking his several attempts to do so. No doubt the offers of the Trustees had something to do with Pierson's willingness to move, as, with his large and growing family, his financial prospects as a settled Rector of the Collegiate School at Saybrook promised better than his small pay of £60 as the Killingworth minister. Yet I imagine that his interest in science, which was greater than usually could be found in the Colony at the time, and his firm belief in the possibilities of the School, were even stronger inducements. In the hope of securing a release from his congregation, he bought the six acres at Saybrook, named in his inventory, and the Trustees voted him £100 to build a house thereon, if he would remove. But the opposition of his people had resulted in a deadlock that had lasted until his unexpected death.

Not only did they oppose his removal, but the good Killingworth people had even raised serious objections to the continuance of the School there, and to their minister giving any of his time to it. All of which doubtless had kept Rector Pierson in a sad flutter and state of indecision. He had even found it necessary to write a letter to his congregation. In this he says that he "perceives a misapprehension" among them as to "my Answer at New Haven [when he had accepted the Rectorship] to the Rev. trustees of the

The Lord house, Old Saybrook

Collegiate School." The facts were, he said, that they had wanted him to remove to Saybrook and "take the care and conduck of the school," and "remove to the place by them appointed for it." As to this, he says, "I answered as you have heard, that I Durst not Deny a Divine call to attend to that work so far as was consistent with my ministerial work among you." But "Not Discarning a present call thereunto; after much perswasion and pressing to it, my Answer was to act therein as god should open my way." The consent of his people was necessary to his removal to Saybrook, he then said. He might not secure this "generall and joynt consent," but if he did (and the good Rector's business side here rises again) he should "expect your ingagement by sufficient sureties to Reimburse and according to agreement, without which I shall not part with the house and without this ingagement I shall not think I have a sufficient expression of your consent to my removal." This letter "to the inhabitants of Killingworth" was dated September 21, 1705. As might have been expected, it did not at all meet with the "joynt consent" of the canny Killingworth deacons. They had voted, with the rest of the townsfolk, to give him as their minister the "town house." This Pierson, desiring to leave for Saybrook, now proposed to keep permanently. So their answer had not been unexpected. "We do declare," say they, "that it is our opinion that it is not, or like to be consistent with your ministerial worke amongst us to attend sd school as heirherto," and "we shall not endeavor to act in that matter any firther than we have allready Don."

The unfortunate Rector, thus impaled upon the two horns of this unexpected dilemma, had found himself agreed, on the one hand, to be the Collegiate School Rector and to settle in Saybrook (where he had now invested in land with that idea in mind) and, on the other, under contract to remain as the pastor of the Killingworth people who were now proceeding to tell the Trustees to take their school out of the village and secure another Rector.

Matters had thus remained for the first four years of Mr. Pierson's Rectorship. In 1706 they came to a natural crisis. In that year the Trustees (on the Rector's "request") voted to ask the town of Killingworth to allow "the Collegiate School to be & remain hear under the care & conduct of the Rev. Mr. Pierson." The town's reply was an abrupt one. It was not "to allowe that the School should be kept hear as it has been." The Killingworth village worthies, however, seem to have been willing to reconsider this action, doubtless on Mr. Pierson's final urging. For, early in the winter of 1705-1706, they made "choyce of Decon Griswold, Robert Lane, Sarjts Shether, Stevens and John Crane," as a "Comity to consider of, and draw up sum terms or proposalls for the town to consider of with Respect to the allowance of the Collegiate School Being hear under the care and conduct of Mr. Pierson." It was while these "proposalls" were being laid before his flock by Rector Pierson that his death had occurred.

II

Conditions in the Colony found the Trustees unprepared to elect a new resident Rector after Mr. Pierson's death,— a fact which goes to show, I think, the rather complete dependence of the enterprise up to that time upon Abraham Pierson. Nothing had come of the effort to secure subscriptions from the Colony, and there was therefore little or no money in Treasurer Alling's hands in New Haven with which to settle a competent master. The problem was temporarily solved by the acceptance by the Rev. Samuel Andrew, now forty-six years old, of the Rectorship *pro tem*, and of the charge of a part of the scholars,—the Senior classes,—at his parsonage in Milford. The Killingworth establishment was broken up, and Phineas Fiske, of the Class of 1704, who had the previous year succeeded John Hart as Tutor, went over, bag and baggage and with the remaining scholars, to Saybrook, probably at first to the house of the now elderly Rev. Thomas Buckingham, who must have agreed to give a general oversight to them. That this was a highly fortunate circumstance for the Collegiate School may be gathered from even the little we know of this Saybrook minister. He was, apparently, energetic when it fell upon him to take action for the good of his community, as was shown in his galloping about to rouse the village when Andros arrived. From an appealing letter to Governor Saltonstall, asking him to approach in his stead Governor Winthrop for a gift to the School ("I have neither

Skill nor Corage in manageing such affairs," he wrote), it
is likely that he was less energetic in business matters. But
he was "kindly in his manner, dignified and scholarly, and
his councils were received with deference both by the tutors
and the students." It is said that the Collegiate School
youths "loved him like a father." He practically filled the
place of Rector Pierson until his death two years later,
though Samuel Andrew was the nominal head of the
academy.

Samuel Andrew's acceptance of this responsibility was
no doubt encouraged by James Pierpont. Yet the Rev. Mr.
Andrew was well adapted for the position, so far as the
educational side went. He had been a Tutor and Fellow at
Harvard, and had been forced to assume the chief responsibilities of that college during the unsettled administrations
of Presidents Oakes and Rogers. In that capacity he had
been Tutor to James Pierpont, Samuel Russel, and Noadiah
Russell of the Class of 1681, and to Joseph Webb of the
Class of 1684,—all of whom were now fellow Trustees of
the Collegiate School with him. As matters were to turn
out, Mr. Andrew was to remain Rector *pro tem* for the
next twelve years; during that period, while a good
teacher, he showed no great aptitude for the administrative
side of his office.

Under these unsatisfactory conditions, the divided Collegiate School jogged along for the next few years, losing
ground rather steadily, until for a series of four years but
two or three scholars were graduated annually, and the
Trustees found themselves facing serious difficulties.

That Saybrook Point was not a particularly good place
for such a school was soon to become apparent. The long
sandy road that led across the marshes to Old Saybrook
Point continued to the water front, where there was safe
anchorage and a shelving beach. There were probably

less than twenty houses, at this time, on and about the six squares of Gardiner's early town, and about as many more to the north and on the mainland. The Collegiate School scholars must have become well acquainted with the landmarks of the Point: with Lion Gardiner's old windmill, the Black Horse Inn, the ruins of the first earth fort and the stone and woodwork of the second fort facing the Sound, with Lady Fenwick's tomb, and the sunny open Green in the middle of the village, across which, from the main village street on the west side, could be seen Mr. Buckingham's parsonage under its elm trees.

During this time we do not even know, however, where the declining academy was housed. The small Calvinistic library had likely remained in Mr. Buckingham's Saybrook parsonage study and, for a time at least, Sir Fiske (as the Tutor's title was) probably held his classes there, the few scholars boarding about the village as best they could. Treasurer Nathaniel Lynde had early offered his house and lot, facing east on the town Green and across it from the minister's. The deed, however, had not been passed, but now, in 1708, when the School appeared to have definitely settled at Saybrook, it was duly executed, and the Trustees came into possession of the Lynde property.

Tradition has it that this house of Nathaniel Lynde was a unique structure, some "eighty feet long" (very likely made up of a main structure and a wing, as many of the well-to-do merchants of the day built), with sanded oak-plank floors, oil-paper windows, and great stone fireplaces. Saybrook stories have it that this elongated structure, or "college house," was the dormitory of the two tutors, Sir Fiske and James Hale, and likewise the scholars' recitation hall. While he was tutor there, Phineas Fiske married a Saybrook girl, the daughter of the village blacksmith of Essex, and no doubt set up his Penates in some upper rooms

The Collegiate
School at
Saybrook ❖

of this Lynde establishment.[1] In 1709, however, James
Hale retired, and Azariah Mather, the son of the aged
Windsor Trustee, and four years graduated, took his place,
preaching between his college duties at the Saybrook Meeting-house after the death of the Rev. Thomas Buckingham
in that year. When he resigned in the following year, to
become the regular Saybrook minister, Joseph Noyes, a
year out of the Collegiate School, became his successor.
Noyes, in the time to come, was to be one of the most important factors in early Yale history. He was the son of
old James Noyes of Stonington and nephew of Moses
Noyes of Lyme, who had also by this time become a Trustee.
He "had made himself very much master of the learning
taught at College in that day." Upon the retirement as
Tutor of Phineas Fiske, in 1713, Sir Joseph Noyes, assisted
by his classmate, William Russell (a son of Noadiah Russell), became the mainstay of the struggling School, and
continued as such until he became the successor of James
Pierpont in New Haven two years later and married his
daughter.

During these years the Treasurer of the School found it
one of his chief duties,—perhaps his most onerous one,—
to feed the dozen or twenty youths who came for their instruction to the Lynde college-house. Treasurer Alling
commissioned Captain Browne of the "Speedwell" for a
number of these necessaries.[2] Thus fifty bushels of wheat
and as many more of rye were shipped from New Haven
to Boston to raise money for this purpose in 1707, and a

[1] Apocryphal legends concerning this house are to the effect that it was
built for the Collegiate School and was one story high. But the evidence
is that it was a building that had come into Lynde's possession, and was
given by him to the School.

[2] Professor Dexter has published, in the New Haven Colony Historical
Society Papers, an exhaustive account of Captain Browne's business.

couple of casks of "green wine" went to the School, or the
"college," as Captain Browne called it. More green wine
was purchased later, and twenty yards of stuff for bed
curtains (probably for Tutor Mather and his bride), and
some brass rings, a pewter basin, a pound of alum, a pound
of nutmegs, and seventeen yards of silk crêpe for gowns
for the Tutors. A year later Captain Browne sold some
goods for a hogshead of rum, costing £12 16s., for the
scholars. John Dixwell of Boston, the silversmith, had
been acting as an agent for the School, and the proceeds of
a sale of corn and rye in the Boston market are paid over
by him. Some blue calico is ordered,—the first mention of
that color in Yale annals,—a hair-sieve, a brass skillet, a
steel candlestick, and some lace thread. Captain Browne's
later business for Treasurer Alling appears largely to have
consisted in carrying grain to Boston, the value of which
was paid over by School agents there besides Dixwell.

III

I suppose that it was about this time that the course of
study was made four years.[1] The School year began and
ended at the Saybrook Commencements in September, and
there were no long vacations. From a letter written about
this time, we find that the Senior classes closed their studies
when the hot weather came on in mid-July, and then appeared before the Tutors and such of the Trustees as could
come to Saybrook, to be "proved and approved" for pres-

---

[1] The course had been set for four years for a first and three years for a
second degree at the Saybrook organization of the Trustees. It had, however, been voted that if any of the scholars "shall demand Their Diploma or
Licence at the Expiration of 3 years and from thence of 2 full years," they
could have it if they were duly qualified. Practically all of the first students of the Collegiate School took their bachelor's degree under this special
arrangement.

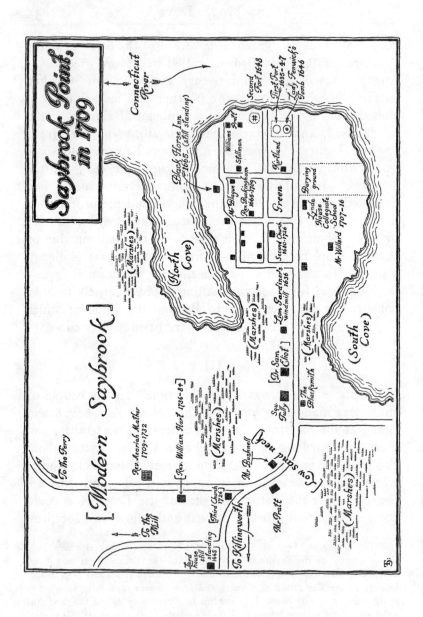

Saybrook Point, in 1709

[Modern Saybrook]

Connecticut River

To the Ferry

To the Mill

Rev. Azariah Mather 1709-1732

[Rev. William Hart 1736-8+]

[Third Church 1726]

Lord house still standing 1665

To Killingworth

Mr Pratt

Mr Bushnell

[Cow sand neck]

(Marshes)

(Marshes)

(Marshes)

(Marshes)

(Marshes)

(Marshes)

North Cove

South Cove

Squ Tully

[Dr Sam Eliot]

The Blacksmith

Lion Gardiner's windmill 1636

Black Horse Inn :-1665. (still standing)

Mr Pratt

Williams Point

Stillman

Kirtland

Mr Buckingham 1665-1703

Mr Bogue

Green

Second Church 1680-1726

Burying ground

Lynde House Collegiate School 1707-16

Mr Willard

Second Fort 1648

First Fort 1635-47

Lady Fenwick's Tomb 1646

entation as candidates for their degrees. Joseph Noyes in 1714 writes to Rector Andrew to this effect, and proceeds to ask Mr. Andrew to "appoint them their commencement work," that is, the Latin theses on assigned theological and metaphysical topics which, as at Harvard, they were publicly to pronounce upon their graduation. When the September Commencements came, there were small gatherings at Mr. Buckingham's house, and, after his death, probably in the village Meeting-house, over which Rector Andrew presided.

While these Commencements had been very quiet at first, in order to permit the Collegiate School to get under way without attracting uncomfortable notice in London, the fear of this interference had rapidly died out by 1710, and the Trustees had voted to allow a little more publicity to them. So that I suppose that now these annual Collegiate School events were of some small Colony interest, attended by perhaps a score of near-by coast and river-town ministers, by many of the Saybrook and Essex and Lyme villagers, and even, on occasion, by the Governor himself.

Benjamin Lord of the Class of 1714, later to be a Tutor for a brief time in the School, years afterward described those early Commencements. They were held in the Saybrook Meeting-house. The Rector presided, flanked, in the deacons' seats, no doubt, by such Trustees as could come, in their full-bottomed wigs, white bands, black coats and smallclothes, black stockings and shoes with silver buckles. Long sessions were held, both morning and afternoon of the great day. Prayers began and closed these ceremonies, and between times the "disputations" were held, in Latin. Toward evening the Commencement closed with the granting of the degrees. Says Benjamin Lord: "The Rector gave degrees much in the present form (no *pro modo Anglice* then) ; when he came to ye words *hunc Librum,* he gave ye candidates a little book into their hands, which they returned for ye next, for they came up only two by two; no Diaplomas were delivered then. The Rector previous to the giving of Degrees ask'd the consent of the Trustees, saying, *placetne vobis,* etc., to which they answered, *placet, placet.*"[1]

Of the thirteen boys who had been given their Bachelor of Arts degrees under Abraham Pierson's direction, eleven had either returned to him for graduate study in theology or had immediately set about preparation for the pulpit by placing themselves under their home-town ministers, these being in most cases, of course, Trustees of the Collegiate School. During the succeeding ten years the proportion of ministers to laymen among the graduates was hardly smaller, thirty out of the forty-two graduates of that period going into the ministry.[2] So that the purpose of the founders, to supply a home ministry through the Collegiate School, was beginning to be carried out. What sort of a place the Connecticut at this time was, into which these Collegiate School youths went for their life work, and what were its social and educational limitations, may now be briefly considered.

[1] The earliest Collegiate School diploma granted for a Bachelor's Degree that has been preserved is that of John Hart of the Class of 1703. It reads:

Omnibus et Singulis Has praesentes perlecturis Salutem in Deo. Vobis Notum sit, quod Iohannem Hart Candidatum, Primum in Artibus gradum competentem, tam probavimus, quam approbavimus: quem Examine sufficiente praevio approbatum, Nobis placet Titulo Graduq Artium Liberalium Baccalaurei; adornare et condecorare. Cuj[s] hoc Instrumentum in membrano scriptum Testimonium sit. A Gymnasio Academico Connecticutensi 17 Calend. Octobr. 1703.

ABRAH. PIERSON, Rect.

MOSES NOYES   THOMAS BUCKINGHAM
NOADIAH RUSSEL
Inspectores.

[2] This proportion would be larger if one counts in the number who studied theology but did not become ministers.

CHAPTER III

THE CONNECTICUT COLONY IN 1701-1714

I

ECTOR PIERSON'S cider and tobacco doubtless had played their part
in the hospitality which, as was the
case with all of the country ministers
of the day, he showed to passers-by on
the Boston Post-road. And no doubt
these occasions were infrequent enough
to the Killingworth minister, as they
were to Thomas Buckingham and the Collegiate School
Tutors at Saybrook in the years just after his death. Com-
panionship after their kind was not within easy reach for

the educated men of Connecticut of Rector Pierson's day. For we should remember, in calling to mind these times, that there was then a wide gap between the intellectual interests of the educated college man and the rest of his community. Scholars were few and far between, and were men of mark. Forming a small social circle about them were the well-to-do farmers and merchants, often traveled men and chosen to be Deputies in the General Court. But below these came the general run of the population, small farmers and hired men, country bumpkins, slaves, and village riffraff of narrow mental horizons and uncouth ways. We find this great mass of the common people of the Colony at that date, graphically portrayed by the Boston school-ma'am, Madam Knight. Of the upper class she remarks that "many of them are good, Sociable people, and I hope Religious too; but a little too much Independent in their principals." She found them living "Generally very well and comfortable in their families. But too Indulgent (especially the farmers) to their slaves: suffering too great familiarity from them, permitting them to sit at Table and eat with them (as they say to save time), and into the dish goes the black hoof as freely as the white hand." The merchants, or small village storekeepers, the sprightly Boston traveler found, had high social standing and were looked up to with great awe by the country people who came in to trade and run up bills. These "merchants" seem to have carried matters with a high hand. "They rate (says Madam Knight) their Goods according to the time and spetia they pay in: viz. Pay, mony. Pay as mony, and trusting. Pay is Grain, Pork, Beef, &c. at the prices set by the General Court that Year: mony is pieces of Eight, Ryalls, or Boston or Bay shillings (as they call them), or Good hard money, as sometimes silver coin is termed by them; also Wampum, viz. Indian beads which serves for change. Pay

as mony is provisions, as aforesaid one Third cheaper than
as the Assembly or General Court sets it; and Trust as they
and the mercht agree for time."

Hardly a better picture of Rector Pierson's times could
come down to us than such a little scene as this good lady
describes as occurring at a New Haven tradesman's shop.
"Being at a merchants house," she writes in 1704, "in comes
a tall country fellow, wth his alfogees full of Tobacco; for
they seldom Loose their Cudd, but keep Chewing and
Spitting as long as they'r eyes are open,—he advanc't to
the midle of the Room, makes an Awkward Nodd, and
spitting a Large deal of Aromatick Tincture, he gave a
scrape with his shovel like shoo, leaving a small shovel full
of dirt on the floor, made a full stop, Hugging his own
pretty Body with his hands under his arms, Stood staring
rown'd him, like a Catt let out of a Baskett. At last, like
the creature Balaam Rode on, he opened his mouth and
said: have you any Ribinen for Hat-bands to sell I pray?
The Questions and Answers about the pay being past, the
Ribin is bro't and opened. Bumpkin Simpers, cryes its con-
founded Gay I vow; and beckning to the door, in comes
Jone Tawdry, dropping about 50 curtsees, and stands by
him: he shows her the Ribin. *Law, You,* sais shee, *its right
Gent,* do You take it, *tis dreadfully pretty.* Then she en-
quires, *have You any hood silk I pray?* wch being brought
and bought, Have You any *thred silk to sew it wth* says
shee, wch being accomodated wth they Departed. They
Generaly stand after they come in a great while speachless,
and sometimes dont say a word till they are askt what they
want." The village storekeepers on such occasions seem to
have given the purchasers no choice, but bring out what is
ordered.

And we have still another cue from Madam Knight about
the Connecticut people of 1701. They were, she con-

sidered, generally rather clever, though provincial. "These people," she wrote, "have as Large a portion of mother witt, and sometimes a Larger, than those who have bin brought up in Citties; But for want of emprovements, Render themselves almost Ridiculos, as above. They are generaly very plain in their dress, throuout all ye Colony, as I saw, and follow one another in their modes; that You may know where they belong, especialy the women, meet them where you will."

While Madam Knight, fresh from Londonized Boston, had found Connecticut people more sedately dressed and provincial in their fashions, a few of the leading people were now dressing in rather more garish costumes than their Puritan fathers. The country-folk were plain enough, though a deserting soldier just before this time was advertised as wearing a periwig. Wigs, however, were now the universal custom throughout New England, and no doubt were worn by the more progressive provincials in Connecticut. Long, square-cut coats were in style, with great cuffs, and, for the more elegant dandies, gold- and silver-embroidered lapels. The earlier high Puritan hats had gone out for lower crowned but still broad-brimmed cloth or fur hats. Embroidered waistcoats were coming in. The women of the day, in spite of the Rev. Solomon Stoddard's thunderous denunciations from remote Northampton, were beginning to wear hooped petticoats of "tabby" silks, charmingly colored and embroidered, as well as the soft flowered dimities of Pierpont's early New Haven day fashions. We have seen how Governor Fitz-John Winthrop, of New London, had been one of the most famous of Connecticut dandies. He had been succeeded in 1707 as Governor by his pastor, Gurdon Saltonstall, but Winthrop's official sanction to the Boston styles (which he kept in touch with through a tremendously serious correspondence on the modes with his nephew, a Boston macaroni of the times) must have had its effect on the respectable and well-to-do Connecticut gentlemen of his circles. Muffs were still the fashion for both men and women, and in 1712 the London notion of necklaces and neck-scarfs was coming in. Great wearers of fancy gloves and of innumerable rings were these good Connecticut folk of the Collegiate School's early years. Rings were still not given at marriages, in conformity with Puritan prejudices, but they were, in extraordinary profusion, at funerals, where they were considered such perquisites that Judge Sewall sometimes set it down in his diary as a great disappointment if he arrived too late to receive one. I imagine that the zest for fashionable clothes was a considerable factor in the daily lives of the Connecticut folk of these Saybrook days of the Collegiate School. Perhaps this was one more phase of the pendulum-swing away from the early Puritan rigidity that was showing itself now in other things besides the importation of London fashions, games and dances. Benjamin Tompson, the "learned schoolmaster & physician," who preceded Ezekiel Cheever in the Charlestown Town School, had showed some of the current conservative feeling about this change of manners in his "New England's Crisis":

> Deep-skirted doublets, puritanick capes,
> Which now would render men like upright apes,
> Was comlier wear, our wiser fathers thought,
> Than the cast fashions from all Europe brought.
> 'Twas in those dayes an honest grace would hold
> Till an hot pudding grew at heart a cold.
> And men had better stomachs at religion,
> Than I to capon, turkey-cock, or pigeon;

to which he harmoniously added, as a gentle barb against the gossiping ladies:

When honest sisters met to pray, not prate,
About their own and not their neighbor's state.

And Timothy Woodbridge, now one of the Collegiate School Trustees, had had his say about the changes in manners, also in verse. We have in a complimentary poem to a Boston minister this poetical effort of the Hartford minister and Collegiate School Trustee:

Here be rare lessons set for us to read,
That offsprings are of such a goodly breed,
The dead ones here so much alive are made,
We think them speaking from blest Eden's shade.
Hark how they check the madness of this age,
The growth of pride, fierce lust and worldly rage;
They tell we shall to clam-banks come again,
If heaven still doth scourge us all in vain.

II

It was among people of this provincial and yet fashionable sort, and for the higher education of their sons, that the Collegiate School had been founded, and had selected its course of studies.

And this was, naturally, as limited in its interests as was the intellectual horizon of the Colony itself. The leaders in the New England settlements had, indeed, been well-educated men. Among the numerous Cambridge graduates and the fewer Oxford men of the original settlers had been men who, even in the old country, had high reputations for learning and ability. Their successors, however, had not had their advantages, but had received the education that the limited intellectual resources, both in tutors and books, of the pioneer life of the colonies afforded.

And this, compared either with the contemporaneous university education in England, or with the broader range of studies which were later on to be adopted at home, was

Governor Treat's house in Milford 1699

narrow enough. Absorbed in the political and religious struggles of these pioneer days, harassed by the French and Indian wars, their energies taken up by the hard life of the plantations, the common run of this sturdy New England people had had little time, if inclination, for keeping abreast with the intellectual currents abroad. We have seen how, in Connecticut, even the common schools had been neglected. This had been true throughout New England. The most that Harvard (supported, as it was, by the larger circle of English-university-bred men of Massachusetts), the single New England college up to this time, had been able to do had been to carry its youth through pretty elementary studies of the three ancient languages, through elementary arithmetic and some surveying, and a course in logic and a metaphysics which was still cobwebbed in long outgrown systems. Calvinistic theology and a quaintly unsophisticated study of natural laws called "Physicks," completed the higher education of this early day. The best-educated men of the time were thus limited to an extremely narrow and outgrown intellectual order.[1] The general run of the people were not educated at all beyond a reading knowledge of their own tongue—and even then not in all cases. The briefest survey of the intellectual horizon of 1701 will show how restricted it was.

So far as an interest in literature went, there was little enough of it in the New England of Rector Pierson and his fellow Trustees. As had been natural, the first books that had been written here had been reports by the best-educated of the first settlers on conditions in New England, and accounts of happenings, for the benefit of friends left at home. Winthrop's engaging letters to his wife, and Bradford's history, were of this period. Then had followed a long series of theological treatises, such as John Norton's widely-read "Orthodox Evangelist," Thomas Hooker's "The Soul's Implantation," John Cotton's famous "The Bloody Tenant Washed and Made White in the Blood of the Lamb," Roger Williams' "George Fox Digged out of his Burrowes," and Cotton Mather's enormous product of four hundred treatises, sermons, pamphlets, witchcraft arguments, his now quite absurd "Remarkable Providences" and his encyclopedic "Magnalia." The great "Complete Body of Divinity," of Vice-President Willard of Harvard, expounding the stern Calvinism of the latter 17th Century, was the most pretentious and important of these. In addition, countless "Election Sermons," tracts, "Execution Ser-

---

[1] This was also largely true of the England of the early 18th Century. Locke, for instance, was not a factor in English university education until some time later.

mons" (in which the condemned was rhetorically flayed as
he awaited the rope), and controversial pamphlets, such as
filled the air when the "Half-way Covenant" argument was
on, many of them printed in New England, formed the
staple intellectual pabulum of the educated class.   The
lists of books in New England private libraries of that
day show to what an extent this sort of theological publication comprised the reading of the time.   To these
were added similar works from England, till we seem to see
nothing but theology read about the hearth-fires of these
early Colony leaders.   John Dunton, in 1686, had enthusiastically imported a lot of English books that he expected to
turn a penny on, but says that he and his books were about
as popular in Boston as "Sour ale in Summer."   There were
plenty of booksellers in Boston, and most of them became
rich, and all were dandies.   But their sales were to the
ministers mostly, and of theological works.

Inventories of the time show the small range of books in
Connecticut libraries.   I came across such a list in the
inventory of a Milford estate in the New Haven probate
records of 1700.   The usual household belongings are
given—"cubbards," state tables, a looking-glass, a "great
looking glass," "one negro girl, £30," etc.—and then comes
a catalogue of "som books," mostly folios.   Here were
listed "Fox acts & monuments, Perkins his works, Cooper's
Dictionary, Fox Martyrs 2 vols., Gonerall History of
Turks, Doctrine of ye Gospels, Ciceros works in Latine,
Scapula's Lexicon in Greek & Latine, Christian's Dialogue,
Wilson's Smaller Christian Dictionary, Bundani Questions,
Prim about perseverence, Baxter's Confession of his Faith,
Majors Physiologia, Coles English Dictionary, Compleat
Horsman or exact Farior, Sibbs soul Conflict, appologie of
ye Church of England, the logician's Schoolmaster, Epit-
omie of ye art of husbandry, beames of former light,

Infant Baptisme, a Latine bible, a brief instructions ye worship of God, Calipoia, ye whole book spalms, ye portraiture of Charles 1st, Catalines conspiracy, Burrough of a gracious spiritt," and an "antidote against distractions." Richard Rosewell, the Collegiate School treasurer previous to John Alling, left a "Dixonary, history book," and "1 small book." One Thomas Cooke of Guilford, dying in 1700, left "a book cald ye exposition of ye 10 commandments, the practical Catechisme, ye 10 virgins, a Book titled Faith & good Works all, a parchment called ye Church history, ye Estate of Britain, an old psalm book a book of Sam. Willards, a book titled a good conscience, an old book called ye passion of Christ, ye assembly of divines, a book Sion in distress a book of Sr William Phipps, a book of Thomas Taylors a Latton Book in ox, a paper covered book titled dead Faith, a Boza bible [John Boyse's Translation of The Apocrypha?] and 2 old bibles."

There was, to be sure, some crudely imaginative literature written during this period, though I fancy that most of it had scant audiences. But this was faintly poetical, at the best, and was deeply tinctured with the prevailing fear of God and hope of a very tangible Hereafter. And it took the form of metrical elegies and epitaphs, of "two-penny jeering gigges," or acrostics, as often as it did of more sustained flights of poetry. Isaac Watts' lines,

> Gentle Ithuriel led him round the skies;
> The buildings struck him with immense surprise,

are not more ridiculous to modern readers than the amazing mass of theological verse that came out of contemporaneous New England. Considering that they might proceed so far in their reforming of the Church of England ritual as to sing psalms, the first book issued in New England had been the "Bay Psalm Book," printed on the Harvard press by

Stephen Daye, a ne'er-do-well fellow, who fell into evil ways and was clapped in jail. This badly printed collection of religious doggerel, with amended versions, went through thirty editions. Containing such lines as

> O Happie hee shall surely bee
> that taketh up, that eke
> thy little ones against the stones
> doth into pieces break,

this extraordinary set of Meeting-house songs, together with Sternhold and Hopkins rendering, furnished the New England congregations, as, indeed, New England households, with their religious verse far past the date of the founding of the Collegiate School, and no doubt was used by the scholars.

Timothy Woodbridge probably considered that he was assisting in the moral return of Connecticut, at least to the clam banks of the original Puritan simplicity. But his poetry does not commend his imaginative genius very much to us. This Collegiate School Trustee, however, never sank to quite the abysmal depths of nonsense that Governor Wolcott of Connecticut fell into in his fifteen hundred lines commemorating his predecessor's securing of the Colony charter:

> Religion was the cause; Divinity
> Having declar'd the gospel shine should be
> Extensive as the sun's diurnal shine;
> This mov'd our Founders to this great design.

But the particular star in New England's early poetry was Michael Wigglesworth who, as we have seen, had escaped an early death in New Haven, to become the poetical exponent of all the gloom and despair and agonized spiritual torments of his times.

Wigglesworth was known, of course, to the Collegiate School founders, as were doubtless his poems. "Homely and coarse as his muse is," said a critic of 1829 of his verses, "her voice probably sunk into the hearts of those who listened to her rude melody, leaving there an impression, deeper than any which the numbers of a Byron, a Southey, or a Moore may ever produce." And this was probably true. The ordinary New England folk of the early 18th Century were no nice discriminators in matters of literary taste. They were not readers, and knew little or nothing of the new Queen Anne fashions in books in London. They were still engrossed by the theological disputes of the day in their own narrow circles, and the best of them were spending most of their energy in finding ways of stemming the ebb of the early religious tide rather than in cultivating the graces of life. To them, Michael Wigglesworth's lumbering miles of earnest but unconsciously puerile verses were in the literary field what the sermons and tracts on their scant bookshelves were to them in the matter of solid thinking. Wigglesworth's "Day of Doom" is of course his most noted work.

> Wallowing in all kinds of sin,
>   Vile wretches lay secure;
> The best of men had scarcely then
>   Their lamps kept in good ure.

The final Judgment Day arrives. The Almighty appears,

> With mighty voice, and hideous noise,
>   More terrible than thunder,

and the erstwhile inhabitants of the earth are called before him for judgment. Violent arguments begin between lost souls and God.

> "But Lord," say they, "we went astray,
>   And did more wickedly,

> By means of those whom thou hast chose,
>   Salvation heirs to be."
> To whom the judge. "what you allege,
>   Doth nothing help the case;
> But makes appear how vile you were,
>   And rendereth you more base."

The damned are hastily packed off to their eternal torments, argument or no argument, doubtless to the terror of fireside families to whom the heads of households rolled forth the awful verses.

> Then to the bar, all they drew near
>   Who died in infancy,
> And never had or good or bad
>   Effected personally,
> But from the womb unto the tomb,
>   Were straightway carried, . . .

These infants propound the following extenuating circumstances:

> "But Adam's guilt our souls hath spilt,
>   His fault is charged on us;
> And that alone hath overthrown,
>   And utterly undone us . . .
> How could we sin that had not been
>   Or how is his sin our
> Without consent, which to prevent,
>   We never had a power?"

> Then answered the judge most dread,
>   "God doth such doom forbid,
> That men should die eternally
>   For what they never did.
> But what you call old Adam's fall,
>   And only his trespass,
> You call amiss to call it his,
>   Both his and yours it was.

He was design'd of all mankind
    To be a public head,
A common root, whence all should shoot,
    And stood in all their stead.
He stood and fell, did ill or well,
    Not for himself alone,
But for you all, who now his fall
    And trespass would disown."

Wigglesworth's God proceeds in this vein before the unbaptized infants for numerous stanzas, and concludes:

" A crime it is, therefore in bliss
    You may not hope to dwell
But unto you I shall allow
    The easiest room in hell."

It must have been a heartening ending of this doleful business, to the church members of Abraham Pierson's day, for Wigglesworth to wind up his stupendous mass of doggerel with a fascinating picture of the joyful reception in Heaven of the "saints" themselves, church members in good standing in the village Meeting-house.

Perhaps we can have no worse example, however, of the poetical genius of those days than in the verses of Nicholas Noyes, that persistent disciple of the foppish punning style of an earlier day in London. Noyes' poems are a very good example of the sort of poetry that was accepted by his New England contemporaries. In his "Consolatory Poem" to Cotton Mather, for whom he wrote some prefatory jingles for the latter's "Magnalia," the Reverend Noyes wrote:

Yea, who would live among catarrhs
Contagion, pains, and strifes, and wars,
That might go up above the stars,
And live in health, and peace, and bliss,
Had in that world, but wish'd in this?

This sort of poetry appears to have been about the best that the New England of the Collegiate School's early days afforded.

III

In science we find the contemporaries of the Collegiate School founders steeped in the supernatural, and untouched by the great intellectual awakening in England that had followed Bacon and which was now being brilliantly carried on by Sir Isaac Newton, Locke, Halley, and Cotes. It was said that there was but one copy of Bacon's "Advancement of Learning" in all New England a decade after the Collegiate School was founded. Rumors of a new field of intellectual life had, no doubt, filtered into the colonies. But to the orthodox leaders of the day this departure meant only the threatening advent of a new theology, as had so well been proven in the Latitudinarian movement in Boston. As such, it was sternly to be avoided. So that, by 1700, as little was known of Isaac Newton and John Locke, or even Bacon, in science, as was known of Dryden and Steele and Addison in literature. If the metaphysics that was taught at the Collegiate School was to be of the traditional and long outgrown scholastic systems of the earlier Reformation writers, and if the theology was the strictest and most primitive Calvinism, the "Physicks" was of equal antiquity and a half-century behind more enlightened England's. The New England people of the early 18th Century were still at the intellectual stage of their Puritan forefathers of the early 17th Century. Rector Pierson's classes began the educational history of Yale in a devout belief in a Calvinistic hell, in supernatural agencies, and that the sun moved round the earth.

Rector Pierson's manuscript "Physicks" would doubtless give us a highly entertaining view of the scientific notions of his times, could we discover a copy of it. But we have an idea of what it was like, from the Harvard text-book of the day, a manuscript copy of which, in the handwriting of a Harvard student of 1708, was found a few years ago under an ancient flooring in Faneuil Hall in Boston. Each paragraph in this little Harvard text-book defined some natural phenomenon. It concerned "falling stars" and why they are "inflamed;" "airy meteors;" "irregular winds," the dew. Sleep is caused, we read, by "steames of food, and blood ascending into ye Brain, by whose coldness they are said to be condens'd into moisture, which obstructs ye passage of ye Spirits that they can't freely permeate to ye Organs of Senses"; dreams are "an adjunct of Sleep," "which in ye active fancy's entertaining itself (whilst it has nothing else to do) with ye Phantasms laid up in ye memory." The Harvard "Physicks" of 1703-1707 (and

A Madison House of 1700

no doubt Rector Pierson's) taught that animals were distinguishable from mankind largely through their lack of reason, "though some learned men are enclined to think that religion not reason is ye essential difference between man and brute." This treatise also had to do with medicine, astronomy, and simple measuring (such as of "ye cask both at ye bung' head"), and "fortification."

Rector Pierson's teachings could hardly have been very different from those in this old Harvard Latin manuscript, as indeed both probably came from a common and earlier Harvard source, and in turn from the English university teaching of 1600.

It will be recalled that Noadiah Russell, of the board of Trustees, had been making almanacs in old Ipswich but a few years before this time. His opinions on the phenomena of nature no doubt coincided with much that Abraham Pierson was now teaching. Some of them are worth quoting. "Concerning Lightning and Thunder" this Collegiate School Trustee had written: "Lightning is an exalation hot and dry, as also hot and moist; which being elevated by the sun to the middle region of the air, is there included or shut up within a cloud and cannot ascend; but by an antiperistasis grows hotter and is enkindled, attenuated, and so seeks for more room, which it not finding in the cloud, violently rends the same, breaks out of it and continues burning so long that it comes to the very ground. By its rending the cloud there is caused a most dreadful noise or rumbling, and this we call thunder. So that thunder is improperly reckoned among the kind or species of meteors." And Trustee Russell proceeds: "With this lightning" [a "second sort" which "consists of a more fat and thick exalation"] "there happens to be (yet seldom) a stone, that is called a thunderbolt, which braketh forth with the exalation (as a bullet out of a gun) and breaks into pieces whatever it meets. When it strikes

the ground, it is reported to go not above five feet deep."
Noadiah Russell's published facts about lightning contain
even more curious observations. He says: "If lightning kills
one in his sleep, he dyes with his eyes opened. The reason
is because it just wakes him and kills him before he can shut
his eyes again. If it kills one waking, his eyes will be found
to be shut, because it so amaseth him, that he winketh and
dyes before he can open his eyes again. *Caution* [adds this
sponsor for the intellectual life of early Yale]. It is not
good to stand looking on the lightning for any time, for, if
it hurts no other way, yet it may dry up or so waste the
chrystalline humor of the eyes that it may cause the sight
to perish, or it may swell the face, making it to break out
with scabs, caused by a kind of poyson in the exalation which
the pores of the face and eyes do admit."

It was under such educational auspices, and at such a
stage in Connecticut's intellectual progress, that the Collegiate School of Pierpont and Pierson, of Andrew and Buckingham and Woodbridge and Sir Joseph Noyes, Tutor, was
now developing. As we shall see, circumstances, a few
years later, were to bring a new mental stimulus to this pro-
vincialism, and happily introduce at least a little of the
broader intellectual life of England to the struggling
academy. But for the first decade and more of the Collegiate School's career, it continued to give the orthodox
education of the times, untouched by what was going on in
the outside English-speaking world, and remote from its
cultural influence.

Governor
Gurdon
Saltonstall

CHAPTER IV

THE SAYBROOK PLATFORM

I

WE have seen how in the last years of the 17th Century, the majority sentiment among the ministers of the Colony had slowly been forming in favor of a stronger church consolidation than had been the independent Congregational tradition to that time, so as to stem the rising tide of irreligion. We have seen how this had led to agitation for that proposed church control of the Collegiate School which had been advised by the Mathers. And we have seen how the Pierpont party had rather adroitly evaded that possibility, how they had changed the sections of the Addington and Sewall charter draft that tended in that direction, and how they had secured a charter which, until 1792 (when the State secured representation on the Board of Trustees in return for a grant of money), was to make the Connecticut college independent either of the church or state.

But I do not suppose that we should conclude from this last-mentioned fact that the Pierpont party were averse to a better organization of the churches. Abraham Pierson was avowedly of Presbyterian leanings, and James Noyes (like his father) was a moderate Presbyterian. The Fairfield County ministers likewise leaned that way. That James Pierpont was prepared for a step forward in the churches is likely, though he had been opposed to forming such an organization in connection with the Collegiate School. Saltonstall, I imagine, and Woodbridge had wished to see that School begun under organized church auspices. But this had not been done. Now, however, that the School had been established as an independent institution, there was left to be undertaken the effort to bring it and the Colony churches into a working relation with each other. Such a scheme had been under discussion by the Massachusetts conservatives, as a last despairing effort to stem the tide of the new theology. It was now, in 1703-1705, broached in Connecticut.

The Trustees, meeting in March of the former year at East Guilford (now Madison), prepared a petition to their fellow Connecticut ministers calling attention to the Confession of Faith which had been adopted in 1680 by the New England Synod meeting at Boston, and suggesting that Connecticut concur with Massachusetts by asking their own General Assembly officially to recommend it to the Connecticut Colony churches. Timothy Woodbridge made his first appearance as a Trustee at this meeting, having finally left Boston. Whether his appearance, fresh from a year's sojourn near the Mathers in Boston, had anything to do with the action taken we do not know, but it certainly was agreeable to him. The Savoy Confession approved by the Boston Synod had not been unanimously adopted throughout the Colony, so that the purpose of this action was to secure an orthodox creed for the Connecticut churches. And I suppose that it had another purpose also. Church of England parishes had for some years been established in Boston, where they were received with coldness by the conservative Congregationalists and cordiality by the new Brattle-Coleman party. An Episcopal Church had, indeed, been sought in Stratford in 1690. But Episcopacy had not as yet made progress in Connecticut. In 1701, however, the Society for the Propagation of the Gospel in Foreign Parts had been chartered in London, and missionaries of the Church of England had been sent to New England. One of those, George Keith, had passed through Connecticut and had been "civally entertained" by the broadminded Gurdon Saltonstall, who not only permitted the missionary to preach in his Puritan pulpit but expressed to him "his good affection to the Church of England." The growth of Episcopacy in Connecticut now began, and I imagine that its threat of coming inroads upon the Congregational churches may have had no small part in suggesting to the Collegiate School (as a similar situation had suggested a similar effort at Harvard) that Connecticut Congregationalism put itself in readiness to combat it, at least so far as adopting a Colony Congregational creed was concerned. It appears that this movement met with good success and that "the churches and ministers of the several counties met in a consociated council, and gave their assent to the Westminster and Savoy Confessions of Faith. It seems [adds Connecticut's historian Trumbull] that at this council they also drew up certain rules of ecclesiastical union in discipline, as preparatory to a general synod, which they still had in contemplation."

However this may have been, nothing resulted from this

last-mentioned proposal until five years later. The Rev. Gurdon Saltonstall of New London then appears on that public stage where for the next seventeen years he was to be so important a figure.

Contemporary references go to show that Saltonstall was probably the most celebrated preacher of his day, as he certainly was one of the most versatile. On his death, in his seventeenth year as Governor of Connecticut, he was referred to in the Boston paper as "a profound Divine, a Great Judge in the Law, and a consummate statesman; He had made Excellent observations in Natural Philosophy, and had a peculiar Genius and Skill in the Mathematics; Not to mention his lighter Studies of Philology, History, Geography, &c., in each of which he excell'd enough, to have made an other Man, very Famous: His Person, Mien and Aspect were equally attractive of Love, Esteem and Admiration." As a public speaker, Gurdon Saltonstall received from his contemporaries the highest praise of any of his colleagues. He "charmed" his hearers, it was said of him, "in such a Strange and Wonderfull manner, that when he has sometimes spoken for Hours together, there has appeared nothing but Satisfaction, Delight and Rapture, till they have all complain'd, that he Left off, & Robb'd them of their Happiness too soon." Saltonstall, with these unusual intellectual attainments, was "very much Fixt, in the Establish'd Religion, of New-England, after a long, strict and critical Enquiry, into the Principles of it." Cotton Mather's encomiums in Saltonstall's case were even more highly colored than usual, but they give us a glimpse of the man himself. He had, said Mather, "an Agreeable Aspect: The Silver Basket of a comely Body, carrying in it the Golden Apples of a well-furnished and well-disposed Soul; And a venerable Presence charming with Familiar Condescensions. We will not call him a Star [concludes Cotton

Mather, soaring upwards from his customary rhetorical heights] but even a Constellation of the most fulgid Endowments."

During the last years of his Governorship, Fitz-John Winthrop had been more or less incapacitated, and had turned over to his young minister much of the Colony's business, especially, it was said, his official correspondence, though he doubtless continued his epistles on fashion himself. His death, in November, 1707, left the Colony in a difficult situation. Serious troubles over the Rhode Island and Massachusetts boundaries were still unsettled. Governor Dudley of the latter Colony had for several years been attempting to get control of Connecticut, and had repeatedly attacked its charter before the Attorney Generals of both King William and Queen Anne. A suit was now pending on the last of these charges. The French and Indian War was rising on the horizon. In all of these matters Saltonstall had been a close adviser of Governor Winthrop, and, it was said, was the only man in the Colony who knew the standing of the suit brought by Dudley, having, in fact, written the Connecticut brief in reply to it. Under these circumstances, he was judged to be the most capable successor to Winthrop who could be found. A month after Winthrop's death, therefore, the Assembly, meeting in special session, repealed a law that the Governor must be elected from the Magistrates, and chose the New London minister Saltonstall, his election being ratified by the freemen the following May.

Almost the first official act of Governor Saltonstall was to bring before the Assembly a document calling for a synod of the Colony churches to arrange for an ecclesiastical establishment.

Now this action of Saltonstall's was a serious step to take. The similar effort in Massachusetts had ignominiously failed, and this new suggestion was especially serious because of the form which Saltonstall originally gave to it. In this he had proposed by legislative enactment to command the ministers to meet and draw up a form of church discipline, which then might be imposed upon the Colony churches by the Assembly. This meddling by the Assembly in church affairs had long been a sore point in Connecticut church history. The more moderate Presbyterians of the Colony (among whom Pierpont seems to have taken the lead), together with the laymen in the Assembly who wished the churches to retain their independence, were stoutly opposed to it. There was a sharp collision between the two parties. The Deputies succeeded in altering the first draft so that the final Act, as passed, called for county ministers' meetings indeed, but with "messengers" to be present chosen by the laity, and permitted these conventions to elect delegates as they saw fit,—two or more to a county,—to a Colony synod to be held at Saybrook at the next Collegiate School Commencement.

This action suggests a significant factor in the whole Saybrook Platform episode. Though it did not succeed, here again was an effort to secure governmental authority over the churches, with its resulting threat of governmental control over the acts of the Collegiate School. While the episode shows Governor Saltonstall as a firm believer in a centralized Colony authority over the religious state of the people, it likewise shows Pierpont again as the one who proposed to keep the two apart, and to rescue the struggling academy of which he had been the original promoter from state or even church control.

II

This is not the place to give more than a brief review of the Saybrook Synod and its famous platform, and note its

Governor Saltonstall's ·:· chair ·:·

connection with the affairs of the Collegiate School. This, of course, was considerable. I presume that James Pierpont, who assumed the lead at this synod, was in sympathy with it. But that he did not go as far as did Governor Saltonstall is entirely substantiated by the traditions of the meeting. Pierpont was undoubtedly looking out for his infant Collegiate School as much as he was for the state of religion in the Colony; he was, therefore, interested in securing a Colony creed for both church and school rather than in a Presbyterian organization of the churches.[1]

It was on the eighth of September, 1708, that the seventh annual Collegiate School Commencement was held at the Saybrook Meeting-house. The Synod convened the day following. Tradition has it that this meeting, famous in Connecticut history, was held in the large lower room of the Lynde house, which the day before had finally come into the

[1] Standard studies of these may be found in Dr. Leonard Bacon's long and minute account in his "Contributions to the Ecclesiastical History of Connecticut," published in 1861, and in his chapter on Pierpont in his "Thirteen Historical Discourses." Trumbull's History also contains an exhaustive statement, and Professor Williston Walker has treated it at length in his "Creeds and Platforms of Congregationalism."

formal possession of the School. There was probably a small attendance, though the interest in the proposed Platform may have brought a larger assembly of ministers and laymen than usually attended the Commencements. As it happened, nine of the twelve Trustees of the Collegiate School had been elected delegates to this meeting: James Noyes of Stonington, Thomas Buckingham of Saybrook, Moses Noyes of Lyme, Samuel Andrew of Milford (then, of course, Rector in title of the School), Timothy Woodbridge of Hartford, Samuel Russel of Branford, little Noadiah Russell of Middletown, John Davenport of Stamford, and James Pierpont of New Haven. New Haven County alone sent no laymen "messengers." The Saybrook Synod, therefore, was practically the Board of Trustees of the Collegiate School.

The business of this famous Synod was threefold: the adoption of a Confession of Faith and of a form of church government, and rules for the latter. The Synod seems to have come down at once to a test of strength between two extremes; the one, represented by Pierpont, taking it for granted that the churches already had a Confession and needed now only the public announcement of it by the Assembly and some loose form of church association; the other, representing the Saltonstall party, that the Synod should send a Confession and organization plan to the Assembly, which should then impose it upon the churches. Tradition has it that the first draft was drawn up by James Pierpont, but that it was far from the extreme views of the agitators for a change, and a most conservative document. The upshot of the discussion was a compromise. Pierpont's original draft was so amended and changed that it gave some appearance of following the more radical views. Yet, as passed, it left the Assembly only the business of "public testimony thereunto as the faith of the churches of this

Colony," and framed an organization which, for years afterwards, was to be interpreted by the various church associations as they saw fit. The several counties (which were to have distinct "consociations," all four being represented in a "General Association" by ministerial delegates) came to differ very greatly from each other in the practical application of it.[1]

The important result to the Collegiate School of the Saybrook Synod of 1708 was that after the year 1722 (and the custom extended far into the 18th Century) every officer of the Collegiate School and of Yale College was under the necessity of publicly accepting the Confession of Faith adopted at it, and that that stern Calvinistic faith thus became the officially adopted creed of the School and was strictly taught to its scholars.

The Saybrook Platform of 1708 was the final act in the long effort to establish Puritanism in Connecticut. And it was a successful one. The Assembly, to be sure, adopted an act of toleration in its October session at New Haven immediately following, as it now could well afford to. Under that Act dissenters from the now standardized Congregational church were permitted to enjoy a similar religious liberty to that granted by William and Mary to dissenters from the Church of England, though they still were taxed to help support the Colony church. But the Saybrook Platform squarely set Connecticut and the coming Yale College back into the traditional mould. Changed as it was and modified from the primitive religion of John Davenport and Thomas Hooker, the accepted religious faith and theology

[1] Hartford and New London Counties accepted the Saybrook Platform as it was passed, Fairfield took a more extreme Presbyterian interpretation of it, and New Haven appears to have taken a middle way. The Saybrook Platform remained in force until 1784, and, with decreasing strictness, till 1850, or thereabouts.

of Connecticut people was henceforth, for generations, to remain in the traditional lines. While Massachusetts and Harvard were tending in the opposite direction, the establishment of the Collegiate School and now the adoption of the Saybrook Platform undoubtedly made Connecticut conservative and, in time, were to have a retarding effect upon the intellectual broadening of her people. The "Great Awakening" of Jonathan Edwards' day, and the still later popular modification of Edwards' stern Calvinism by the first Timothy Dwight, as well as the "New England Theology" of the early 19th Century, all went back, for their source, to the Congregationalism of the Saybrook Platform.

III

Thus much it is necessary to recall of the church history of these early 18th Century days in order to understand the solidly orthodox ground upon which the Collegiate School was now founded. Protected by these theological fortifications against the insidious attacks of the prevalent heresies of the day, and domiciled at Saybrook, the Trustees of that School no doubt considered that the close of the first decade of the little academy found matters in a satisfactory condition so far as orthodoxy went, and that it could now develop into the institution it had been planned to be.

By 1712, however, a new combination of unexpected circumstances was to arise which was to upset these hopeful expectations and all but wreck the infant academy. These grew out of the traditional trouble which Connecticut had had in educational matters,—the financial difficulties of the Connecticut people, and the poverty-stricken treasury of the Collegiate School itself.

I have told how the Assembly had encouraged the School by appropriating a small annual sum to it. This had

Saltonstall's Connecticut Troops in Boston in 1710

been used to pay most of the Rector's salary, leaving the Tutors to be paid largely from the tuition of the lower classes. As at Harvard, this tuition was payable in "country pay," the common legal tender of the times, consisting of farm products and firewood, occasional live stock, and country-store merchandise. But the total income of the School from all sources was limited enough. While Treasurer Alling had the deeds to the Killingly acres of Major Fitch, and, supposedly, to some acres near Saybrook, we do not hear anything about an income from these sources. Established on an independent basis, it is probable that the founders at first had expected to secure financial help from individuals in the Colony. Two years after the founding, in fact, this was attempted. The Trustees had asked the Assembly for permission to circulate a "brief" throughout the Colony for private subscriptions. But, though this permission was cheerfully given, nothing appears to have come from it.   The French and Indian War was then at its hottest, and doubtless the Connecticut folk had all that they could manage in meeting their share of the resulting taxes and levies for military costs and men.   Governor Salton-stall, in 1710, had gone to Boston with three hundred Connecticut soldiers, whose support was a public problem.   So that by 1712 the financial condition of the School was at a low ebb, and the Trustees were forced to appeal to the Colony treasury for aid.   The Assembly, considering this appeal and the general educational situation, at their session in the New Haven Meeting-house in October of that year, rose to the occasion by passing a general Act for "the encouragement of learning," carrying an appropriation for one year of £100 to the Collegiate School "for maintaining a Rector and tutors," instead of the £120 in "country pay" "formerly granted."

But even this Colony aid did not help matters.   The School was rapidly weakening.   There were but two Seniors in 1712, and three Juniors.   The outlook was bad enough for Rector Andrew in Milford and his sole resident Tutor at Saybrook, Sir Noyes.   An appeal was made to the Assembly to remit taxes for the Collegiate School scholars, and to relieve them from military duty, and this was passed. The immediate result seems to have been a sudden increase to nine in the Freshman Class of 1714, though the two succeeding classes fell off again to three youths each.

It was at this low pass that the leaders of the School put their heads together and began to look about them for outside help.

G. Saltonstall

Jeremiah Dummer

CHAPTER V

THE GIFTS OF BOOKS

I

UP to this time the Connecticut political leaders, so far as England was concerned, had been fully occupied in defending their charter rights against their neighbors, and had just managed to slip by the numerous obstacles set up by the jealous Dudley of Boston and the New York Royal Governors.

Under these circumstances, anything like official efforts to interest English leaders in Connecticut matters had not been feasible. So far as the Collegiate School was concerned, the long train of public events in the Colony, beginning with the setting up of the original independent republics, had had its logical outcome. The Connecticut Assembly had hesitated about incurring Royal wrath by independently "founding" a college, and the School itself had begun its own existence under the most quiet public circumstances possible. But now James Pierpont, taking upon his shoulders the fast-slipping fortunes of the Collegiate School, broke the long tradition of aloofness from England, by writing in the Collegiate School's behalf to the Massachusetts Colony Agent in London, one Jeremiah Dummer.

This was in 1711. Dummer was then eleven years out of Harvard, and a resident of London. His personal address was so good and his manners so engaging that he had become a man of some social prominence in the London society of the day. As the friend and social protégé of that Lord Bolingbroke who was Secretary of State under William and Mary, he became acquainted with all of the bigwigs of London literary and political society, and, even after his noble patron had been impeached and deprived of his title, was hail-fellow-well-met with most of them, and apparently used this connection to the advantage of his distant home Province of Massachusetts.

It was to this fashionable young Colonial agent that, as we have seen, James Pierpont had written regarding his family connection with the English Pierreponts. He had, moreover, in that letter, incidentally asked Dummer to see what he could do for the struggling Collegiate School. The correspondence, thus inaugurated, was to bear important results. Dummer's reply to this first letter from the New Haven minister is an interesting Yale document. He had mentioned Pierpont's name in London, telling people that he was "the head of a College,"—no doubt thereby causing the momentary raising of an eyebrow or two among the coffee-house fashionables of the town, as to what outlandish institution had been started in that Puritan Province by the barbarous name of "Connecticut." And he had set about with his usual energy to buttonhole his wealthy friends, and see what he could do for it.

It had so happened that one Elihu Yale, London capitalist and bigwig, had just come to the attention of James Pierpont through an unusual happening. In narrating the early days in Davenport's New Haven, I referred to the family connection between Theophilus Eaton and the Denbighshire Yales. It will be recalled that Governor Eaton married the widow Yale, who brought her two sons, David and Thomas, and daughter Anne (who married Edward Hopkins) with her to New Haven in the Davenport party; how David Yale's fairly large fortune had placed him on the first tax-list of New Haven, and how he had early left the sinking New Haven Colony for Boston, where, it would appear, Elihu Yale was born, probably in 1649. The young Elihu had gone back to London with his father. He had there been put to school, first to the "Merchant Tailor's" and then to Milton's friend's,—Master Dugard's in Coleman Street (under the shadow of Davenport's old church walls),—and, on reaching his maturity, had adventurously gone out with the East India Company to Madras, where he had become the Company's agent, and Governor of the English trading post, Fort St. George. Amassing, by more or less shady means it would appear, a large fortune for his day there, he had returned to London in 1699, and was now living in Queen's Square, Great Ormond Street, in a highly fashionable style, amid the magnificent Oriental plunder of his Madras days. By 1710 Elihu Yale,—then about sixty-one years old,—was looking forward to the end of his earthly life and settling his affairs. Childless, he desired a legal heir to his great estate, and was casting about him for one. A promising candidate appearing in the fifteen-year-old David Yale, son of the great man's rural cousin, Thomas, who had remained at North Haven, Con-

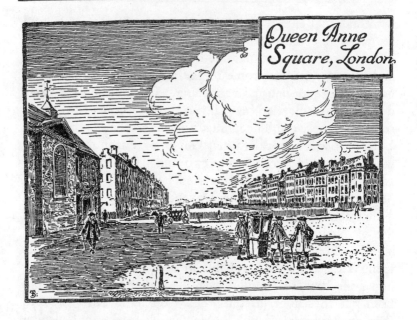

Queen Anne Square, London

necticut, Elihu Yale had sent for him. Pierpont could hardly escape hearing of this. Recognizing in Elihu Yale a logical benefactor of the struggling Collegiate School, he mentions the possibility to Jeremiah Dummer. For Dummer's letter of March 16, 1711 (obviously in reply to this suggestion), is to the effect that "As to Mr. Yale, I doubt I can do anything with him at present, he being very much put out of humour on the account of his losing twenty thousand pounds by Sir Stephen Evans, who lately failed, and thereunto retiring to Sr Caesar Childs in the Country hanged himself with a Bedcord."

Two months later, however, in spite of this untoward occurrence, Dummer had so bestirred himself as to broach the matter with Governor Yale. His letter to Pierpont, May 22, 1711, is to this effect: "Here [he writes] is Mr. Yale, formerly Governor of Fort St. George in the Indies, who has got a prodigious estate, and now by Mr. Dixwell sends for a relation of his from Connecticut to make him his heir, having no son. He told me lately [so the hustling Colony agent had invaded Great Ormond Street] that he intended to bestow a charity upon some college in Oxford, under certain restrictions which he mentioned. But I think he should much rather do it to your college, seeing he is a New England and I think a Connecticut man. If therefore when his kinsman comes over, youl write him a proper letter on that subject, I will take care to press it home." Young David Yale was in due season lifted bodily out of rural North Haven and, in his best leather breeches and country waistcoat, piloted across the sea by a "Mr. Dixwell" to become heir to the great Governor Yale's estates. Something fell out amiss in his relations with his wealthy relative, however, and he was packed home again by the next Boston sailing, to live the remainder of his life on his North Haven farm, and receive, in an honorary degree which the College gave him in 1724, his only tangible reward in the business. No doubt James Pierpont wrote a "proper letter" to the crusty old Governor when the boy was sent over, but nothing came of it for some time, the whole affair seemingly having begun wrong with the future famous patron of the College.

Dummer, however, had become active in other quarters than Elihu Yale's. In that first letter of 1711 he had said that he was "doing what I can to gain Dr. Salmon's Library, which is a fine one indeed, and worth six of that at Harvard College. The only object he makes is, that all Universities follow too much the Study of Heathen learning and corrupt ye doctrine of the Gospel. I told him that your College is a young child that he may bring up to his hand [wherein Dummer took a rather large liberty, as far-away agents often will], & form it to his own model, upon which he has sent you a long story of directions for the students, inclosed in this pacquet, & directed to you. I have not had time to read 'em, tho' he gave me the letter open. I believe it will be well for you to answer it."

I imagine that James Pierpont's reply to the venerable Dr. Salmon's "long story of directions" was not entirely businesslike, so far as Jeremiah Dummer's business-man's view of what it should have been were concerned. For in January, 1713, Dummer writes to the New Haven minister: " 'Tis with regret I must now acquaint you that all my labour and pains with Dr. Salmon are at an end. For when I had brought him to consent to give his Library to your Colledge, an apoplexy took him off before he had time to make a New Will. And so an Old one took place, made several years since, by which he gave that great valuable Library to an Absolute stranger, that he had seen once or twice and took a fancy to. I have endeavored to retrieve this great loss, by begging a Library for you among my friends, & tho' my acquaintance with men of Learning & Estate is very generall, yet I did not expect to succeed so well in this Charitable enterprise, as I now find I am like to doe. For I have got together a pretty parcel of books already, for you to begin with, & I hope in a Years time to send you a very valuable collection with the names of the Benefactors."

II

Under these promising circumstances, James Pierpont bestirred himself to secure for his Collegiate School as permanent a hold as he could upon the apron strings of this enterprising and valuable ally. The Collegiate School, however, had no funds with which to pay the proper commissions to Dummer. So I imagine that Pierpont was one of the first to suggest to Saltonstall that the Colony make Dummer its accredited and salaried London agent, as

Massachusetts had done. Governor Saltonstall must have
fallen in with this plan, for, at the same session of the General Assembly where the increased grant was made to the
Collegiate School, young Jeremiah Dummer was officially
appointed the first resident Colony Agent at London.

This was in October, 1712, and the receipt of the commission reawakened the already thoroughly-fired zeal of
the young gentleman, and led directly to renewed correspondence with James Pierpont and to the forwarding of
the first great modern library that had as yet crossed the
ocean to New England.

James Pierpont, the paucity of new books in the College
library in mind, seems to have been fully aware of the
importance of this promised gift, and to have spared no
pains to help Dummer collect it. He now evidently secures
the signature of others of the Trustees, and possibly of

Plasgrono, Elihu Yale's Wrexham house

Governor Saltonstall, to a strong appeal for books, and sends it to London, at about the time, probably, of the dispatch of Dummer's Connecticut Colony commission. Dummer's reply, in May, 1713, is as follows: "The Library I am collecting for your Colledge comes on well, Sr Richard Blackmoore (to whom I delivered the Committees letter) brought me in his own Chariot all his works, in four Volumes in folio, & Mr. Yale has done something, tho' very little considering his Estate and particular relation to your Collony. I have almost as many Benefactors as books, which makes the collection troublesome as well as expensive. Sr John Davy will give me nothing, notwithstanding his promises but it may be he intends to send what books he gives himself. If he does, it is the same thing to me. I hope you have received what I sent by Capt Holland."[1]

Dummer's mention of Sir John Davie in this letter no doubt had to do with still another effort of James Pierpont to enlist English donations, and calls to mind a pleasant little romance that goes back to Pierpont's college days at Harvard for its beginning. In that Harvard Class of 1681, in which were James Pierpont, Noadiah Russell, and Samuel Russel, now Trustees of the Collegiate School, had been one John Davie, the impecunious younger son of Sir Humphrey Davie, who had settled on Beacon Hill in Boston and whose baronetcy and rich estate in England had descended to an elder son. John Davie had taken a farm just outside of New London in what is now Groton, and had successively been town clerk, rate collector, constable, and rate recorder. He had thus been a suburban member of Gurdon Saltonstall's New London congregation, and could

---

[1] A letter from Dummer to Timothy Woodbridge says that he had sent over "books & globes" by a previous sailing, and that he should "be glad to hear how your Young Academy grows, & whether you have built a convenient receptacle for your library, that I may send you Some proper Ornaments to furnish it."

hardly have been unaware of the efforts of his minister and two classmates, Pierpont and Russel, to found the Collegiate School. The story has it that it was on a hot summer morning in 1707 that a messenger with a packet of imposing-looking legal documents arrived in New London from Boston, looking for him. Davie, so the story goes, was hoeing corn when the messenger rode into his village street, and was having a bout with a country neighbor named Packer to see which could hill the most corn in the least time. As the messenger approached Davie (says Harvard's biographer, Sibley), "who was barefoot and with his shirt-sleeves and trousers rolled up, he inquired his name, and on receiving the answer struck him on the shoulder, and, raising his hat, exclaimed, 'I salute you, Sir John Davie!' " The newly created Baronet lost no time in accepting the documents and in leaving his astonished and impressed neighbor with the hoeing. He married Gurdon Saltonstall's younger sister, hastily left for Boston, dined with the Massachusetts Governor, and sailed for England to claim his title and lands, the income from which, it was said, came to some four or five thousand pounds a year. Farmer Packer, visiting England some years later, searched out his old Groton neighbor, and found him living in style in Devonshire, where he was high sheriff, and where the Connecticut visitor was royally entertained by him. Sir John Davie, so the story goes, told his old friend that for all his sudden wealth and baronial estates, "he had been happier eating one dish for dinner," and that "corn-beans." His death some years later would perhaps not have occurred from "gout in the head" had he remained a simple Connecticut farmer.

Doubtless Saltonstall joined James Pierpont in recalling the Collegiate School's needs to this great man, their common former friend. For, as Dummer had expected, Sir John Davie sent over some books on his own account. These arrived some time during the year 1714, and turned out to be six boxes full,—about two hundred volumes in all,—but mostly theological and therefore not a particularly valuable addition to the already overburdened divinity files of the scant Collegiate School library in the Saybrook parsonage.

But Jeremiah Dummer's long effort to collect a library that would be valuable now suddenly bore fruit. At the September Commencement, 1714, James Pierpont laid before the Trustees a letter from Colonel Alford of Boston, which had been sent to Tutor Noyes, informing him that nine boxes of books had arrived from London and that these were now on their way by freight (no doubt on some sailing vessel) to Saybrook.

These nine boxes contained, as every reader of old Yale history knows, the first part of a very considerable library which, when the second installment arrived, brought the total up to the imposing number of seven hundred volumes, —one of the largest book collections in the New England colonies. Samuel Johnson, of Guilford, was a Senior at the Collegiate School when these books arrived. He was afterwards to become a Tutor and, largely through the influence of these books, remodel his whole intellectual life and become an Episcopalian and first president of King's College, afterwards Columbia University. He says of this collection that "we had a very valuable and considerable Library of choice Books sent to us." And valuable and choice they were, and well chosen by the cosmopolitan Dummer. The catalogue of them is well known. Among them were "All the Tatlers and Spectators, being eleven volumes, in Royal paper neatly bound and gilt," presented by Richard Steele himself. Sir Isaac Newton had received Dummer and handed him from his shelves the second edition of his just-published and famous "Principia," which he had brought out in 1687 and in which he had announced

The Arrival of
the Dummer Books
at Saybrook

the discovery of the law of gravitation which he had made years previously when a professor at Cambridge. He also gave a copy of his "Optics," the Greek "Thesaurus" of Stephanus, and another Greek commentary. Dr. Bentley, late the King's Librarian, graciously gave his own works. Sir Isaac's successor in the Lucasian Professorship in Mathematics at Cambridge, William Whiston, churchman and scientist (who was later to lose his worldly standing through his heretical theological opinions), gave a copy of his famous speculative study, wherein he urged that water instead of fire, as had previously been taught, had been the agency by which cosmical changes had been wrought. The famous churchman, Dean Kennet, gave his own books. Halley, the astronomer, who had at Greenwich Observatory followed Flamsteed with remarkably progressive studies of the tides, comets, and terrestrial magnetism, gave his own edition of Apollonius.

The list of these Dummer books is a long one, and shows the extraordinary work which Dummer must have done on it. Besides these famous books there were numerous sermons, several cantankerous Episcopal tracts, and a broadly-chosen list of standard English classics, including the works of Chaucer, Spenser, Milton, Ben Jonson, Bacon's "Essays," Butler's "Hudibras," Temple, and Cowley,—Shakespeare not appearing. Dummer had given a large number of these himself, and, besides securing the interest of many of the leading literary and scientific men of the day, had looked up everybody who might have a particular interest in Connecticut. He had thus visited the now elderly Sir Edmund Andros, whose adventures at New Haven and Hartford we have chronicled, laid the Collegiate School's needs before him, and come away with a three-volume translation of Josephus. Andros also gave Dummer a copy of Sir Thomas Browne's then old "Pseudodoxia Epidemica," which must

have opened the eyes of the minister-chirurgeons of the
Colony by its exposure of the superstitions which the famous
author of the "Religio Medici" saw his fellow medical men
still accepting.   The former Royal Governor, whose heart
must have mellowed toward his erstwhile independent Connecticut subjects, had also donated an Armenian Dictionary,
quite the oddest volume in the collection.   Sir Francis
Nicholson, who had succeeded Andros, likewise gave some
books.   And we have seen how Sir Richard Blackmore, the
Poet-Laureate, who had just disastrously concluded his
attempted continuation of Steele's "Guardian" in "The Lay
Monk," had gratified Dummer by coming to his lodgings
in his own chariot, and giving four volumes of his works.
Governor Yale put in from thirty to forty volumes, also,
but, as Dummer had said, "very little considering his
Estate."

   When we recall the tiny collection of dusty theological
folios which up to this time had constituted the library of
the Collegiate School at Saybrook, we may easily imagine
how "valuable and choice" this broadly-chosen gift was.
From the first immigration, hardly any current English
books had come into the Colony.   In but a few cases (as in
Chaplain Thomas Buckingham's of Hartford, who carried
Milton's "Comus" with him when he went to the French
and Indian War in 1711, with the Bible and a psalm book),
do we find contemporary English books.   All of the scientific and literary life of the England of the day, as we have
seen, had been a sealed book to provincial Connecticut.   It
is doubtful whether Abraham Pierson had known more
about Sir Isaac Newton's work than his gravitation theory,
as it is likely that his "Physicks" had fallen somewhere between the long-discarded Ptolemaic theory and Copernicus.
And so this great modern collection of books, bringing the
last work of the foremost English thinkers and literary men

to the little village of Saybrook, must have been an epoch-making event.

And so it was to prove, in at least two most important ways to the little provincial academy. Dummer's library was to produce a new intellectual start in life for at least a small group of young Connecticut scholars and ministers, and end in having an effect on the School's teachings, and it was to bring about a situation, for the School itself, which shortly calls for attention.

III

The death of James Pierpont, which unexpectedly occurred but a month after his efforts to secure the Dummer books had succeeded, marks the end of this second period in the Collegiate School's history. Old Judge Sewall wrote in his diary when the news reached Boston, that it was "a very great Blow to that Colony and to all New England." While we have to rely upon such references as these to form a notion of what James Pierpont was like, they were doubtless the popular impression. In the ancient pages of the Boston *News-Letter* for 1714 we find him referred to as "having served his Generation not only as a minister, but [as was a common fashion of the times] also been a great blessing as a physician; and of singular use as there was occasion, to the government by his wise and wholesome counsel." Cotton Mather, whose encomiums on New England divines were more or less colored by his personal relations with them, and who was given to highly enthusiastic portraits when he felt the inclination, refers to him as "The most Valuable Mr. James Pierpont." Of him, writes Mather, "I may use the Terms which *Paterculus* used of One that was in true Goodness inferior to him, *Vir in tantum Laudandus, in quantum Virtus ipsa intelligi Potesti.*" And he goes on to say that Pierpont "has left us a few

Weeks ago; but left with us a fragrant and lasting Memory of a very Meritorious Character. How memorable for his rare Discretion; his bright Holiness; the Spirit of his Ministry, and Savour of his Publick Oblations; his Extensive Genius which inclined him and enabled him, to Do Good unto Many; the various Instances wherein our Glorious Lord made him a Blessing to his Church, his Neighborhood, his Colony! New-haven becomes a Hadadrimmon, upon his Expiration. Every Heart there is in his Tomb, every tongue his Epitaph!" Which was true. No other man had done as much as he to found the School or to maintain it during these first thirteen years of repeated discouragements and all but obliteration. He, as no other one connected with these beginnings of the future Yale, was its "founder" and first pilot. He had conceived the idea, secured public support for it, steered it through its first crisis and thus forever past possibilities of the church and state control, drawn its charter so that it should not wholly be a theological seminary, organized it, selected its first Rector, secured for it a Colony church creed and yet succeeded in keeping that church out of it, found Colony financial support (however meager) for it, and now had raised a modern library for it out of intellectual England. More fortunate, however, than old John Davenport, he had lived to see his Colony college an established fact, rickety as was its support from the public and surrounded by dangers of outside interference as it still was when he died. Had he lived another decade, I fancy that we should have a more satisfactory story to tell than will appear in the following chapter. Among the names of the leaders in Yale history, that of James Pierpont stands, with John Davenport's, at the forefront of those to whom the institution owes its existence.

CHAPTER VI

THE STRUGGLE FOR A SITE

I

HE period of two or three years which we are now to review, was to be the most disturbing and, in many ways, the most critical, in the whole history of the Collegiate School. And I suppose that, if it had not been for the guiding hand of Governor Salton- stall, matters during them would have come to a sorry pass. For these few years were to see the Trustees divide into three factions over the location of the School, the leadership pass into new hands, the scholars become dissatisfied, the Colony General Assembly under- take to get control of the School's affairs, and a nearly successful effort made to split the little academy into two parts and all but wreck it. Anything like a detailed chron- icle of these complicated factors would be a tedious business. But we should be able to follow the general currents of events, and thereby come to a clear understanding of the outcome.

Most of this trouble arose, oddly enough, from the suc- cess which James Pierpont had had in securing the Dummer library. The arrival of these books, bringing the total number of volumes in the School's possession up to nearly one thousand, made it necessary to house them safely and in a more public fashion than had been the case with the few original books of the founders. So that some sort of a permanent college building was necessary. Without funds with which to build such a house, James Pierpont appears to have led his fellow Trustees in another effort to secure Colony aid for it. The Dummer books had been sent to Saybrook, as we have seen, in September, 1714. In October, the Trustees presented the facts to the General Assembly, in session again in the Meeting-house at New Haven, and asked for money with which to erect a house for them. With Governor Saltonstall's support, a petition was drawn up by the Trustees, and an Act "for the building of a proper house for the Collegiate School" presented. This Act passed the Upper House, with Saltonstall's approval, carrying an appropriation of £200 for the purpose. But the Lower House declined to concur, and the bill was laid on the table.

Pierpont's death came the month after this division in the Assembly. Had this not occurred, I fancy that the train of consequences of this appeal to the Colony treasury would not have been just what they were. For the appeal, as events were to show, had been a mistake. In it the start had been made toward inviting legislative action on a very vital matter to the School. The death of James Pierpont removed the one man who could have restrained this action, and left the field free to others who were ready to forward it.

So that when the Trustees met in May, 1715, they had a serious problem before them, and found themselves without the steady hand of Pierpont to guide them in it. At this meeting they again advanced his project of a Colony gift of a proper house for their new books. At the Assembly meeting in Hartford which immediately followed, the Lower House this time received the project with more sympathy. It now agreed willingly enough to the plan for a College house, but voted that the money for it should be raised by a popular subscription among "the well-affected to religion and learning among us." The Upper House, and Governor Saltonstall, however, added a rider carrying a £100 appropriation from the Colony itself, and, the Deputies again refusing to spend the Colony money, the project again fell through. Again brought up at the October session, 1715, an unexpected event resulted in an actual money appropriation by concurrent action of the two houses. It had so happened that the old boundary dispute between Massachusetts and Connecticut finally had been settled, and some 106,000 acres granted to Connecticut. The public sale of this land was expected to provide the Colony with a large sum. With this expectation in mind, the Assembly saw a way to provide the needed money for the house desired by the School and at the same time not dig into the depleted Colony treasury itself. It was voted, therefore, to give £500 to a building for the Collegiate School, as soon as the sale was made.

With this substantial encouragement, the Trustees at once set about determining upon their use of the money. At a special meeting held in April, 1716, it was therefore voted to invest the coming £500 in a "proper building" for the scholars and books, and that a Rector's house should "with all convenient speed be erected."[1] The site for these two buildings was to be Saybrook. In addition it was voted to

---

[1] This vote was as follows: "The Trustees considering the great necessity yt ye Collegiate School in this place Be Put into such Circumstances as may giue greater Encouragement to all yt are desirous of ye Improument of their Sons in ye academical Learning have unanimously agreed and Resolved yt ye five hundred Pounds Granted By ye Colony to this Schóol together with such other sums as may be gained for the Erecting of such Building as ye occasion of the School Requires Be forthwith Improved to ye End that a suitable house for ye Entertainment of ye Schollars with Chambers and Studies as well as a hall and Library as also a convenient Building for ye use of a Rector near adjoining thereunto Be with all convenient Speed Erected and suitably finished."

find "a gentleman of suitable age and Learning" for Rector, "who shall Live in ye house provided for that End and shall have ye advantage of Boarding all ye Schollars vnder graduates Belonging to sd School." A Tutor was also to "Be constantly Maintained" and domiciled "in one of the Chambers of ye College."

II

In order to understand the remarkable turn which events took immediately after this decision, it will be necessary to recall the progress of another factor in the situation which was now forming,—the attitude of the Collegiate School scholars themselves toward the establishment.

We left the Collegiate School where the Senior classes were being instructed at Samuel Andrew's parsonage in Milford, and the three lower classes probably at the Lynde house in Saybrook, under the youthful Joseph Noyes and William Russell, classmates at the School in 1709, and sons, respectively, of the two Trustees, James Noyes of Stonington and Noadiah Russell of Middletown. With the arrival of the great Dummer library and the promising outcome of the Trustees' efforts to secure a house and a resident Rector, the attendance had increased. The ten scholars in the four classes in 1710 had jumped to twenty-five in 1716. And, until the Trustees passed their vote in the latter year, locating the new house at Saybrook, I suppose that there was no inkling of the serious troubles which were at once to arise from it. But these were brewing.

It will be recalled that, in the letters to the "founders" from Cotton Mather and his father, in 1701, the advice had strongly been given that the School should not be established upon "a collegiate way of living," as the term was then,—that is, not in a college house. The Mathers advised that the students should "board here and there in the town, where they can." In this way much money would be saved in "college" buildings, etc., "only," Cotton Mather had added, "let not the scholars board in any families but such as the pastor and other officers of the church may under their hands allow, as fit (in regard to their exemplary piety) for that service of boarding young men that are to be the hope of the flock." The School authorities were to look out for this, and also to see that the boarding-house keepers did not "oppress the students in the matter" of pay (as the tribe has not infrequently done in college history).

Both for reasons of policy and of finance, the Collegiate School had been begun on this necessarily small basis. But the experiment had not proved a success. The Saybrook families who were willing to take in the energetic youngsters in the School in 1716 were not numerous. Only one of the scholars lived in Saybrook and one in Lyme, so that there were twenty-three boys who had to find lodgings in the village. Many of them had to board, therefore, in the northern part of the town, where a few scattered farms then stood where Saybrook proper is today. These youths had a mile or more walk down across the wind-swept neck to Saybrook Point for the early morning prayers that opened the School day.

Furthermore, the teaching by the two young Tutors could have been anything but first-class, and of course far below what could at that time have been had at Harvard under the progressive President Leverett and his four Tutors, Flynt, Holyoke (afterwards to be president), Robie, and Sever. That this was an important matter goes without saying, when we consider the seriousness with which typical Collegiate School students undertook their college careers. To the ordinary run of intelligent and ambitious country boys (and from such the Collegiate School at this period drew most of its scholars) the education to be received at the Colony college was the one great opportunity of their lives. Once graduated, and in possession of that limited general knowledge of the classics yet special fluency in Latin composition and quotation which marked the educated man and gave him his social standing, such a youth had his career open to him, either in the pulpit (with the comparatively good income of the day) or in public life and business. So that going to college was then a great event, for which the family of the fortunate youth would scrimp as they would for no other good fortune. The result was that when these scholars had arrived at Killingworth or Saybrook, they ambitiously set about getting their full money's worth from the Tutors, and were inclined to be unruly if they failed to get it.

Samuel Johnson, later to be one of the leading intellectual lights in the country, had been a typical boy of this sort. Johnson was born in a country deacon's family in Guilford. His father was a "cloth dresser," and "fulled" the rough cloth sent to him,—much of which was usually worn in those days unsheared or pressed. Young Johnson had shown "an inquisitive mind" as early as six years of age; finding a Hebrew commentary at this time, he became filled with a yearning to understand it, and learned it from his grandfather. Full of ambition to know more of the scant book-knowledge of the times, he went to the town school,— then kept by the youthful Jared Eliot, later to become one of the most famous scientific men of his day. On Eliot's leaving, the young scholar was sent to North Middletown, where he found himself better educated than his teacher. Returning to Guilford, he luckily found an English-educated classical scholar, who prepared him to enter the Saybrook Academy at the age of fourteen. Yet the Saybrook teaching was poorer than the precocious Johnson had expected,— it was no doubt the experience of others besides young Johnson that Tutor Noyes knew less of Hebrew than they themselves. This fact necessitated Samuel Johnson's hard application to it on his own account outside of School hours and led, in the cases of many of his fellow students, to a growing dissatisfaction with the poor quality of the Collegiate School teaching. A very good sidelight on this is to be found in the letter from Benjamin Lord. "Who were the chief orators in my day," he writes, "I'm ye less able to say as oratory was but little known, studied, or famed, to what it is now [1779]. Indeed, Composition and Language were then scarcely enô in vogue to excite ambition where there might be a genius for it; but if any, Dr. Johnson was the man that look'd that way. As for the Mathematics, we recited and studied but little more than the rudiments of it, some of ye plainest things in it. Our advantages in that day were too low for any man to rise high in any branches of literature." To many of the scholars, this intellectual poverty was a serious matter.

And another thing must have added to this discontent, Tutor Noyes, while actively interested in the success of the School, and for many years to be one of its staunchest friends and supporters, was a theologian of the primitive New England school even thus early in his career. I suppose that he must have been a rather helpless sort of intellectual leader for the intellectually-ravenous young men under his care. Old parishioners of his remarked, years later, that he was an "unanimating and unpopular" preacher. So he no doubt was quite as uninspiring as a teacher. He certainly, all his life, showed none of that religious warmth which was to become the great feature of the revival under Jonathan Edwards and Whitefield. So we may presume that he was equally cold toward such things during his days as the Saybrook college Tutor. Samuel Johnson had become mildly interested in that most heretical of religious movements of his day, Episcopacy, when a boy at Guilford, and, at Saybrook, was beginning to lean toward the Church of England ritual. Two classmates, Daniel Browne and James Wetmore, became inclined in the same direction when they began with Johnson to read the books in the new Dummer library. *Benj Lord* And, as others of the scholars under Tutor Noyes were later to become leaders against him in the "New Light" movement in the Congregational church itself, I imagine that in his theology, as in his Hebrew, he did not entirely meet the situation.

Their uncomfortable boarding arrangements, the poor teaching of Noyes, and the necessity of finishing their course far away from the Dummer books at Milford under Rector Andrew, had therefore been bringing the Collegiate School youths to the point where they were becoming openly dissatisfied with the education which the School was giving them. When the Trustees met in April, 1716, Sir Noyes had, indeed, been succeeded by Samuel Russell and Benjamin Lord, both just graduated. But both were young. The clamor of the discontented scholars had now become more urgent than before, and the Trustees had to act concerning it. It was therefore voted to add a third Tutor, in Samuel Smith of Glastonbury, three years out of the School, and to permit the Seniors of that year to finish their course where they pleased, at Rector Andrew's or elsewhere as was most convenient to them. As Samuel Johnson says, "Immediately upon this, many of the scholars repaired to their respective homes and where they might have instruction to their minds, a considerable number of them gathering at Wethersfield."

Just settled at this latter place was a young Harvard graduate, one Elisha Williams. He was a well-educated man, five years the senior of the oldest Collegiate School student. He was related to the families of John Cotton

and Governor Bradstreet, so that he was well born in addition,—a considerable factor in Colonial society in those
days. There appears to have been no objection by the seacoast Trustees at this time to this young man's assuming
voluntary charge of such of the Seniors as wanted to go to
him. But the immediate results of this easy compliance by
the Trustees were to be disastrous in the extreme.

III

Up to this time the Collegiate School had somehow or
other managed to scrape along, in spite of financial difficulties, poor teaching, and the Saybrook inconveniences.
Much of this had been due to Governor Saltonstall's continued interest and good advice. But, as we have seen, much
more had been due to James Pierpont. His death seems to
have removed the balance wheel among the Trustees. A
new element, hitherto in the background, now came to the
front. Pierpont had been the fifth of the original eleven
Trustees to pass off the stage up to this time. So that, when
the Trustees met to make a new start in expectation of the
Colony's £500, they presented a new combination of per-
sonalities. Old James Noyes and Samuel Mather were
still Trustees, though both were giving small attention to
the School's affairs. Of the other original Trustees,
Timothy Woodbridge, Samuel Andrew, Samuel Russel, and
Joseph Webb remained. Old Israel Chauncy, however, had
been succeeded by the now elderly Moses Noyes of Lyme,
Thomas Buckingham by young Thomas Ruggles of Guilford, Noadiah Russell by John Davenport of Stamford, and
now James Pierpont had been followed by young Thomas
Buckingham of Hartford. Among these Trustees, Pierpont's leadership had fallen upon no one natural leader.
This leadership there are evidences that Timothy Wood-

bridge now attempted to assume, to be shortly opposed in that effort, however, by the newcomer, John Davenport.

During the difficulties that at once arose in consequence of this factional disturbance, old Samuel Andrew, Rector *pro tem,* appears not to have taken a leading part or exerted what little authority he had. The Reverend Andrew, scholar that he was (he was given an honorary M.A. by Harvard during his Rectorship), lacked the qualities of public leadership which we have seen shown, in their different ways, by such contemporaries as James Pierpont, Timothy Woodbridge, Gurdon Saltonstall and John Davenport. Describing him, years later, an old parishioner said that he had "great powers of mind. He was, however, intellectual and theological, rather than religious. He was one of the ablest scholars in all New England." It appears from another ancient source that Rector Andrew was not in the least inclined to social intercourse. "He spent most of his time in his study," it was said of him. "He never made it a practice [as was the necessary business of parsons in those primitive days] to visit and converse with his people. Seldom was he known to leave his study on a week day, even to attend a funeral." All the visiting of the Milford sick and poor had to be done by the elder and deacons. With the future of the Collegiate School in such scholarly yet impractical hands, little could have been expected by his fellow Trustees except troubles of various sorts.[1]

And these difficulties now came on with a rush. It will be recalled that the Trustees had voted to build the proposed new college house at Saybrook. When the General Assembly met at Hartford the next month, Timothy Woodbridge and young Thomas Buckingham, the two active

[1] Samuel Andrew's continuance in the Rectorship appears to have been through no choice of his own. A letter by him, a facsimile of which appears on page 334, shows that he remained in office solely to save the School from being abandoned as the result of the controversy among the Trustees.

Hartford Trustees, brought in a memorial for themselves and "in the name of many others," requesting the General Assembly to override the Trustees' vote fixing the college at Saybrook, and to order it permanently placed at Hartford.

This sudden move must have been received by the remaining Trustees with astonishment. There had been no indication that such an attempt had been in mind until the presentation of this memorial. In fact, both Timothy Woodbridge and Thomas Buckingham had been at the April meeting and, so far as we have any record, voted with the others for the Saybrook site. When we consider all the previous history of this site controversy, however, the action of the two Hartford Trustees appears natural enough, if it was unprecedented and mischief-making. As we will recall, there had been a deadlock on this question from the moment that the original promoters of the School had broached the subject to the Colony at large. Hence the Collegiate School site had not been decided when the charter was granted. It had been because of this deadlock, with all the possibilities of trouble that would have ensued if the New Haven desire had been pushed at that time, that Pierpont had attached himself to the New London County faction and agreed upon a compromise for Saybrook. We will recall how Saltonstall, then the New London minister, no doubt sided with old James Noyes and Thomas Buckingham of Saybrook on this, and how Governor Fitz-John Winthrop had thrown his influence for that village, and, in fact, was prepared to make a will in favor of the School if Saybrook was chosen.[1] And, in spite of Saybrook's distance

---

[1] Rev. James Noyes was originally for Saybrook as the permanent college site because he believed that Governor Winthrop's £100 bequest could be

from the western towns of the Colony, the Fairfield County Trustees had followed Pierpont in vøting for it. Matters had gone along well enough while Pierson was in charge, and until now for the nine years that had elapsed since his death. Pierpont seems finally to have settled his mind on the question and to have remained to his death a Saybrook-site man, if for the one purpose of not reopening the old question and having the college go elsewhere.

The Hartford faction had also accepted the Saybrook site, though, I imagine, with reservations. But events had now changed their attitude. The scholars were scattered over the Colony. And now there was a £500 Colony grant for a "college house." Any controversy over the site had hitherto been useless, because there was no permanent establishment possible anywhere. But now there was an actual sum of money in sight, and the town where the college house was to be erected from it would necessarily become the permanent Collegiate School site.

But another and more personal reason existed. Of the twenty-five boys whom we have seen becoming discontented with the poor teaching at Saybrook, thirteen came from up the river, or from inland towns of Hartford County, and one had come from Springfield. Of these thirteen, four were in families in the churches of Timothy Woodbridge and young Thomas Buckingham, and one of these was the son of Buckingham himself. The latter was a Harvard graduate, and no doubt was but little impressed by the small educational facilities at Saybrook and desired his son to have better. The arrival of young Elisha Williams at near-by Wethersfield for the study of divinity gave Buckingham this opportunity, for no doubt Williams had become well known to him, if indeed he had not come to Wood-

secured in no other way. After Winthrop's death Noyes no longer felt so strongly for that location.

bridge and Buckingham for his theological instruction. There is evidence that Buckingham had now renewed Timothy Woodbridge's interest in securing the Collegiate School for Hartford, and had been the instigator, through his son, of much of the troubles which the Saybrook scholars had been making over their Tutors and Rector Andrew. In his manuscript account of these years, Tutor Samuel Johnson makes it clear that he believed this to be so. The "Murmuring of the Unruly & Ungoverned Schollars," he says, "advanced to a Great heigth blown up (as was on but too good Grounds thought) by some Gentlemen up on Connecticut River, & also by some belonging to Saybrook Town, who wished not well either of the School's being at Saybrook, or to the Tutors or both. As also great fault was found with SayBrook as a place not Suitable for the School, & thus the Tutors were disgraced & the Town became odious throughout the Colony—& this mutiny could not be heald tho many Gentlemen took pains with the Schollars for that End."

The bombshell which Buckingham and Woodbridge now dropped into the Trustees' camp caused "a mighty commotion," as well it may have. It was the first public breach in the hitherto publicly friendly relations of the Trustees, and it took the question of the Collegiate School site out of that body's hands, and placed it, for the moment, in those of the General Assembly. Yet there was much support from the people of the river towns for this change. Among other gentry, Samuel Welles, a wealthy Hartford citizen, signed the petition. This document set forth "the present declining and unhappy circumstances in which the School lies, and the apparent hazard of its being utterly extinguished, unless some speedy remedy be applied." The location at Hartford being such a remedy, the petition added that money would be subscribed if such a course were taken, and that many neighboring citizens of Massachusetts would contribute and send their sons to it. The memorial requested Assembly action on the petition, in the form of a committee to hear the question. The Assembly promptly acted on this request and summoned the Trustees to appear before such a committee on May 22.

IV

The division among the Trustees, as a result of this "unaccountable" action of the Hartford members (as Samuel Johnson dubs it) at once resolved itself into three factions. Timothy Woodbridge and Thomas Buckingham of Hartford, with old Samuel Mather of Windsor (now entirely incapacitated for business), composed the river-town group. James and Moses Noyes stood solidly for Saybrook. A third group, though siding with the latter at this time (May, 1716), comprised the remaining five Trustees: Samuel Andrew of Milford, Samuel Russel of Branford, Joseph Webb of Fairfield, John Davenport of Stamford, and Thomas Ruggles of Guilford. In answer to the Assembly summons, six of the Trustees attended the committee hearing. Mather still remained away, and the three senior members of the seacoast group refused to appear on the ground that the summons was not legal; the Colony legislature, said they, had no power to call the Collegiate School Trustees together. No doubt there was a lively time at this public meeting over the School site. The seacoast-faction, led by John Davenport, who was now rapidly coming to the front as Pierpont's successor among them, carried the day. The Assembly's committee agreed to give the Trustees until the following October to get together on the site for the new college house; "unless," says Samuel Johnson in his account of the proceedings, "they could universally agree on the next Commencement where the

School should be built, then they would desire the Assembly to nominate a place for it."

V

The summer of 1716 now intervened, bringing with it such an agitation of the Collegiate School site question as had never before been seen in the history of the academy. By this time the New Haven party undoubtedly felt that Saybrook eventually would have to be given up, a feeling that must have been accentuated when smallpox broke out in that village during the summer and the remnant of the scholars left at Saybrook had to move in a hurry to East Guilford (now Madison), where the former Tutor, now Rev. John Hart, received some of them, the others going, we are told, to the house of Tutor Johnson's father, the cloth-dressing emporium of Guilford.

With a few of the Seniors at Milford under Andrew, most of them at Wethersfield under the unofficial Williams, and some at East Guilford under Benjamin Lord and John Hart (Samuel Smith having declined to serve, probably through the Hartford Trustees' influence), matters now were certainly in a bad way for James Pierpont's Collegiate School. I suppose that, however low the little academy had sunk before, at no time in its history did it fall to quite the depth that it did during this summer of 1716. Certainly the Fates had their hands set against the Connecticut college project. Everybody, however, was working strenuously to appear at Commencement the next September, prepared to force their claims. Lively canvasses for money contributions now began. The two Hartford Trustees, content with the impression which they had made on the Assembly, appear not to have succeeded, if indeed they attempted, to raise money for the School to establish itself there. But the Saybrook and New Haven factions were very busy indeed. While old James Noyes could not have been very active, I imagine that his brother Moses was, as no doubt were several Saybrook residents. By September there had been raised pledges amounting to £1,200 or more,—a large sum for those days,—if the School should remain there.

And it is now that the ancient New Haven claim for the Collegiate School took the tangible turn that it had lacked up to this time. Treasurer Alling no doubt took a leading hand in this movement, as did Rev. Joseph Noyes, who had just become the successor to James Pierpont in the square, wooden Meeting-house on the New Haven Market-place. Their canvass was an unexpectedly successful one. Nearly £2,000 were subscribed by some sixty-three people. And the Town of New Haven did something as well. On July 30 it voted, probably urged by Alling and Noyes, to give eight acres of land "at the end of the town" if the Trustees would settle the School there.

At Commencement that September, the Trustees came together at Saybrook for their first meeting after the explosion of the two Hartford members. Both Woodbridge and Buckingham were there, and we may well believe that high words resulted between them and such a fiery representative of the others as John Davenport of Stamford. The senior Trustees,—the Noyces ambo, and probably Andrew and Russel,—seem to have made every effort to secure an agreement on Saybrook, but without unanimous results. The vote stood five to two for this, Woodbridge and Buckingham firmly holding out. The matter was put to an adjourned meeting, to be held,—the Trustees still voting five to two on even that question,—in New Haven the week before the Assembly met there a month later.

In this action we can now clearly see how matters were

forming. Up to this time the seacoast Trustees had been
entirely willing to remain at Saybrook. As we have seen,
they had voted with the two Noyes brothers to that effect.
But this was not a popular decision for the Colony at large,
and, with Hartford as the probable alternative in case the
Assembly acted, these Trustees now appear to have swung
in a body, under Davenport, for the alternative New Haven
proposition. This suggestion was now, it would appear,
pressed on the two Saybrook adherents, the Noyes brothers,
through Joseph Noyes. This young man, whatever we may
think of him in his later attitude toward the College affairs,
at this point added himself to the succession of the first John
Davenport and of James Pierpont (to whose daughter,
Abigail, he was engaged to be married at this time), by
securing the action which was finally to bring the Colony
College of his predecessors to New Haven. It was by his
efforts with his father and uncle, as tradition has it, that,
when the Trustees met in New Haven October 17, 1716,
the vote for New Haven as the site for the College, still five
to two, became seven to two, and a de-
cision. Young Noyes had won over his
father, James Noyes, and his uncle,
Moses Noyes, who, as moderator at the meeting, stated that
New Haven was his second choice.

There is every indication in the reports in the University
archives that this Trustees' meeting was a lively one, and
that ecclesiastical fur flew throughout the evidently prolonged session. The first question was to confirm the previous vote to remove the School to New Haven. Trustees
Ruggles, Davenport, Webb, Russel, and Andrew voted
"Yea"; "against it Mr. Buckingham & Mr. Woodbridg."
Moses Noyes, Moderator, was for Saybrook first, but then
for New Haven. The meeting then broke up for a three-
day interim. Woodbridge promptly opened the adjourned

Rev. Azariah Mather's house in Saybrook

session with a proposition to leave the question to the
Assembly, where he had good reason to believe he could
carry the Deputies at least against New Haven.   Ruggles,
Davenport, Webb, Russel, and Andrew,—the "seaside"
Trustees,—voted him down, Buckingham alone standing
with him, though old Mr. Noyes was willing.   The question
was temporarily dropped for the election of Samuel Smith
of Glastonbury as Tutor.   The seaside Trustees voted this,
Buckingham and Woodbridge being noncommittal.   Samuel
Johnson was also proposed by the seasiders.   Woodbridge
was against it "because of" his "Newark call."   The site
question was then reintroduced.   The majority five voted to
begin at once a "Collegiate School" and Rector's house in
New Haven.   Noyes "suspended."   "Mr. Buckingham
chuseth Silence.   Mr. Woodbridg saith nay."   Voted.   It
is proposed to ask the Governor to help in the "architechtonick part of the buildings."   The five agree, "Mr. Buckingham chuseth not to act.   Mr. Woodbridge hath nothing

agt advice." The five seaside Trustees then vote to demand the £500 Colony money until then in the hands of Buckingham and Woodbridge, the two latter not voting. The meeting is now in full command of the five seacoast Trustees, and they carry everything before them. Samuel Andrew is chosen Rector "for the present" over the silence of the two Hartford ministers; Sir Johnson appears and accepts his Tutorship; the building committee for the College house is named from among the majority; it is voted formally to inform the students of the change of location of the School to New Haven; Samuel Russel is asked to write to Boston for the "Books & Globes given to the Collegiate School" by Dummer, and to hand them over to the Rev. Joseph Noyes; old Moses Noyes of Lyme is voted the responsibility of the books still at Saybrook; Tutor Samuel Russel is ordered to bring the "Colledg-Records" from Saybrook to New Haven; the Senior Tutor is made "Library-keeper." Throughout all of these formalities, which in the total firmly established the Collegiate School at New Haven, neither Woodbridge nor Buckingham took part in the voting. The seacoast Trustees were in high feather. John Davenport roundly signed the famous minutes afterwards as scribe and dispatched them to old James Noyes at Stonington, who "perused & well considered the above 32 voats" and signed them. Moses Noyes later wavered in his allegiance to this decision to remove to New Haven and, somewhat shakingly, joined the two Hartford Trustees in their later efforts to undo by Assembly act the decision. But the remaining six, including James Noyes, stuck by their guns, though they felt it necessary to reaffirm each of these historic votes at their next meeting.

And thus it was that New Haven secured the Collegiate School. As a sop to the discomfited Hartford Trustees, Stephen Buckingham, a young Harvard graduate then minister at Norwalk, was elected a Trustee. A relative of Thomas Buckingham of Hartford, and the son of one of the original Trustees, Stephen Buckingham had been *Stephen Buckingham* one of the five Colony ministers to receive the degree of Master of Arts at the first Collegiate School Commencement in 1702. His election filled out the last of the number of eleven Trustees, which had been vacant from the first. In order to bring order out of chaos in the teaching force of the School, young Samuel Johnson was chosen Tutor, and Samuel Smith again invited to teach, though the latter appointment was again refused. The Reverend Noyes agreed to help Tutor Johnson, and, until a permanent Rector could be chosen, it was voted to have Samuel Russel, Webb, Davenport, and Ruggles alternate in quarterly visits to the School on behalf of the triumphant majority.[1]

So the first Collegiate School teaching in New Haven began, thirteen youths coming to town, and doubtless boarding where they could while going to Mr. Noyes' house down Elm Street for instruction.[2] Fourteen remained, however, at Wethersfield, and three or four went back to Saybrook, where the Rev. Azariah Mather, lifelong irreconcilable to the removal from Saybrook, taught them at his parsonage, or at the abandoned Lynde house and where the great Dummer library still remained.

[1] A grandiloquent letter from the Trustees to Jeremiah Dummer, in 1717, speaks of New Haven as "the Large & Pleasant Town of New-haven to be the kind Alumna to bear in her Arms, & cherish in her Bosom the Infant Nursery of Learning in Our Government."

[2] Rev. Joseph Noyes, according to maps of New Haven drawn in 1724 and 1748, lived in Governor Eaton's old mansion of the New Haven church-state days.

CHAPTER VII

THE BEGINNINGS AT NEW HAVEN

I

T might well have seemed that the division in the School had healed, and that now all was fair sailing.

But the river-town scholars remained at Wethersfield under Elisha Williams, and to them were added ten Freshmen, of whom six were Hartford County boys, including among the latter the famous Jonathan Edwards from East Windsor, who had just entered at New Haven, but who had left on account of dissatisfaction with Tutor Johnson. For the next two and a half years, the Collegiate School existed as a tripartite institution. Samuel Andrew remained Rector *pro tem* throughout this period, apparently unable to bring his academy together or to heal the difficulties among his Trustees, if, indeed, he made any extraordinary efforts to do so. With Timothy Woodbridge still looking for every opportunity to stop the movement to establish the School at New Haven and supporting the Wethersfield defection as a lever in that effort, and John Davenport of Stamford leading the seacoast Trustees to keep the School at New Haven, these two or three years must have seen plenty of excitement. In spite of the hopeful prospects for a college house at New Haven, the whole enterprise promised again, in 1717, to come to an ignominious and disastrous end.

It will assist us best, I fancy, in visualizing what was left of the Collegiate School life during these years, to become acquainted first with the New Haven conditions, and then the situation at Wethersfield, and then recall the final fight of the Hartford faction. We may thus arrive at the end of the long struggle which, through unexpected aid, finally and permanently settled the academy at New Haven.

II

Tradition has it that the vote of the majority of the Trustees to remove the Collegiate School to New Haven was based on the understanding that two good town lots, one for the college and one for the Rector's house, should be at the disposal of the School.

These two lots were at the southwest corner of the old Market-place, where Osborn Hall and College Street Hall now stand. The former, desired by the Trustees for the "College house," was known at the time as "Mrs. Hester Coster's lot." It was some 205 by 274 feet, at the present corner of College and Chapel Streets. In the original division of the Colony land, this lot had been granted to one Joshua Atwater, a London merchant, who had been Treasurer of the New Haven Jurisdiction. On it he had built a large house facing the wooded Market-place. This he had sold to William Tuttle, one of his fellow settlers and a careless sort of person, whose troubles over fencing his "Indian's land" had previously caused a town vote in favor of the Indians, "that we may not have such complaints of cattle and hogs spoiling their corn, which they say makes their squaws and children cry." Tuttle in turn had sold it, just after the arrival of James Pierpont to be the town minister, to a Mrs. Hester Coster, a devout member of

Pierpont's church, and she, dying in 1691, had willed the lot to the church and ordered its income used to support the "lectures" which we have seen James Pierpont giving in the neighborhood.

The original Atwater mansion having become untenantable by 1716, and the income from it negligible, the church deacons willingly agreed to the Reverend Noyes' proposal that they dispose of the old Atwater lot to the Collegiate School, whose Trustees had decided upon it as the best site for their enterprise. An acre and a quarter of it was accordingly sold to the School "for twenty six pounds current money."

The site for the proposed Rector's house, facing the Coster lot across what is now Chapel Street, and across College Street from Captain Miles' Tavern, had originally been the homestead of the Rev. William Hooke. He, also, had left it to the New Haven church, and it was at this time an ancient farmhouse, in poor repair, set back from the present Chapel Street in its garden and orchard. This also was sold to the Trustees.

With these two well-situated lots, facing each other across the shady main street of the upper town, the Trustees immediately set about building their "College house" on the first of them. The School treasury contained an accumulation of some £125 at this time, and, so the historian Trumbull tells us, the first £250 of the Colony grant was now actually in hand. Regardless of the Hartford opposition, it had been voted to put this money, and what was paid in from the New Haven pledges, immediately into the proposed building, the haste no doubt being in order to clinch the New Haven site by erecting a building on it as soon as possible. All this had been in October, 1716. The New Haven support had been increased in December by the appropriation of land in the "Yorkshire quarter," and now, in January, 1717, actual building began, in the face of renewed attacks by the Hartford Trustees which we shall refer to later. A building committee,—consisting of Rector Andrew and Trustees Russel, Webb, Davenport, and Ruggles,—had been appointed, and this committee now found itself in possession of elaborate notions as to "the architechtonick part of the buildings," from Governor Saltonstall, whose great mansion on the shores of what is now Lake Saltonstall had been the wonder and admiration of the entire Colony.[1] Henry Caner, a Boston carpenter who had made a reputation by his recent repairs on King's Chapel, was given the contract, and by September, 1717, the Collegiate School's first building was well under way.

During these two years, 1716-1717, the New Haven main part of the Collegiate School had been getting along as best it could, without a library, and with the dozen or more scholars boarding about town, probably coming to Samuel Johnson's lodgings or Mr. Noyes' house for instruction, and

[1] Governor Saltonstall's house in East Haven was one of the finest in Connecticut. Mr. Thomas R. Trowbridge described it years ago, from personal knowledge, as a house that had evidently been "intended for the residence of a wealthy and important personage." "A broad hall and massive oaken stairway," he wrote, "was the feature of the broad central hall." Triangular cupboards were in the corners of the lower rooms. There were brass finishings throughout the house, and much wainscoting. There was an old English-style hiding place back of the chimney. The "room of state" was on the lower floor, and here hung, "for nearly one hundred and twenty years, the famous 'Leathern tapestry,' representing a stag hunt in a forest, with a large and imposing retinue of huntsmen, horses, and hounds; it covered the four sides of the room and was imported from England. These 'leather' hangings were famous throughout the state, and for years were gazed at with admiration by our primitive ancestors, such magnificence rarely being seen in those days. Some pieces of this 'tapestry' are in the possession of the descendants of the Governor still." Other pieces are in the Connecticut Historical Society rooms at Hartford, but the great part of this "tapestry" fell the victim of visitors' knives, and a good deal more of it finally became parts of the saddles and wagon seats of the neighboring farmers.

The Saltonstall House

attending the Reverend Noyes' Meeting-house on Sabbath days. The regularly-appointed assistant to Sir Johnson, Samuel Smith of Windsor, having steadily declined to come to New Haven, the senior Tutor was sent by the Trustees to Wethersfield to reconcile him to the majority party, but to no purpose. So that Samuel Johnson, well equipped as he was to take the responsibility, found it necessary to have the Reverend Noyes take some of his classes, and get along as best he could with the others.

This low condition of the original faction of the divided Collegiate School would undoubtedly have sunk to even greater depths had it not been for the character and the intellectual power of Samuel Johnson, its youthful Tutor. Yet even he was depressed. "Things looked dark & melancholy," he afterwards wrote of this period, "& even spightful & malicious." The full burden of the task of meeting this situation devolved upon him, practically alone.

We have already made this young man's acquaintance. He was a hard student, and a scholar and theologian of an unusually open mind for his day. And he had the additional advantage of being, so tradition goes, a man of exceptional gifts as a leader of young men,—though Jonathan Edwards did not think so. He had probably brought over to New Haven at least a handful of the more important volumes of the Dummer collection, still housed at Saybrook, for the indications are that during these two years he was giving a great deal of study to them. One of these books, Sir Isaac Newton's personal gift of his own works, appears to have been particularly interesting to him. His biographer, Dr. Chandler, says that as soon as he had put his hands on this unknown treasure, young Johnson had become fired with an ambition to master the great Englishman's scientific theories, startling as they must have seemed to the starved intellect of this young New England Congregational minister. But

Johnson had never been a mathematical prodigy, and he found the scant knowledge that he had imbibed under Tutors Noyes and Fiske insufficient for the purpose. So he had begun, just out of the Collegiate School and the single Tutor in it, to make up for what he had lost. During these first two years Johnson had proceeded to inform himself in mathematics with such success that Newton's "Principia" and "Optics" became, we are told, at least intelligible to him, and certainly revised his scientific idea. from the bottom up.

In September, 1717, the first Collegiate School Commencement was held at New Haven, no doubt in the Reverend Noyes' Meeting-house on the public square, with Rector Andrew in the pulpit and Governor Saltonstall beside him. Four boys were graduated. Samuel Johnson on this occasion received the degree of Master of Arts, and the Trustees, meeting after the public ceremonies, no doubt at Mr. Noyes' parsonage, gave him an assistant in the person of Rev. Joseph Moss of Derby, who with the Reverend Noyes now took the Seniors, the three lower classes being taught by Johnson alone. During the college year 1717-1718, this arrangement was maintained as well as it could be under such disadvantageous circumstances. But by the end of that year the new "College house" was nearly ready, and Samuel Johnson, as we shall see, moved into it.

III

During all this time, Elisha Williams had been maintaining another section of the Collegiate School at his farmhouse just outside of Wethersfield. Details are lacking of this Wethersfield enterprise, so that we do not know how it was managed, where the scholars boarded, or what different course of study, if any, from that at New Haven, was given.

Tutor Samuel Johnson

I imagine, however, that the youths who went up daily over the rough back-country roads to the Williams' village farmhouse found themselves in an intellectual atmosphere that was charged with energy. For Elisha Williams was no ordinary man. He seems to have been of a restless temperament, full of vim and tireless mental activity, and, withal, a young man of rather unusual qualities and a winning manner. There was something in him of his ancestors, John Cotton and Governor Bradstreet. He had adventurously voyaged to Nova Scotia after leaving Harvard to preach to the fishermen. He was now studying divinity and helping out his finances by working his farm. He was elected by his town a Deputy at the Assembly in 1717, holding the clerkship of the Lower House for several sessions. He was to have, in 1719, a severe illness and become "sanctified" by it to such an extent as to quit politics for the ministry and become the parson at Newington. In 1739, he was to enter Colony politics again, with his eye on the Governorship, and become a judge of the Superior Court. His roving disposition and great energy were then to take him, as chaplain of the Connecticut troops, in the audacious and successful attack on Louisburg, out of which he was to come colonel of a Connecticut regiment and commander-in-chief of the Colony forces in the following campaign in Canada. Business regarding his troops' pay taking him to England in 1749, he was to be presented in London society to a beauty of the day,—a Miss Scott,—by Dr. Doddridge as "another praying colonel" and marry her out of hand, to the discomfiture of the great man, who was currently believed to be a suppliant for the lady's affections himself. With this fine lady—

> Too lovely maid, possess'd of every Art
> To charm the fancy and command the heart

(Dr. Doddridge had written of her)—Colonel Williams was to return to New England, and, after filling further public offices, to die at that Wethersfield farm at which, as a youth, he had taught the dissenting scholars of Samuel Johnson's Collegiate School.

If the truth were known, this first and highly irregular proceeding under Elisha Williams at Wethersfield was an educational success. Judging by his results at Yale College a little later, and the admiration felt for him by such ambitious students as young Jonathan Edwards, Williams must have had a thoroughgoing academy there, small as it was. In 1719 he bought the Wadhams house on the southeast side of Broad Street, between (according to the old Wethersfield records) the houses of John Warner and Richard Montague. The Rev. Stephen Mix was the minister there at this time, and is said to have assisted in the teaching: a Wethersfield antiquarian is of the opinion that some of the recitations of the Collegiate School scholars may have been in his parsonage. It was a common custom of the times to own Negro or Indian slaves. The Rev. Timothy Woodbridge of Hartford owned an Indian boy, John Waubin, whom he "publickly engaged" to bring up "in the Christian religion." This Collegiate School Trustee also had Negro slaves, for a few years later he was to sell a thirteen-year-old Negro boy named "Thorn" "in plain and open market," and his wife was given another named "Tom." The Rev. Elisha Williams owned a squaw Indian slave during his Wethersfield Collegiate School days. This squaw had a son, "Ambo," born in 1715. "Ambo" was to grow to become a soldier in the War of 1756 and march against the French in Eliphalet Whittlesey's company with seven others of his kind. When the Collegiate School was at Wethersfield a female child, "Desire," was born to Williams' slave squaw, thus adding another interesting member of the Tutor's household.

IV

It would be too long a story to narrate here the continued series of efforts which the two Hartford Trustees, Woodbridge and Thomas Buckingham (aided by Stephen Buckingham), made to settle the School at Hartford during this period from May, 1716, to June, 1719. Looked at from one point of view, this was a most disturbing and unfortunate affair. Voting as they did, for Saybrook, it had been a highly extraordinary thing for Woodbridge and Buckingham to bolt, as one might say, the Trustee's unanimous action, and ask the General Assembly to undo it. And it was an extraordinary act, certainly, to abet the Saybrook scholars in their dissatisfaction (as all traditions unite

Milford. July. 23. 1717.

The above letter by Rector Andrew, which shows his aloofness from the School and indicates his desire to be relieved of its management, runs as follows: "Worthy Sr Haveing received two Letters from yourselfe about your Classes takeing their second degree this Commencement I could not speedily answer to the first, whether there would be any such time, or when or where it would be, if there was any such thing; as to the other inquiry, whether it would be expedient for any of yourselves to seek a second degree at such a time, it was not meet for me to direct in that matter, your own inclination to it must guide and direct you; the place where the Commencement may be, can be no discouragement to some, and I know not why it should be to any, seeing New Haven cant be Judged inferior to Saybrook, unless because the last's being the birthplace of some should give it the prheminence in that Judgment; but it seemed most probable to me, that my possible concernment in the matter might be the greatest

in saying that they did) and defection to Wethersfield. It
was a peculiar act, for Trustees of the Colony college, to
set up a rival establishment at Wethersfield, and practically
place an outsider, in Elisha Williams, over it as of equal
rank with Rector Andrew of Milford. It is difficult to
understand why the effort to remove the School to Hartford was kept up so long, even after the new college building
had been erected at New Haven.

Yet there would probably appear more extenuating circumstances than we now have in mind, were we to know
more about the conditions that prompted these various and,
to the majority Trustees, treasonable acts. I imagine that
local pride had had something to do with this, as well as
the traditional jealousies between Hartford and New
Haven public leaders. And I suppose that a dynamic man
like Woodbridge found little that was to his fancy in such
a highly respectable and scholarly, but, withal, inactive
person as his former Harvard classmate, the good Rector
Andrew of Milford. On the whole, I think a thorough
study of this whole period might show that the polished and

discouragement together with the unsettled state of the school, and the great
opposition against New Haven; as to myselfe I have Laboured with the
Trustees, that a more suitable person might be improved to give degrees,
not being ambitious either of the Honour or advantage, and should have
absolutely refused, if it had not been such a time, wherein differences among
ourselves might have blasted our present design; it is something difficult for
me to offer Questions, which have not been formerly disputed, but I shall
offer the enclosed to your selves, from which you may choose such as are
best pleasing, which have not been Lately debated avoiding to the best of
your remembrance; for my memory is too brittle to keep long in mind things
of such a nature, being concerned with greater matters; with all the regards
to the Revd Mr. Noyes and yourselfe, praying that the only wise God would
bless your Labours for the advancement of religion and Learning among the
students, in the Collegiate school at New Haven, I am, worthy sr
                              your very humble servant
                                                SAMUEL ANDREW
Milford, July. 23. 1717."

cultivated Hartford leader had never been of the New Haven persuasion in many things, theological and educational, and was entirely ready, when the first opportunity came, to swing the Collegiate School over to his neighborhood and to his own way of thinking. He had not been one of the originators of the enterprise; he had been at Secretary Addington's elbow when that lawyer had drawn up the church-control plan for the School's founding that Pierpont had refused; he was away from Connecticut during the period of the first meetings of the Trustees; he had waited until the death of Pierpont before he had taken an active interest in the School. The three-year flurry which he now caused in the Collegiate School's life was undoubtedly largely for the best of reasons, so far as his view of them was concerned. That he did not succeed in wrecking the institution was, however, due to no fault of his, but to fortuitous circumstances of another and quite unexpected variety. A brief review of the Reverend Woodbridge's efforts to side-track the Collegiate School to Hartford, culminating in the final secure establishment of the institution at New Haven, will bring us out into the last and most satisfactory period which these rambling chronicles of Yale's early days have described.

V

The majority vote of the Trustees to settle at New Haven, clinched as it was by the decision to build the "College house" at once, had appeared, by October, 1716, to end the Hartford disaffection. But Woodbridge and Buckingham did not so look at it. Two months later they were behind the calling of a Hartford town meeting, at which a public petition was drawn up ordering the Hartford Deputies in the next Assembly to oppose the New Haven site and secure action which should locate the School where the Assembly desired. This decision the two Hartford ministers no doubt expected would be for their own town. The seacoast Trustees made a vigorous reply to this renewed petition. This was written, so it was said, by Jonathan Law of Milford, the son-in-law of Rector Andrew and later to be Governor of the Colony. It argued that New Haven, being further from Massachusetts (and thus Harvard) than the Connecticut River section, was the best location in the Colony for a college which was intended to serve Connecticut interests; that it was the center of the life of the Long Island coast towns, which included the most important villages in the Colony, and that New Haven had offered the largest financial support. But the main contention of this paper by Judge Law harked back to the fundamental theory upon which the Collegiate School had been established. This was a characteristic New Haven claim,—the independence of the Trustees from Colony legislative interference. We have seen how this had been firmly secured by that preliminary informal "founding" at Branford by the original promoters of the college scheme. We have seen how the senior Trustees had applied that theory by refusing to obey the summons of the Assembly committee the previous year to bring their troubles to the public bar. There was to come a time when, under Rector Clap, this principle was to be the storm-center of a most important struggle between the College and the Colony. It was now announced with clearness and vigor. The Trustees, this statement said, were empowered by their charter to decide all matters connected with the School. If what they did was legally done by majority vote, the General Assembly had no interest in it, and certainly had no business championing the minority side.

In April, 1717, all of the Trustees but Mather, Woodbridge, and Thomas Buckingham met in New Haven and

chose one John Prout, a recent graduate of the School and
"Naval Officer" for the New Haven port, as Treasurer to
succeed Judge Alling (who had died just after he had
secured the New Haven money offers for the School). They
now reaffirmed the vote to build the new "College house"
on the Coster lot whether the absent Hartford members
liked it or not. The Coster lot had now been purchased,
the ancient Atwater mansion on it torn down, and at the
New Haven faction Commencement in September, 1717, the
long frame of the new house had been raised by Caner,
and the work pushed so that something tangible could be
shown to the general Assembly at its October meeting.
Elisha Williams, now beginning that public career which
we sketched in a preceding page, was a deputy from
Wethersfield to this General Court, and, on its organization
in Rev. Mr. Noyes' Meeting-house on the New Haven
public square, became its clerk. His influence, and the
lobbying which he and the Hartford Trustees had done
among the magistrates and Deputies, now had their result.
On the arrival of the members of the Assembly in New
Haven on October 10, 1717, they had seen, with astonishment, the rough framework of the new Collegiate School
building rising skyward through the oaks and elms of the
upper Market-place. As some of the members of that
Assembly considered that the site of the School had not yet
been legally fixed anywhere, least of all at New Haven, I
fancy that there was much excitement over this businesslike
procedure of the majority of the Trustees, and some heat
as well. This at once showed itself in the vote of both
Houses, taken no doubt with much wrath at the Meeting-
house to the accompaniment of the hammering of Caner's
carpenters across the Market-place, that the Collegiate
School Trustees should immediately appear and explain
their unexpected and outrageous proceedings.

Building the College House

This peremptory summons, considering the state of mind of the General Assembly, could hardly be neglected, and so the seacoast Trustees girded themselves for what they proposed to be their final fight for New Haven. All but old Samuel Mather and the latest member, Rev. Stephen Buckingham of Norwalk, attended a special Trustees' meeting called for this purpose just as the Assembly was adjourning. It must have been a spicy session, for both Woodbridge and Thomas Buckingham were there, and John Davenport rode over from Stamford, armed, as the saying goes, for the fray. No doubt the great periwigs of these reverend Trustees shook with the heat of this final trial of strength between the warring factions, and their ministerial black silk gowns fluttered vigorously as Trustee after Trustee stood up (perhaps in Captain Miles' upper room) and carried on the battle. The result was to be expected. A majority and a minority report were drawn up. The first, signed by James Noyes (who drew it), Rector Andrew, Russel, Webb, Davenport, and Ruggles, stood emphatically for New Haven. The minority paper, which, as "Some Observations," was presented the next day, was signed by Woodbridge and Thomas Buckingham, and counted in Stephen Buckingham (who was not present), the bedridden Samuel Mather, and Moses Noyes. To the claim of the majority that the legislature had no legal right to interfere in a question settled by a majority of the Trustees, this Hartford answer was that it had not been settled by a majority, Thomas Ruggles of Guilford having been illegally elected a Trustee when he was under the minimum age of forty. By counting Ruggles out (a highly specious bit of reasoning, as the Hartford Trustees had never raised the point before, and had voted at meetings at which Ruggles had been present), and counting on their side two Trustees

who had not been present, the attempt was made to show
that there had been no such majority.

It was at this somewhat critical juncture that Governor
Saltonstall again stepped into the breach and used his
influence to solve the mooted question. The Lower House,
indeed, voted that the School should at once be set up at
Middletown (evidently an effort at a compromise). But
the Upper House, led by Governor Saltonstall, took the
ground that the site question was not one for the Assembly
to settle at all, and that Jonathan Law's argument that the
Trustees alone had that power, was a sound one. And so
the heated controversy cooled down once more, with the
honors still on the side of the New Haven faction. But it
at once flared up again, the Assembly still in session, owing
to the presentation of an exhaustive and decidedly aggressive paper by the New Haven-site Trustees, replying to the
"Observations" of the two Hartford members. The attack
on the actions of the Hartford Trustees, in this paper, was
made with much vigor. The upshot was a special hearing
set for both sides by the Assembly.

This final act in the long drawn-out controversy was
described at the time by young Samuel Johnson, who had dismissed his classes for the day and gone over to the Meeting-
house to see what happened. Governor Saltonstall, according to Sir Johnson, led off the business by a speech from
James Pierpont's old pulpit, in which he told of "his sorrow
to see the difference," and defined the method of procedure
at this public meeting, which he hoped would definitely
settle the question. The Rev. John Davenport, speaking
for the "Seaside Trustees," then narrated the history of the
whole imbroglio, "and vindicated the same, showing likewise
the irregular and factious management up the River, and
specially of the petition proffered to the General Court" by
Woodbridge and Thomas Buckingham the year before,

which had brought on all the trouble. I fancy that John Davenport used all of his colony-wide famous pulpit power in this presentation of the majority's case, and that he stirred matters up considerably. Timothy Woodbridge, suave and polite, but no doubt fired with more than his usual energy, replied, supporting "what they had done up the River." Davenport answered this with much strength of statement, and carried the day. "And so the dispute ended," writes the reporter Johnson. There was some argument by a Deputy or two that the charter called for unanimous action in such a matter, but this was refuted by Davenport and made the small impression it probably deserved. "The Upper House," says Johnson, "all as one man agreed that they would advise the Trustees settling the School at New Haven to go on with it, esteeming their cause just and good, and they sent it down to the Lower House, where there was great throes and pangs and controversies and mighty strugglings; at length they put it to a vote and there were [36 to 30] for the side of New Haven."

"And thus at length," proceeds Tutor Johnson, "the upriver party had their will, in having the School settled by the General Court, though sorely against their will, at New Haven, but many owned themselves fairly beat."

But the end was not yet. When the Assembly met at Hartford the following May (1718) Woodbridge again broached the subject. The Lower House, which throughout these proceedings appears to have reflected the popular opinion perhaps more than the Upper House and Saltonstall, "considering the great dissatisfaction of the country in general," voted to divide the annual £200 Colony grant for the support of the Tutors between those "at Wethersfield, Saybrook, and New Haven, according to the proportion of scholars under their tuition." Saltonstall saw to it, however, that this highly unfortunate bill was not passed by the Upper

House, and the New Haven faction was thus again left to carry on the School as it saw fit.

But the Wethersfield school was still, somehow or other, maintained (probably by the tuition of the fourteen scholars still at Elisha Williams' farmhouse) and what was left of the Collegiate School went about its regular daily business in New Haven under Tutors Samuel Johnson and Daniel Browne, the Seniors going to Rev. Joseph Noyes for instruction, and Rector Andrew riding over from Milford for Commencements. It no doubt seemed to those playing their parts at this juncture, that this situation was likely to prove a permanent one, and that, unless something unexpected happened, there would be two Collegiate Schools in the Colony, one at New Haven, supported by the Governor and magistrates and with the School funds and building now all but erected,—the other at Wethersfield, under a rival group of tutors, supported by the evidently irreconcilable Hartford Trustees and the House of Deputies.

Joh. Davenport

CHAPTER VIII

"YALE COLLEGE" AT NEW HAVEN

I

UT more funds were needed, if the college house and the proposed President's house were to be paid for and finished, and so, late in October, 1717, the successful New Haven party among the Trustees immediately set about discovering some way in which they might advance the financial interests of the academy, now that they had carried their point as to its site.

The only place to look for this help was apparently again in England. And among the possible English friends of the School old Governor Elihu Yale still loomed as the most promising, as his uncle, Edward Hopkins, had to John Davenport just sixty years before. A letter was now dispatched to the crusty old gentleman, a manuscript draft of which is still among the University papers. This is worth quoting. "The affair of our School," says this quaint document, "hath been in a Condition of Pregnancy: Painfull with a witness have been the Throwes therof in this General Assembly; But We just now hear, that after the Violent Pangs threatening the Very life of the Babe, Divine Providence as a kind Obstetrix hath mercifully brought the Babe into the World, & behold A Man-child is born, whereat We all Rejoyce." This scriptural-obstetrical epistle no doubt finally reached Elihu Yale in London and astonished him greatly.

Jeremiah Dummer was still the Colony agent in London at this time, and still a prominent figure, if his activities did not entirely commend themselves to some of the more snobbish of the London fashionables. Negotiations were therefore again opened with this indefatigable gentleman. The Trustees send him a letter of thanks for his book collection. In this they take occasion to report progress as they had to Governor Yale. "We are in hopes of having shortly perfected a splendid Collegiate House," they write, "which was raised on the 11th instant. We behold its fair aspect [evidently not all of the poetical flights of the day were monopolized by Wigglesworth or Nicholas Noyes], in the Market-place of New Haven, mounted in an eminent place thereof, in length ten rods, in breadth twenty-one feet, and near thirty feet upright, a spacious hall, and an equally spacious library, all in a little time to be splendidly completed." This rhetorical outburst duly arrived at Dummer's London lodgings[1] and, suggesting as it did further efforts to raise money on the part of the Colony agent, had, as we shall see, its immediate effect upon Elihu Yale, already in receipt of a special and equally flowery letter of his own.

But other agencies were likewise at work for the School in this connection. Our old acquaintance, the Rev. Cotton

---

[1] Dummer writes in reply to a letter, in February, 1717, that he is "sorry I cannot yet Send you the rest of the books with the Catalogue, but I hope to do it by the fall, having a promise of Several large benefactions not yet come in." He adds that he would like to have "some Oration at your Commencement take notice of what Books you have already receiv'd (I mean in General words) & acknowledge your obligations to yor Friends here, & that then a proper paragraph of it might be prepar'd for the Boston Gazett, & the Gazett sent over to me. I could perhaps make use of this contrivance to the great advantage of the Collegd, besides it is a necessary peice of gratitude in you, & as requisite for my acquittal." I do not know that this "proper" acknowledgment ever appeared in the Boston papers.

Mather of Boston, was now again in a hostile state of mind toward Harvard College, this time largely because John Leverett had been elected President instead of himself, and because the progressive Leverett was introducing supporters of the new theology into Harvard's councils. Cotton Mather had for these reasons peevishly been staying away from meetings of the Harvard Corporation for some time, and was now entirely out of sympathy with that institution and (if we may believe President Quincy) very much alive again to the possibilities of the Connecticut Collegiate School taking Harvard's place as the orthodox New England college.

While Cotton Mather's renewed interest in the Connecticut college's affairs was to be a considerable factor in the unexpected turn which matters were shortly to take in its fortunes, it was natural enough. To such adherents of the old New England Congregationalism as the Mathers, the steady progress of Harvard College, through Increase Mather's final years and Vice-President Willard's and now John Leverett's, had been toward an intellectual and religious emancipation which spelled only one thing to the old order. We have seen how the two Mathers had interested themselves in the Collegiate School's beginnings. The establishment of the Connecticut school, however different it was from the Mathers' suggestions, had undoubtedly resulted in one satisfactory thing, to men of their way of thinking. It had very decidedly resulted in keeping Connecticut to the traditional and conservative paths that their own Massachusetts was forsaking. Placed by its charter in the hands of a self-perpetuating body of Connecticut ministers of their own and the old Massachusetts sort, the Collegiate School had been set back still further into the old order by the adoption in the Saybrook Platform of that Colony Congregational creed and organization which

Massachusetts had failed to get. So that, with President Leverett developing Harvard by 1718 along new and, to Cotton Mather, highly dangerous lines, it was natural that the latter should again have turned to Connecticut and interested himself in its School's welfare. Writing in that voluminous diary in which he recorded his religious experiences, Cotton Mather unburdened himself as follows: "What shall I do for the welfare of this College at New Haven? I am inclinable to write unto a wealthy East-India merchant at London, who may be disposed on Several Accounts to do for that Society and Colony." This he now did. For we find the Rev. Cotton Mather suddenly taking it upon himself to write to Elihu Yale (he maintained a large correspondence with English leaders concerning many New England matters), suggesting still further generosity. After one of his most verbose and rhetorical flights, Cotton Mather proceeds to inform Governor Yale that "New England is now so far improved as to have the best part of two hundred meeting-houses." The spiritual state of the congregations of these Meeting-houses is thereupon parenthetically prayed for at his usual length by Mather, who then leads up through that channel (the previous career of Governor Yale to the contrary notwithstanding) to urge upon the great London merchant "his serious regard unto the account which we are to give of our stewardship." And then, no doubt to Elihu Yale's surprise, Mather applies all of this argument, not to a money gift to that Harvard College of which the writer was a Fellow, but to the little Collegiate School at New Haven with which he had no official connection whatever. "You have, sir," says Mather, in his best style, "been most kindly inquisitive what you may do for such a people. . . . The Colony of Connecticut, having for some years had a College at Saybrook without a collegious way of living for it, have lately begun to erect a large edifice for it in the town of New Haven. The charge of that expensive building is not yet all paid [evidently Mather knew intimately of the conditions there], nor are there yet funds of revenues for salaries to the Professors and Instructors to the society. Sir, though you have your felicities in your family, which I pray God continue and multiply, yet certainly, if what is forming at New Haven might wear the name of Yale College, it would be better than a name of sons and daughters. And your munificence might easily obtain for you such a commemoration and perpetuation of your valuable name, which would indeed be much better than an Egyptian pyramid."

This epistle was an extraordinary one, when it is remembered that the Trustees of the Collegiate School, so far as we know, had given its writer no authority to go to Elihu Yale, and certainly none to concoct a name for it on his own account at Boston. Mather (who was little given to worrying about his own errors) himself probably realized this. In writing to Governor Saltonstall a little later, he refers to the matter in saying, "I confess, that it was a great and inexcusable presumption in me, to make myself so far the godfather of the beloved infant as to propose a name for it. But I assured myself, that if a succession of solid and lasting benefits might be entailed upon it your Honor and the Honorable Trustees would pardon me, and the proposal would be complied withal. It is a thousand pities [he adds] that the dear infant should be in danger of being strangled in the birth, by a dissension of your good people about the place where it shall be nourished in the wilderness. But probably the Yalean assistance to New Haven will prove a decisive circumstance, which will dispose all to an acquiescence there."

While the real piety of most of the people of that day can hardly be denied,—certainly the almost fanatical religious fervor of Cotton Mather cannot be,—I imagine that it was more or less a fashionable affectation with many others, just as, a generation later, it was fashionable to be anything but pious. Cotton Mather's sincere piety was well established, but I do not suppose that the Yalean was. And so Cotton Mather had used the fashionable literary plea of the times with the great London capitalist, that it would not "be any disadvantage upon your person or family, for a good people to make mention of you in their prayers unto the glorious Lord, as one who has loved their nation, and supported and strengthened the seminary from whence they expect the supply of their synagogues." Mather then committed the soul of Governor Yale to the tender mercies of Jeremiah Dummer, "an excellent friend, our agent, who has been a tender, prudent, active, and useful patron of the infant College at Connecticut," as in truth he had been. Dummer, he suggests, will wait upon Mr. Yale at his palatial house in Great Ormond Street, and take anything that he would be willing to give, in order to have the first building of the "dear infant" Collegiate School baptized with his name.

Dummer, with a redoubled burst of his extraordinary energy, promptly undertook this renewed attack on the coffers of Governor Yale. Yet he seems to have had special reason for this loyalty to the Collegiate School. Though still the Massachusetts Colony agent, he had recently been displaced by one Henry Newman as the Harvard College London representative. It was possibly for that reason that Dummer was shortly to be found contriving to divert gifts from Harvard to the Connecticut School on his own account, though President Quincy suspiciously suggests that Cotton Mather was behind him in that effort also. Thomas Hollis of London was then beginning his great benefactions to Harvard, and letters from him to one of the Harvard Fellows at this period show that Dummer tried hard to get him to shift his interest to the Collegiate School of Connecticut. Governor Saltonstall himself sent letters through Dummer to Hollis for this purpose, as, indeed, he had a good right to do. But references by Hollis to some anonymous Boston adviser of this course led Quincy to the possibly correct notion that this "underhanded" person was none other than our good friend Cotton Mather again. Be that as it may, the scheme fell through, and Harvard properly counts the Hollis family gifts, dating from this time, among its greatest early donations.

II

Though the Wethersfield school was in full operation during the summer of 1718, in spite of the Assembly's decision to let the majority Trustees have their way, the New Haven party had steadily proceeded with the building of the new "College house" on the Coster lot, and, just before Commencement in September of that year, were completing it, Governor Saltonstall looking in now and then on its architechtonick side from his home in East Haven.

Yet that situation was still far from satisfactory. The Hartford faction showed no inclinations whatever to drop their claim on the School. The Wethersfield scholars had not responded to repeated invitations to join the regular classes under Samuel Johnson and the ministers, Noyes and Moss, at New Haven. Nor was there quite enough money in hand with which to pay the contractor for the new building. The possibility was a good one that it could not be finished at all without help. It was for this last reason that Dummer had received urgent requests to push Governor Yale's inclinations as hard as he properly could.

That great man had meantime read (doubtless with much amusement) the fulsome letter of Cotton Mather, and the physiological description of the Collegiate School's beginnings that had been forwarded by the Trustees. We may fancy that Mather's suggestion that Yale's name would be given to the new "College house" had appealed to him, whether the prospect of prayers for his soul had or not. Yet it was a small matter at the most to the great man. Thomas Hollis wrote that he himself had never heard of the New Haven institution, and, though it had of course been pressed on the attention of the bigwigs of London by Jeremiah Dummer but a few years previously, I suppose that most of them had by this time forgotten about it. To Elihu Yale it was so small an affair that it was likely enough that he had never thought of it between Dummer's calls, and that it was in quite an offhand way that he had finally lent an ear to that agent's persistent arguments, and agreed to help it.

Compared to his reputed wealth, the gift that Elihu Yale now made to Dummer was extremely small. We do not know the precise value of Yale's estate at this time; but one of his three daughters left some £20,000 years later, so that it must have been considerable. To Dummer, within three or four months after he had received the Mather letter, Governor Yale finally gave goods estimated by him at £800 in value. These, shipped in three great bales from London in June, 1718, and arriving at Boston in due season in the care of former Lieutenant Governor Tailor, were found to consist of an odd assortment of wares, readily, however, turned into hard cash in the Boston market. Part of this consignment contained "25 pieces of garlix, 18 pieces of calico, 17 pieces of stuff (worsted goods), 12 pieces Spanish poplin, 5 pieces plain muslin, 3 pieces camlot, and 2 of black and white silk crape" (out of the black crêpe

Elihu Yale

were made the customary scholars' and ministers' gowns of the time). The whole lot was within the next three years sold for a total sum of £562 12s. sterling, the largest private donation to the College for the next hundred years and over.

The news of this gift, of the greatest possible importance to the Collegiate School Trustees at this particular moment, happily reached New Haven just before the September Commencement of 1718. Dame Fortune's face had turned.

If Governor Yale could have been present to understand the value of his contribution to the provincial school, he might easily have come to a new realization of the comparative importance of things on this mundane sphere. For what was next to nothing to him, living in his plundered splendor in his great London house, was everything to the struggling academy in far-off and primitive New Haven. For these Trustees, the last of the money needed with which to pay for the new "College house" was now all but in hand. The Yale gift marked the successful end of all their efforts and of those who had stood by them and who had supported the New Haven establishment.

Immediately after the receipt of the news of this gift, the Commencement Trustees' meeting was held for the first time in the new "College hall," now all but completed.

III

This great college house, which until now we have merely seen as it was building, was an extraordinary structure. Standing on the ancient Atwater lot of John Davenport's Colony days, it had been erected about where Osborn Hall now stands, fifty feet from College and thirty-four from Chapel Streets, facing the former. It was a much elongated and pinched-together edifice, 165 feet on the present College Street by 22 on Chapel.[1] It was three stories

[1] Durfee Hall is 181 feet by 40; South Middle (now Connecticut Hall) 105 by 40; Old South was 100 by 40, while North Middle and Old North were about the size of South Middle. The depth of this first Yale College building, 22 feet, while so given by President Clap, would appear to be underestimated, were it not for the fact that the Trustees so gave it in their letter to Dummer later on. The drawing by Mr. Diedricksen of this building follows these dimensions and produces an entirely different looking structure from the traditional Greenwood engraving, which was entirely out of drawing and with incorrect proportions, though probably based on correct items.

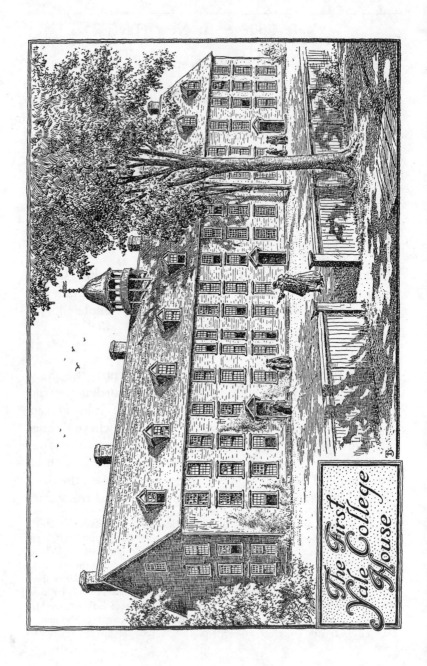

The First Yale College House

high, with "50 Studies in convenient Chambers," and had a kitchen ell on the ground floor on Chapel Street. It was built entirely of wood, and, on the Wadsworth New Haven map of 1748, appears to have been painted blue, as were many of the village houses by that time. James Buck, bookseller, "at ye Spectacles" in Queen Street, Boston, had a plate drawn by one J. Greenwood and engraved by T. Johnston, of this first Yale building, some twenty-five or more years later. I imagine that this ancient drawing will have to be taken with some salt, unless Governor Saltonstall's "architechtonick" gifts were of a much lower order than his Harvard contemporaries'. For the three Harvard buildings of the same date, forming three sides of a court that was open to the country Cambridge roadway, were much more attractive, if we may believe the representations of them that have come down to us.

Yet this ungainly structure may not have been as barracklike in its actual appearance in 1718 as its extraordinary dimensions would indicate. A returning graduate, in 1787, Professor Dexter finds, bemoaned the razing of this building, saying that it "was by far the most sightly building of any one that belonged to the University, and most advantageously situated. It gave an air of grandeur to the others." These "others" were of course what is now "Connecticut Hall," built in 1752, the Athenæum, built in 1761, and the Commons (later the Chemical Laboratory), built in 1782. A correct representation of it suggests that it may well have been all that Manasseh Cutler said for it in 1787. Taking the ground floor as a type of the three stories, there was, at the south end, a thirty-one-foot "Hall," used as a dining-room and for a time as a chapel. Next north came a nine-foot entry for the staircases. Then came two suites of studies and bedrooms, each suite twenty-one feet long. Then came another entry, and two more suites.

The third entry and a single twenty-one-foot suite ended the structure on the north. Judging from the building directions, there must have been a considerable "over-hang" to the sharply pitched roof. While there exists no floor plan of this elongated structure, we should be able to tell pretty accurately how the rooms were laid out. President Clap, who was an indefatigable note-taker on everything about him, kept a student-room account book when he was president. Therein, on rough sketches of the College House elevation, he would jot down the names of aspirants for rooms at the next college opening, and record the allotments when made. In October, 1746, he made such a sketch. Including the attics, he shows twenty-two suites, each twenty-one or -two feet wide on the front of the building. The names of from one to four students are set down in these spaces on Clap's plan. In addition, he writes names in the stair-entry spaces over each of the three ground-floor doorways,—hall bedrooms for single roomers. So that over sixty scholars could be accommodated in the building. The administrative life of the College centered about the "Hall" and Library at the south end. These were fairly large rooms, with fireplaces at the outer sides. The Trustees met in the Library on the second floor.

This large room, the rest of the structure not being completed, was now thrown open to the Governor and the Upper House for the formal dedication of the building.

IV

And, properly enough, this was a gala occasion. Colonel Tailor rode down from Boston with a retinue to attend it. Governor Gurdon Saltonstall "and his Lady," the Deputy Governor, and all the Superior Court judges were there, while the Colony leaders who were in sympathy with the New Haven location doubtless also attended.

The scene, provincial as it might have seemed to the sophisticated former Boston Lieutenant Governor, must have been a splendid one for New Haven, thus attended by the dignitaries and great folk of the Colony. For the Puritan garb of the Connecticut people long since had passed away. The ministers still wore their white bands and black gowns, their black coats and smallclothes and stockings. But the gentry had by this time come to dress according to the fashionable epoch of the mid-18th Century of Old England. Gold cords were on the gentlemen's hats; their waistcoats were creations of embroidery and colored stuffs; their square-cut coats were even decorated with "frogs" of gold and silver and brocades. Their powdered periwigs and perukes were, in some cases, of enormous size. Their great cuffs ended in ruffles, and their silk stockings were of many hues. The Colony gentlewomen were quite as resplendent in their periwigs and mantles, drawn open to show the charming hooped-petticoat modes of London and Boston. The gay attire of these good folk must have lent much color to the occasion.

Samuel Johnson, still Tutor of the School, has left us a vivid account of these proceedings. The first business of this famous Commencement was the formal dedication of the new College house. At this ceremony, following Cotton Mather's voluntary suggestion to the great man, the Trustees now formally named the new building "Yale College," and a unanimous and probably most enthusiastic vote was proposed and passed, that "Our Collegiate School" itself be "named Yale-College."

And then the formal amenities of the occasion begin. Colonel Tailor, in the prevailingly elegant attire of fashionable Boston, addresses the black-gowned Trustees and resplendently-attired Magistrates with a fine speech, in which he expresses, for the absent donor, his great satisfaction in giving his little "for the perfecting and adorning" of the truly remarkable building in which they are met, etc.

These great events over, the whole Assembly marches to the square Meeting-house in the center of the public square (much as Yale Commencement processions did for over a century later, and as, passing around the modern successor of that early New Haven church, to their own hall, they do today), and there the first Commencement of "Yale College" is held.   There is a prayer, and then a Latin Oration "by the Saluting Orator," young James Pierpont, son of that promoter of the college plan who was first to bring it to Elihu Yale's august attention.   The usual lengthy Latin "Dissertations" are given by the graduating Seniors in their black gowns.   Then the Rev. John Davenport, grandson of the pioneer whose life work for the Colony college had, unknown to him, paved the way for the present great occasion, makes a most polished and splendid "oration in Latin," in which he expresses, in the language of the cultivated men of his day, the thanks of the Trustees "to Almighty God and Mr. Yale under Him for so public a favor and so great a regard to our languishing School" [as Tutor Johnson duly translates it].   Then diplomas are given to eight Seniors and to two candidates for the Master's degree.   After this long ceremony, Governor Saltonstall, erect, strong of figure, vigorous of eye,—in full-bottomed periwig, his long ministerial starched band showing on his many-buttoned and flaring-sleeved coat,—and with all the force and polish for which he was famous through all the colonies and in New York, steps forward in the high pulpit and delivers a Latin speech which, coming from him as the

The
Commencement
at New Haven
in 1718

official head of the Colony, could only mean the final settlement of all disputes, and the beginning of a new era for the long-suffering School. Governor Saltonstall congratulates the Trustees on their success and courage in building the new college house, now named "Yale College"[1] by the grace of God and Governor Yale, and on "the comfortable appearance of things with relation to their School." And the ceremonies close again with prayer, after which the assembly moves out onto the broad tree-shaded Market-place, assured that all the troubles of the Collegiate School are at an end, and that, as "Yale College," its future is sure.

And now the Trustees and the Colony high officials and the former Lieutenant Governor of Massachusetts, and the judges of the Colony Superior Court in their gowns, and such of the Colony Magistrates as are there, return across the Market-place, past the dilapidated old Courthouse and the new Hopkins Grammar School wooden building, to the College Hall, where they are "entertained with a splendid dinner," and the hoop-skirted ladies "at the same time" are "entertained in the Library," the gallant Boston Colonel joining them at the table, after which, as was the custom of the day on such great occasions, they all stand up and sing "the four first verses in the 65th Psalm,"—

> Thy praise alone, O Lord, doth reign
> In Sion thine own hill,—

"and so the day ended."

"Everything," wrote Samuel Johnson, slipping back to his lodgings that night to write down the doings of the

---

[1] "Yale's College," the Trustees informed the absent Cotton Mather, was the name of the new building. While the College house itself was "Yale College," the School became by that act popularly known by the patron's name and was so rechristened by the Trustees at this time.

day, "was managed with so much order and splendor that the fame of it extremely disheartened the opposers and made opposition fall before it." For which consummation, no doubt, the Trustees had much to thank Governor Saltonstall.

Yet the Trustees did not stop at this final success of their long efforts. Meeting in business session on the great day, they had proceeded to vote that the College library should be brought into the new "Yale College," and that Rector Andrew should write to "Mr. Henry Flynt [then the mainstay of the teaching force at Harvard, but later to show himself hardly adapted for the undertaking] to obtain from him some good encouragement that he will accept the offer of a Rector's post in our Yale-College, our eyes being on him for Rector." A "Steward" was appointed in charge of the scholars' rooms and board, and a tutor to assist Samuel Johnson.

On October 8, 1718, several of the rooms in the new college house were ready for use, and Samuel Johnson had his goods brought over to it from his lodgings and the new assistant Tutor, Daniel Browne, moved into it from his father's house in West Haven. And I suppose that within a few weeks the handful of students were given their rooms by the new "Steward," and that by November the College was in full operation under the eye of the Rev. Mr. Noyes, the local minister. At about this time all of the Wethersfield scholars also arrived, bag and baggage, Jonathan Edwards, now a Junior, among them. But they returned in a month to Elisha Williams, evidently still dissatisfied with the teaching, leaving seventeen scholars with Johnson. Though we do not now know the precise reason for their action, I imagine that the failure of the Trustees to secure Tutor Flynt of Harvard for the Rectorship had something to do with it. He, fortunately for Yale

College, had declined to leave Cambridge, and it would appear that no further immediate efforts were made to select another man. Rector Andrew still remained the nominal head of the establishment.

V

So, in spite of the settlement of the site question by the opportune gift of Elihu Yale, the Hartford Trustees still stuck to their guns.

Yet there was now nothing left of this long-standing opposition except the determination of Woodbridge and Buckingham to keep it up. Even the Lower House now fell into line with the march of events, and deserted the Hartford faction. The General Assembly of October, 1718, was as usual held in New Haven, and its members now decided to patch up all the past differences. The Governor and Upper House on this occasion accepted the invitation of the Trustees to leave Captain Miles' convivial Tavern and hold their sessions in the new College Library, the Lower House sitting, as usual, in the Meeting-house down the hill on the Market-place.

Over the still tangled affairs of the newly-named "Yale College" there was now another long legislative discussion. Yet the situation was plain enough. There had indeed been a long public squabble over the proper site of the Collegiate School, with good arguments for each of the three places that wanted it. But the majority of the Trustees, acting within what the Assembly now agreed was their right, had decided upon New Haven. They had collected much money for it. They had succeeded in securing the munificent gift of the great Governor Yale of London. They had built a splendid "College house." This and the institution itself, in the presence of the chief men of the

Colony, they had named Yale College. And they had proceeded to elect a resident Rector.

On the other hand, the leaders of the Hartford dissension, naturally enough under conditions prevailing some time back, had refused to agree with their fellow Trustees, and were persisting in their Wethersfield enterprise. In fact, they had just granted Collegiate School degrees, before a large country assembly in the Wethersfield Meeting-house. This, it would now appear (as the historian Trumbull solemnly pronounced it just a century later) "could be considered in no other light than that of a great misdemeanor, and highly reprehensible." Yet both Woodbridge and Thomas Buckingham were too important men for even the most irritated of the New Haven party legislators to chastise for all this in public. The Assembly proposed to bring the factions together, and, acting as the Colony Court, order what should be done to this end.

So we find the Assembly voting, with reference to the School, that the public money paid to it for the past year (as had been refused affirmative vote by the Upper House on the last occasion it was proposed) should be divided between the Tutors at all three of the rival schools; that the Wethersfield graduates should be given Yale College degrees "without examination"; that all the Wethersfield scholars should be admitted to Yale College with no questions asked; that these scholars are "ordered" to "come down to New Haven"; and that "said college be carried on, promoted and encouraged at New Haven, and all due care taken for its flourishing." To placate the disgruntled Saybrook and Hartford people for their loss, the Assembly likewise voted that £500 should be appropriated for a fine new Statehouse at Hartford, and that £50 should be given to the Saybrook town school. The Assembly finished its arrangement of the College's affairs by voting that the Governor and his Council, at the request of the Trustees, should give such orders as were necessary "for the removing of the books, belonging to the said college, left at Saybrook, to the library provided for the placing of them at New Haven."

VI

This action, regarding the books, as we have seen, had already been voted by the Trustees, and on October 28, in accordance with the Assembly's command concerning it, Governor Saltonstall and the Council ordered the Secretary of the Colony, one Wyllys of Hartford, to make out the necessary papers for their transfer. A formal demand for the College books was therefore made out by Secretary Wyllys and sent by messenger to Saybrook.

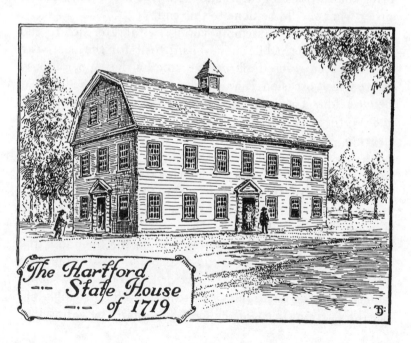

The Hartford State House of 1719

Samuel Johnson, as I have noted, had probably brought over a few of these volumes to New Haven to assist him in his teaching and for his private reading (Sir Isaac Newton's two scientific books among them). But there is evidence that the remainder of the former Collegiate School collection had remained at Saybrook all this time, awaiting the outcome of the struggle over the site, and that these were still at the old Thomas Buckingham parsonage, or at the newly-built house of Daniel Buckingham, his son. How many volumes were thus at Saybrook at this time is not definitely known. But beside the forty or so original books given by the "founders" at the first Saybrook meeting, we have seen some seven hundred arrive from Jeremiah Dummer, and two hundred from Sir John Davie. So that there were more than a thousand books in Daniel Buckingham's house when this Colony order reached him.

Two of the Trustees,—young Thomas Ruggles, the Guilford minister, probably being one of them,—rode over to Saybrook early in November, with a written order for the books from Rector Andrew. To their astonishment young Daniel Buckingham received them coldly, saying that "he did not know that he had any books belonging to 'Yale College,' but when he did, and should receive authentic orders, he would deliver them." It appeared from this refusal by Buckingham that the Saybrook people, in spite of their £50 sop from the Colony treasury, had not accepted the situation and still proposed to fight about it. The Rev. Azariah Mather doubtless had his hand in this turn of events, and I imagine that the Hartford Trustees had theirs. The claim may have been made, for that matter, that the books had been given to "the Collegiate School at Saybrook," which was still flourishing with one scholar at the Reverend Mather's parsonage, and that those responsible for the new "Yale College" at New Haven had no right to them. This in fact was worrying even the New Haven site Trustees, as in a letter to Dummer he was asked to say plainly that he had secured his gifts for the Collegiate School, "wherever the same were finally settled." Dummer later replied to this to the effect that the site of the School was of no consequence to him, though he hoped it would be agreed upon. Young Buckingham evidently took an opposite view, and sent the two Trustees packing. The upshot was another appeal to the Assembly to straighten matters out.

The story of what now developed is well known, as it is one of the amusing episodes in these extremely serious times. Governor Saltonstall, already appealed to more than once to straighten out the tangled conditions of his Colony College, wearily called a Council meeting at Saybrook early in December, and haled young Buckingham before it. But the latter was obstinate. He still refused to give up the Collegiate School books. So the Council ordered the County Sheriff and his constables to go down to Saybrook from Hartford and get them by force.

We may imagine the excitement that this show of Colony official power created in the quiet little Saybrook village. The townspeople, siding naturally with Buckingham and their minister, doubtless leave their farms and shops and crowd up about young Buckingham's house and into it as the sheriff and his constables push their way into the house. (They say that the house itself was barricaded.) Doubtless they jeer loudly as the constables emerge, laden to the chins with the great folios that had been given by the "founders" and the books that Dick Steele and Dr. Bentley and the great Elihu Yale and the Poet-Laureate of England had sent over. Probably they get in the way as much as they can and, as the cold December afternoon wanes, become more and more excited as they see the last of the great

Bringing the College Books to New Haven

volumes deposited in the ox-carts that have been impressed by the sheriff. Night coming, the cartloads of books are kept under guard till they can be taken the next morning across country to Guilford, where Thomas Ruggles was to house them till New Haven wagons could be sent over to get them. But during the night the Saybrook people draw off the guard, turn loose the oxen, upset the carts, carry off such of the books as they happen to fancy, and send out parties to break down the bridges over the creeks west of the village toward Killingworth. When morning comes, the sheriff finds himself left with no helpers, and with as many obstacles as possible put in the way of his doing anything further about the business. But he manages to collect what he can of the débris and the next day arrives safely at Guilford with a quarter of the original library lost for good, and many of the remaining volumes permanently damaged. In his account of this proceeding, Samuel Johnson says that 260 books were lost and 1,000 saved.

This episode marks the end of Old Saybrook's appearance in Yale annals. The old town has added to itself a

new and thriving village on the mainland, has transferred
its chief interests to it, and has slept peacefully throughout
the two centuries that have since elapsed. The early dream
of a great Puritan metropolis, presided over by Pym and
Cromwell, never came true. The Market-place that was
to be a New-World emporium had become the village Green
when this affair of the College books took place. Today,
with a proper memorial of Yale's first days there set up on
the Lynde lot next to the spot where the fair Lady Fenwick
lies buried, the charming old village is very much the same
that it was when the Collegiate School, for nine brief years,
was its chief citizen.

CHAPTER IX

RECTOR CUTLER

I

HE remnant of the Collegiate School books was now in Samuel Johnson's care in the library of the new "Yale College." But the Hartford Trustees still refused to give up their school at Elisha Williams' Wethersfield farmhouse, and Governor Saltonstall took Rector Andrew's reins in his hands and again went at the persistent problem. A formal joint meeting of the Colony Council and the Trustees was called at New Haven for the 11th of March, 1719, to see what could be done. Only four or five of the Trustees attended this meeting, and Woodbridge and Thomas Buckingham were deliberately among the absentees. But Saltonstall proceeded to business.

Of the principal needs of the struggling academy, two had by this time been met in the securing of a library and funds for a "College house," and in the permanent settlement of the site question in favor of New Haven.

There remained, however, the need of a more business-like government than had been the case since Rector Pierson's death twelve years before. The newly-named Yale College needed the right man for resident Rector. Samuel Andrew had never evinced any particular capacity for affairs and, so far as we now can see, had not been a very strong factor in the troublous times which I have been chronicling. He had been assisted by a long succession of young Tutors, some of whom had not been successful as teachers and all of whom had been preparing themselves, while teaching, to become settled ministers elsewhere. The single flash of activity in settling this question, in offering the Rectorship to Tutor Flynt of Harvard, had died out,—fortunately, as it happened,—with his declination. It had been because of this failure that the final refusal of the Hartford Trustees to join the majority had probably been made, and doubtless with good reason.

All of which now resulted in a highly entertaining, if serious, student outbreak. The Assembly had ordered the fourteen Wethersfield students to "come down" to New Haven, and they had come, including Jonathan Edwards. They proved an unruly and rebellious lot. And they proceeded, so Sir Johnson believed, "to unhorse" him from his Tutorship. This "black design" is possibly borne out by the facts. For the Wethersfield scholars at once began to make trouble at the College and in the town, being "very immoral in their Conversation so that they became odious to the people of ye Town," writes Johnson, and to "get together a Collection of faults" with "the public Expositions & Disputations & managements of the Tutors & especially of the two upper Classes which were under me." Johnson says that these complaints were sent clandestinely to Timothy Woodbridge and approved by him as sufficient grounds for further efforts on his part to attack the College, though Woodbridge later on emphatically denied that he had had anything to do with it. And they did not stop there, for "presently thereupon comes 3 of the parents of the Scholars to see how it was, & they designed to have them away." Rector Andrew being hastily sent for, Trustee Samuel Russel already being at the College house, there was a great powwow between the parents and College officers, which resulted in Andrew's supporting Johnson, but asking time from the parents to call a special meeting of his Board. The "3 parents," publicly agreeing to this postponement, privately permitted their sons to leave New Haven. Here was a great to-do, and, as Johnson writes, "The Schollars were going away all so fast" that the Rev. Mr. Noyes had to come into the breach, and agree with the parents to take the Juniors himself and hand over the Seniors to Reverend Moss of Derby. But even this did not help matters, the disaffected parents evidently being ready to take away their sons on any pretext. A week later they returned with horses and all of the scholars of the Wethersfield faction "went away but one." While Timothy Woodbridge may not have been a factor in this situation, I imagine that he received the news of it with satisfaction. At about this time he had written to Benjamin Coleman, a Harvard Fellow, suggesting that the dissatisfied Yale students might finish their course of study at Harvard. He was quite willing, at least, that his own stepson, in the Class of 1718, should do so. Coleman very honestly and frankly replied that he did not think this would be a good thing. It would be "heavily borne" by the New Haven site faction, he said, and he rather advised Woodbridge, whose "generous public spirit" was well known, to quit the struggle. He did not think that Harvard should receive "any number of your Scholars at this critical time," though he was willing that Woodbridge's son should come. Nothing therefore came of this original idea of the Hartford minister, even his stepson continuing at the New Haven College.

But the whole situation was now one which could not be permitted, for the good of the Colony, to continue any longer. At the joint meeting of the Trustees and the Assembly, therefore, Governor Saltonstall brought the problem down to the one issue of a proper head for the

School. The College officers were practically told by the General Assembly to find such a Rector.

Proceeding, with some alacrity, to this end, the Trustees took Mr. Andrew's advice and offered the post, *pro tem* for the moment, to his son-in-law, a young minister then settled over the Stratford Congregational church.

II

This young man, then but thirty-six years of age, was the Rev. Timothy Cutler. He was a Charlestown, Massachusetts, boy, and had been graduated at Harvard under Increase Mather in the year that the Connecticut Collegiate School had been started. He had come to the Stratford Meeting-house from Boston as old Israel Chauncy's successor, in 1709, with a reputation of being "one of the best preachers both colonies afforded." He had married a daughter of Rector Andrew of Milford shortly after settling at near-by Stratford, and was at this time conducting the affairs of his little congregation with success. We have President Stiles' word for it that he was "great in the philosophy, metaphysics, and ethics of his day." He was a fluent user of Latin in conversation and public addresses, and was "of a commanding presence and dignity." And he was a great reader. He had become a close friend of Tutor Samuel Johnson,—but a few years his junior,—and so had found himself a frequent traveler to New Haven to read the books which Johnson had brought over from Saybrook. I suppose, in the light of after-events, that it was the opportunity which the Rectorship offered him, of being closer to these books, which decided him to accept the position.

Asked to relieve him from their church ministry to accept the Rectorship of Yale College, the Stratford people had "passively" submitted "to God" in the matter and

Rector Timothy Cutler

agreed to it, which was more than the Killingworth people had done in Rector Pierson's case. Yet they had asked back the parsonage and "home lot" which he had been given on settling there, as the Killingworth people had wanted in their settlement of the Pierson request; and the Rev. Mr. Cutler had handed it back, as Abraham Pierson had not been willing to. The demand of the Stratford people for £100 to call a new minister seems to have been gladly complied with by a General Assembly that saw itself thus rid of the College trouble. In March, 1719, Rector Cutler arrived at New Haven and began his duties as the new head of the academy.

It naturally had been expected by Governor Saltonstall that this last act in settling the difficulties of the divided Colony college would have brought the two Hartford Trustees into the fold. But for some reason or other, they still held out. Woodbridge, especially, persisted. There is extant a letter from Governor Saltonstall of this date, written to Rev. James Noyes, which throws an interesting light on the Hartford leader's attitude. Woodbridge waylaid the Governor, says the latter, "as I came out of town" on horseback, and buttonholed him on the College site question. Saltonstall tells Noyes that Woodbridge "moved me to desire a Meeting of the Trustees; I told him I could not think It would be of good Consequence for such a Motion to begin with Me." Woodbridge pushed the point and the Governor told him that if he himself "would move, I would give It what Favour I might; and offered him If He would write, to take Care of a Lettr to You, Who would probably discourse with Me about It." This Woodbridge was disinclined to do, and the conversation ended there. Saltonstall added, for Noyes' own information, that he continued to stand with the Trustees and did not propose to "insert my Self into their Affairs, till I see further Reason for It."

If the attitude of these two disaffected Hartford ministers had hitherto passed through the successive stages of local pride, educational ambition for their neighbors' sons, and obstinacy, it now seems to have taken the character of downright pig-headedness. For, in spite of the complete failure of their efforts to get the College for Hartford, and the popularity of the New Haven settlement throughout the Colony, they now made a final move to even up matters with Saltonstall, whose interference in affairs had finally spiked their guns. To this end both Timothy Woodbridge and Thomas Buckingham offered themselves for election as the two Deputies from Hartford in the May election in 1719 that now came on. This extraordinary and unprecedented action could have been but for the one purpose that they now showed in it. For they began a Colony-wide propaganda to secure the defeat of Governor Saltonstall for the next annual term, with the idea that one Gold, at the time Lieutenant Governor, would become head of the Upper House in his place, and, with themselves leading the Lower, undo what had been done regarding the Colony College. But the scheme fell through. There was a great popular rally to the support of Saltonstall at the next election. He was overwhelmingly reëlected Governor, though the two Hartford Trustees got into the Lower House, as they had planned. Woodbridge made the opening prayer of the session, but seems to have made some remark that infuriated the Governor. Saltonstall, long-suffering in his efforts to smooth the ruffled Hartford Trustees, now blazed forth in what was undoubtedly a very proper temper. He caused charges for defamation of character to be brought by a down-river Deputy in the Lower House against the luckless Rev. Timothy Woodbridge. The House sustained these charges and voted to exclude Woodbridge, who vigorously replied, and the Upper House called for a further hearing. Though we do not know the outcome, the Reverend Wood-bridge appears to have from that moment been withdrawn as a factor in the now-concluded Hartford fight. His inter-est in the College while Timothy Cutler was Rector, was sufficient to induce his wife, a wealthy woman by a previous marriage, to give a bell to the College house. Cutler, thanking Madam Woodbridge for it in a letter to her hus-band, says that it was put in place (in 1720) "and gives a very pleasant clear Sound." From that time forth, Timothy Woodbridge was a staunch friend of the College.

It was at this time that Elisha Williams underwent his long sickness which I mentioned in another chapter, and recovered from it so "sanctified" that he decided to leave off teaching and enter the ministry at Newington, just outside of Wethersfield. I presume that this event, together with the Reverend Woodbridge's public scarification in the

Assembly, must have been the prime occasion for the final winding up of the school at his Wethersfield farm that now took place. For in June, 1719, all of the Wethersfield scholars, among them Jonathan Edwards, finally left the Hartford establishment and joined their former Fellows at the new Yale College at New Haven.

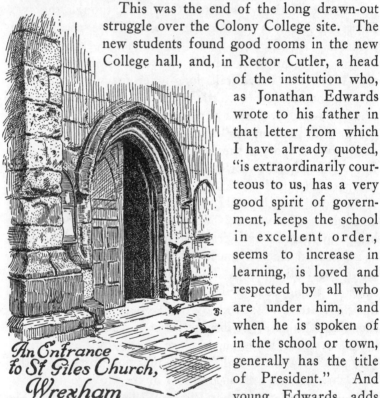

This was the end of the long drawn-out struggle over the Colony College site. The new students found good rooms in the new College hall, and, in Rector Cutler, a head of the institution who, as Jonathan Edwards wrote to his father in that letter from which I have already quoted, "is extraordinarily courteous to us, has a very good spirit of government, keeps the school in excellent order, seems to increase in learning, is loved and respected by all who are under him, and when he is spoken of in the school or town, generally has the title of President." And young Edwards adds

An Entrance to St Giles Church, Wrexham

that he thanks his father for advice given him. "I am," he says, "sensible of the preciousness of my time, . . . and I take very great content under my present tuition, as all the rest of the scholars seem to do under theirs. . . . The scholars all live in very good peace with the people of the town, and there is not a word said about our former carryings on."

III

According to President Clap's later compilation of gifts to the College up to this time, it would appear that, in addition to the books previously mentioned, and the private and public money pledges, the Treasurer of the College had received £50 from Governor Saltonstall, and £10 from his good Lady, two acres of land in New Haven from one Joseph Peck, seven acres in New Haven from Tutor Moss of Derby and seven from his father, eight acres in West Haven from Captain Samuel Smith, and twenty-eight books from Dr. Daniel Turner of London. The General Assembly had voted £300 worth of the new lands, and £40 annually for the next seven years to the College for the Tutors' salaries.

Moreover, there was much talk of further benefactions from Governor Yale, who by this time had received the thanks of the Trustees and an account by them of the ceremonies at the dedication of the "College house" and of their action in naming the institution after him, as Cotton Mather had promised. Jeremiah Dummer had reported the reception of this address by the now aged and infirm capitalist. The old gentleman, it appears, was more than a little pleased by the affair, "saying," writes Dummer, "that he expressed at first some kind of concern whether it was well in him, being a churchman, to promote an Academy of Dissenters. But when he had discoursed the point freely [and no doubt been informed by Dummer, as had been old Doctor Salmon, that the Connecticut ministers probably would change the seminary's theology to suit, if he pressed the point] he appeared convinced that the business of good men is to spread religion and learning among mankind, without being too fondly attached to particular tenets about which the world never was, nor ever will be, agreed." All of which was extremely broad-minded of a former India merchant who had not worried very much about such matters in the process of squeezing that portion of mankind nearest him for his riches. "Besides," puts in Dummer, quoting the great man, who was now a contented and honored pew-holder in a London parish church, "if the discipline of the Church of England be most agreeable to Scripture and primitive practice, there's no better way to make men sensible of it than by giving them good learning." Governor Yale, having eased his Episcopal conscience with this energetic first aid from the elastic-conscienced Dummer, now agreed to give £200 a year to his "Yale College" during the remainder of his life and "to make a settled annual provision to take place after his death." Goods valued at £100 were reported shipped by Dummer two years later. And Dummer constantly pushed ahead for more. "I was with him last night, to refresh his memory about the books, pictures, & other presents which I formerly mentioned to you, but it seems they won't be in order 'till a month hence." These "presents" had been expected to be "Mr. Yale's picture at full length with his nephew's on the same canvas,"[1] which, Dummer said, had been "drawn for a present to your Colledge Hall, and another parcel of Books, part of which he has promis'd me shall be the Royal transactions in seventeen Volumes." Governor Yale had also thought to send over "a pair of Globes," but Dummer had told him that the School already had them, and Yale

---

[1] The Elizabethan Club at the University possesses a full length painting of Elihu Yale with a youth at his side. The age or origin of this portrait has never been determined. The representation of Yale in it, however, is of a man much younger than the one in the Zeeman painting which hangs in the University Dining Hall, and which was done in 1717, according to President Stiles.

had agreed to send instead "some mathematical instru-
ments, & glasses for making philosophical Experiments, as
Microscopes, Telescopes, & other glasses for use as well as
for ornament & curiosity."

"But old gentlemen are forgetful," Dummer writes to
the Trustees. And Governor Yale proved the adage. For
he never proceeded with his annual pledge, nor did he put
the New Haven college in his will. He died intestate on
July 8, 1721, at his house in Great Ormond Street, and
that was the last the Connecticut College heard of him.
Poor Jeremiah Dummer, this second chance having slipped
through his fingers through the untimely arrival of the
Great Reaper, hustled about to see what he could do about
it for several years thereafter. But though he made tremendous efforts to interest Yale's three daughters (one
of whom was married to Dudley Lord North and another
to James Cavendish, uncle of the Duke of Devonshire)
nothing ever came of it. There is a story that Governor
Yale, just before his death, had himself seen to the packing
up of £500 worth of goods to send to the New Haven
Trustees, but that he died before he could manage it. These
goods were duly unpacked and distributed with his estate
to his noble daughters, and to that unmarried Ursula who
survived him.

These fine things were all in prospect in 1719, and I do
not doubt were expected by the Trustees of the new Yale
College. In the meanwhile they needed their Rector's house,
had voted to build it, and were asking Colony aid again for
it. The Upper House again was sympathetic, but the Deputies balked, as usual. Not only did they not wish to give
Colony money outright to the College, but they reported
that there was "too great a spirit of learning in the land"
anyway, and that "more are brought up to it than will be
needed or find improvement" (in which we light upon the

first instance in Yale history of the hard-headed questioning of the value of a college education). But in May, 1721, the Assembly agreed to permit the Trustees again to circulate a "brief" to raise money,—this time for the Rector's house. A Colony collection was taken on the Sabbath day, July 23, which came to £100, paid in small individual contributions from pew-holders in the sixty-five Meeting-houses of the Colony.

But this was not enough, and in October, the Assembly, in passing an Act "for the better Regulating the Duty of Impost upon Rhum," voted that all the money derived from that genial source during the first two years after its enforcement should be paid over toward helping the College build its Rector's house. President Clap lists this as £115 in his itemized account of the College assets in 1722. The house cost was £260, according to the same authority, though other authority is to the effect that the contract with Caner, the "College-house" builder, called for £600, the discrepancy doubtless arising from the terms in which the figures are given.

The Yale family church-yard near Plas-yn Yale

CHAPTER X

THE NEW HAVEN OF TIMOTHY CUTLER

I

 HE twoscore youths who were gathered together under young Timothy Cutler's promising Rectorship in the new Yale College hall in June, 1719, found themselves living in the midst of a village life that had hardly changed from the quiet provincialism of James Pierpont's times, as that, in its turn, had not progressed far beyond John Davenport's.

New Haven's total population was less than a thousand at this time, and there were perhaps a hundred and fifty houses. Except for scattered farms south of the present George Street and north of Grove, and a somewhat closely-built seafaring section east of the present State and Meadow Streets and thus down to the harbor's shore, the village was much the same as when the first efforts had been begun for the Colony college. If we might, in fancy, accompany one of the new College Freshmen about this little village on his first walk of a Sabbath afternoon, we might picture to ourselves, with some approach to vividness, what sort of a place this New Haven of Rector Cutler's day was.

And I suppose that the small compass of the place would be the first thing that would interest such a stranger. Meadows, rye- and oat-fields and stubbly clearings on which the cattle and geese and pigs of the townsfolk pastured, surrounded the original nine squares, except where here and there the woods came in close to the town's outskirts, as was the case in the whole section now traversed by Whitney Avenue and Prospect Hill. No cross lanes had up to this time been cut through the original town streets laid out by John Brockett for Theophilus Eaton's settlers. Country roads had branched off from the western ends of the modern Chapel and Elm Streets and the north end of College, while "Neck Lane" and "Payne's Gate" led off eastward from the north end of what is now State Street. The three creeks on the banks of which Michael Wigglesworth's elders had built their first rude huts in 1638, still led up into the "quarters" from about where the railroad yards are today. One of these rippled along the east side of the modern State Street, its west bank dotted by a few houses belonging to sailmakers, tanners, weavers, and "mariners." A second creek, emerging from the ancient swamp at the southeast corner of the Market-place, still trickled muddily across town and into the State Street rivulet. The broader and deeper creek just south of the present George Street, up which John Davenport's small vessel with its burden of the original settlers had sailed to the College Street corner, was still a sizable stream in 1719, so navigable that boats could land passengers where High Street now joins George, at which place stood a blacksmith's shop in Rector Cutler's day.

All of the original outside eight squares of the village were at this time fringed, as they had been since the settlement, by farmhouses, the interior of these blocks being fenced-in open orchards, meadows and cornfields. Weavers, blacksmiths, joiners, soap-boilers, saddlers, cordwainers, coopers, clothiers, and millers occupied many of these houses, plying their trades, no doubt, there, though the Town-mill was out the present Orange Street near East Rock. But, from the old map of Joseph Brown of 1724,

from which we can reconstruct something of the New
Haven of those days, most of the folk were "husbandmen,"
"yeomen," and "planters." Numerous "deserted" houses,—
relics of Davenport's times,—appear in the outlying streets
on Brown's map, and no doubt many of the homesteads
actively in use were antiquated and weather-beaten survivors
of those older days. James Pierpont's parsonage, fronting
the Market-place behind his two "great elms," was occupied
by his son, now fatuously pursuing the English Pierrepont
earldom. His successor in the village Meeting-house,
Joseph Noyes, lived in the old Eaton mansion down Elm
Street, while Treasurer Prout's house was far down toward
the harbor line on what is now Water Street, as became the
Naval Officer of the Port.

But such a new arrival at the College would have been
more interested in the great Market-place of the town, and
the life about the new Yale College house facing it from
its southwest corner. And he would have found his tower-
ing College hall but a small part of this public center of
New Haven. The square bounded by what are now Chapel,
York, Elm, and College Streets at this time had but eight
houses on it, two or three barns, and a group of surviving
log "Sabbath-day houses" where York and Elm now meet.
On York Street, beside these cabins, lived the two Hotchkiss
families, farmers, and Sam. Chatterton, weaver, who was
domiciled at the Chapel Street corner. One house faced
the present Elm Street, about where Peabody Museum now
stands. On Chapel Street above High, lived one Jonathan
Tuttle, a "planter"; Stephen Ball, soap-maker, had his
odoriferous premises where the Art School now stands.
On College Street, Sam Mix, "yeoman," lived at the
Battell Chapel corner, while two barns and the farmhouse
of one Joshua Tuttle, "husbandman," filled in the present
sites of Farnam, Lawrance, and Welch Halls. On the

The Market-place from the College Yard in 1724

Chapel Street corner, built close to the street lines, and within its low wood fence, was Elihu Yale's magnificent structure that Cotton Mather had prophesied would be a finer affair than an Egyptian pyramid. Three farmhouses faced Chapel Street on the other side from the modern Old Campus, as did three on Elm Street,—Lieutenant Mix, Deputy to the Assembly, living where the Divinity School now stands.

In the midst of all this quiet village life was the great Market-place, still more or less as it had been in the early days of the Colony. Facing it, across the present crowded and busy Chapel Street, were two large and ancient houses, one, at Chapel and College Streets, that had formerly been Captain Miles' Tavern, now belonging to one Mr. Woodhouse, and the other, far down where Chapel and Church now intersect, occupied by the descendants of the ruined Gregson of Captain Lamberton's "Great Shippe" days. Between these, where Temple now crosses Chapel, was a barn. So that the Yale College student of 1719, walking down Chapel Street in his flowing college gown and broad flat hat, had nothing but this barn and gardens and open fields to look at across from the present Green. Four houses stood on the Elm Street side of the Market-place at that time, and as many on Church Street, the great spaces between them being fenced-off meadows and orchards, with the virgin woods and harbor beyond.

The Market-place itself at this time was but little changed from James Pierpont's day. The second Meeting-house had been built in 1668, and enlarged sometime later, as we have seen. It was about in the center of the public square, probably just east of the present Temple Street, and was of wood, with a pyramidal roof, upon the apex of which, in an open belfry, still hung the bell that we have seen purchased for it from a sailorman in the harbor. The Town whipping-post still stood on the College Street side of the Market-place, and just north of it the "gaol." It had been in this same year, 1719, that the two first important changes in the appearance of the old public square had been made. One of these was the erection of a Statehouse. This was now being built at College and Elm Streets, by Caner, whose work on the "College house" had been approved by the townsfolk and Assembly, and who was now living on Chapel Street in an old house facing the present site of the Art School. The new Statehouse was a two-story wooden structure, some forty-five by twenty-two feet in size, with a great chimney at either end, and was to be used by the County courts and by the General Assembly until 1763, when a Boston-style brick Statehouse superseded it between the present Trinity and Center Churches on Temple Street. Just before this time, the Town had voted to build a new house for the Hopkins Grammar School. This was now being built on the College Street side of the Market-place, between the whipping-post and Chapel Street and nearly opposite "Yale College." The old Cheever School, that had been enlarged for the Hopkins Grammar School, was still standing at this time near Elm and Temple Streets (though Brown's map does not show it for some reason or other), and was to be used for an "English school" until 1756, when a brick building took its place. West of the Meeting-house of course lay the village cemetery, making, all in all, with the prison and whipping-post, a cheerful outlook for the scholars in the "College house," and one that no doubt had a salutary effect upon their morals.

II

It may have been the very gloom of these surroundings that helped to throw the College into a great uproar, in

Rector Cutler's second year. There had been a student uprising at Saybrook over the boarding accommodations and the teaching; the Wethersfield group had raised a rumpus over Sir Johnson; in 1721 the entire student body rose in its wrath over the Commons. There seems to have been trouble, from the first, to secure a competent steward and a cook for the College kitchen. In Cutler's first year as Rector the Trustees had "discoursed" with Captain John Munson, the middle-aged steward, over the hiring of a cook. The Widow Hannah Beecher had been offered the place as "standing cook," and the Trustees had voted that "fresh meat be provided for the Schollars Dinner 3 times a Week." But this did not solve the difficulty. Within the year the students were muttering discontents over the food at the long tables in the hall of the College house. Jonathan Edwards was a resident postgraduate student at this time, and a letter to his father tells the story. Suddenly, in February, 1721, the entire undergraduate body as one man agreed to boycott the Commons of Captain Munson and put themselves under bonds of fifteen shillings apiece to stand by each other. When Munson put on the food no one appeared to eat it. Rector Cutler sent for Trustees Andrew and Russel, and haled the undergraduate body into his presence, where he laid down the law with such firmness that he "affrighted the scholars that they unanimously agreed to come into commons again." But this did not end the matter. The students worked themselves up into a great state of rebellion. They committed "some monstrous impieties, and acts of immorality," says Edwards. Especially prominent among these latter crimes were the stealings of "hens, geese, turkies, piggs, meat, wood, &c—unseasonable nightwalking, breaking people's windows, playing at cards, cursing, swearing, and damning, and using all manner of ill language, which never were at such a pitch in the Colledge as they are now." Rector Cutler finally called a Trustees' meeting and expelled some of the ring-leaders.

The affair must have made a considerable stir in the quiet provincial village, where there was not much excite-ment for the College lads except what they could make for themselves. The New Haven townspeople had never recovered from the financial ruin of the famous Dela-ware enterprises, and, as had happened at Saybrook, had never succeeded in carrying out the great trading ambitions of the settlers. The long effort to bring trade to the port, which at one time nearly became successful, had now ebbed again, so that there were now but two coasting vessels and a West Indiaman in the harbor, besides a handful of smaller craft. The people, as we have seen, were all farmers or small merchants and artisans, though there was a doctor (one Mather) living on lower Elm Street. There were no lawyers in those artless days, and the magistrates and justices and judges had to be selected for common sense and what smattering of English common law and knowledge of the Assembly's acts they could muster.

Yet these primitive New Englanders managed to keep abreast of the fashions of the day, so far as they could by the occasional voyages to Boston of that Captain Browne's "Speedwell" which we have heard of on previous pages. The New Haven folks' relations to this seafaring Captain have recently come to light in the pages of his old account book. These were largely in the nature of barter, the towns-people loading Captain Browne's little vessel with wheat and flour from the East Rock mill; corn, rye, and oats from the many farms; pork and bacon, a little beef, and much fresh butter; peas and beans, nuts, beeswax and honey, and sometimes some eggs (a basket or two of which occasion-ally went on to that Madam Knight whom we have seen visiting friends in New Haven). Numerous furs were in these consignments, and there were usually some bales of flax or wool sent on, with maybe some linen or worsted cloths, roughly manufactured at Tutor Johnson's father's place at Guilford, or by the several "clothiers" living in New Haven. Treasurer Alling had been a purchaser, as we have seen, for the Saybrook establishment from Captain Browne, and he, as well as all of the prominent people in the town, used the Captain's services.

Something of the flavor of these ancient Yale days comes back to us in the items which Captain Browne set down in his old account book. He brings back to the village from the Boston emporium such things as silver spoons, silver shoe-buckles, silk handkerchiefs, ivory combs, brass kettles, writing paper, silver chains, gauze fans, jackknives, whalebone for the ladies, pins, gloves, sugar, wineglasses, ribbon, green wines, tankards, hornbooks for the small people, rum, felt hats for the boys, looking-glasses, broadcloth suits for the gentlemen, periwigs, and castor hats of rabbit's fur. The Derby minister, Rev. Joseph Moss, but recently assisting in the College teaching, is a good purchaser from Captain Browne. He buys, so the ancient account book shows, 6,000 nails for his parsonage, a pint of wine, the usual minister's broadcloth coat and black crêpe gown, a Bible, a "great journal," a barrel of gunpowder, 200 pounds of small shot, half a grindstone, a brass kettle costing £5 3s., some glass bottles, a glass inkhorn, a trunk with drawers in it, Madeira wines, a small book called "The Clerk's Guide" (which he needed in order to brush up for his duties as Town Clerk of Derby), and Henry Care's "English Liberties," a ponderously-compiled and amazingly dull legal digest. Several stores, in one of which Madam Knight will

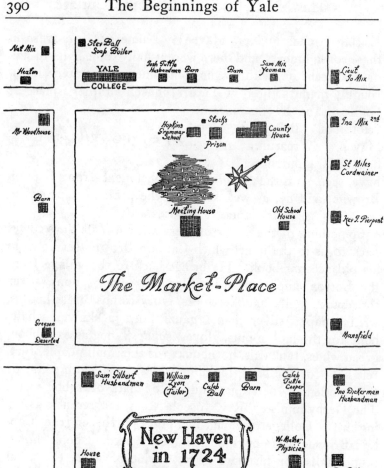

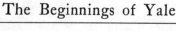

be recalled as observing the country people making their
awkward purchases, were scattered about the New Haven
of this day, where the College scholars on their infrequent
off-afternoons might purchase paper and jackknives.

So that, on the whole, the New Haven folk of this period
lived at least a comfortable life, as Madam Knight found
that they did, and, provincial as it was, not entirely out of

the fashions of Samuel Sewall's Boston. The houses of the more easy-circumstanced of these villagers of Rector Cutler's few New Haven years, were quite comfortable homes. Roaring log fires heated them and homemade "white-amber" candles and imported whale-oil lanterns lighted them. Each house of the better class had its heavy homemade furniture, with here and there an imported Jacobean chair or Dutch table, its pewter mugs and platters and tankards, its warming pans for cold winter nights, and its costly brass kettles. There were no carpets or rugs, to be sure, but the thick oak-slab floors were properly sanded. The great kitchen fireplace, with its yawning cavern where the great kettles and little kettles swung from cranes, was the center of the family life. Here the townsfolk had their neighborly gossip and wines of evenings, and here the occasional dropper-in among the older men had his pipe of tobacco. Rough woolen suits, worsted stockings, broad-brimmed fur or felt hats, low shoes and buckles, and great capes, were the usual garments, except on gala occasions, of the men. The women of the little village kept Captain Browne busy picking out fans, and thimbles, and silver chains, and rings and lockets for them in the Boston market.

But neither the men nor the women appear to have bought many books. Bibles and hornbooks were brought on in plenty, some of them "painted" (with rough-colored pictures). And primers come for the children. But of general literature, as was the case a generation earlier, there appears to have been a great dearth in Captain Browne's accounts. John Flavel's "Husbandry Spiritualized" (a famous English Presbyterian book of the day) is imported by one trader; an old salt ventures to invest in "The Mariner's Compass"; the "Wit's Cabinet, a Companion for Gentlemen and Ladies," a highly moral compilation (containing much useful information on palmistry and dreams), appear among the items; some "Latin books" are bought by Samuel Mix, probably for his boy of eleven; a copy of Bunyan's immortal book is ordered, and "The Experienced Secretary."

If the literary taste of New Haven from 1707 to 1716,—the period covered by Captain Browne's entries,— is to be judged by them, I imagine that very little may be said for it. But Connecticut folk generally, as we have seen, were not readers, and, besides the Scriptures, their psalm books and occasional copies of "sarmons" published by the great men of the Boston pulpits and now and then of London, about define their intellectual efforts. It was left to the ministers in charge of the new College, and to the ambitious scholars under them, to undertake the more exalted flights in the ancient languages and the Scriptural commentaries that comprised the cultivated provincial's education of the day.

Captain Browne's Boston purchases of Bibles, catechisms, and hornbooks for his New Haven patrons, was, I fancy, more significant of the church situation in the Colony at this time than might appear on the surface of things.

For, in spite of Cotton Mather's flowery introduction of the Connecticut folk to Governor Yale, the religious condition among them was again at that low ebb which was the case when James Pierpont was called to John Davenport's pulpit. We have seen how General Assembly and Town Court orders had been passed to stem this religious decline in Pierpont's day, and how the Collegiate School had been projected by Pierpont for the same general purpose as well as for other reasons. We have seen how that School had been given a Congregational creed in the Saybrook Platform, through Pierpont's influence, and how that Platform had been expected to bring order out of chaos in the inter-relations of the churches. All of these enterprises had formed themselves about the common desire of the ministers and lay leaders of the Colony, to hold Connecticut steadfast to the traditional theology and the stern morals that were disappearing in Massachusetts.

But matters had not turned out that way. The disturbing conditions of Queen Anne's War had reacted on the religious state of the people, and had brought it, by 1714,—in spite of the Saybrook Platform,—to so low a pass that legislative action had again been necessary. And so, in that year, the Assembly had requested the Colony ministers to report on the religious situation among their congregations. The receipt of a lugubriously gloomy reply had resulted, the next year, in a blanket act by the Assembly, "for the preventing of such decays in religion." This Act had again demanded the strict enforcement of the old and neglected laws regarding primary education, for the "better observation" of the Sabbath, and against "lying," "swearing," "tippling and drunkenness." And it emphatically ordered that the various town officers should "make diligent inquiry of all householders, how they are stored with bibles." If "any such householder be found without one bible," proceeded this statute, "then the selectman shall warn the said householder forthwith to procure one," to the end that "all families be furnished with a suitable number of orthodox catechisms, and other good books of practical godliness," with special reference to their preparation of their readers for "that great duty, the Lord's supper."

So, just before the Saybrook Collegiate School had become Yale College at New Haven, we find that there had been a Colony-wide effort on the part of the ministers and legislators to bring the religious state of the people back to that orthodoxy from which Massachusetts was rapidly slipping and to the stern moral conduct of their forefathers, and that Bibles and catechisms and hornbooks for the children had been purchased in numbers.

Nor had this effort to regain the religious plane of an earlier day stopped there. One of the chief reasons for the continued attention by the Assembly during these years to the affairs of the Collegiate School had been that upon that institution the Colony leaders had based their chief hopes for a new generation of orthodox religious leaders, both in the pulpit and public life. I do not doubt that Governor Saltonstall, who was one of the most vigorously devout men of the day, had interested himself in the School's affairs very largely for this reason. As we have seen, though not a Trustee, he had even been willing to assume the mantle of James Pierpont's constructive leadership of it. He had succeeded in this. The new Yale College hall now stood in all its cerulean glory among the ancient trees across the lane from the Market-place upper corner. All of the formerly divided groups of scholars were housed in it. He had used his official authority to bring over the Saybrook books. The Rev. Timothy Cutler, young and ambitious, and renowned for his scholarship and his preaching, had finally been chosen by the Trustees for its Rector. Governor Saltonstall no doubt believed that his leadership in the affairs of Yale College had finally brought forth the dawn of a new day. And the Trustees of that college, comfortable in their thoughts of the reëstablished school under Rector Cutler, may well have had the same hopefulness, and have proceeded again to attend to their congregations' spiritual needs without worry over the School for the first time in the history of their ambitious undertaking. To them, the great London book collection now properly set forth upon the shelves of the new Yale Library was to be the start of a new intellectual interest in the orthodox

support of their own devoutly-accepted Calvinism.   Yale
College, under Timothy Cutler, was to become, in truth, to
the Connecticut of the 18th Century, what Harvard College
had been to New England in the 17th.

CHAPTER XI

THE RESULT OF THE BOOKS

I

UT as often happens in this world of ours, things do not always turn out as we have planned. Though affairs, religiously speaking, settled down into more or less the old channel a few years later, a flurry now came on which must have astonished the good Congregational Trustees of the now re-established College and produced a great commotion generally.

Curiously enough, this flurry was the direct result of the receipt of Jeremiah Dummer's great English library, now stored in the new College hall.

These books had now been in the possession of the College for six years. Yet they had hardly been opened, so aloof from the currents of the modern intellectual world that was growing up in England were the Connecticut leaders of this day. And this is a curious thing. For among the Dummer books were the published products of the most progressive thinking of the times, at least so far as concerned theology and science,—the two all-embracing intellectual interests of the period. Stored in a remote house in Saybrook, there had been no effort to make use of them until the Trustees had happened to think of them and request their removal to New Haven. They had been received, and shelved, and that had been the end of them. According to

Tutor Johnson, they had become as if they were not, to the Colony generally and to the College in particular. The black-gowned ministers in charge of them had doubtless viewed with pride their imposing array on the Saybrook parsonage's bookshelves. With a gratified knowledge that the great Calvinistic authorities were well represented, the Trustees had passed over the light frivolities of Dick Steele, the ponderous volumes of current English Episcopalian theology, and the unintelligible tomes of the hardly known Isaac Newton, and had returned to their own small collections of Latin commentaries and mediæval Calvinistic writers, quite satisfied about them.

But, as it had happened, a small group of students and young graduates had undertaken a somewhat surreptitious examination of these books that the Trustees did not bother over. These students were Jared Eliot, 1706, now settled at Killingworth; John Hart, 1703, of East Guilford; Samuel Whittlesey, 1705, of Wallingford; James Wetmore, of North Haven, Daniel Browne and Samuel Johnson, the two Yale College Tutors, all three of the Class of 1714. Going over to Saybrook to read the books, and then to the new College library in New Haven, this little group of men,—all Congregational ministers,—were to find themselves, shortly after 1720, arriving at an intellectual and religious point to which *Jared Eliot* it had hardly been expected by the devout Trustees that the books would bring anybody. It will serve our purpose best to follow what now occurred in the case of Tutor Johnson, who has left us the only account we have of what happened.

We have some time since found this young gentleman studying some of these volumes privately in his lodgings. Poring over them under his flickering candle of evenings after his college day's labors were over, young Johnson seems to have immersed himself in the study of them. Circumscribed, as he had been, by the limits of the education meted out to the Collegiate School youths at Saybrook, this young scholar was now making up for lost time with a vengeance. He had, so he says, been graduated from Saybrook with a very large conceit of his intellectual attainments. He had drawn up an elaborate system "of all the parts of learning within his reach," and considered himself a learned man. But his first plunge into Sir Isaac Newton had shattered this high opinion of himself, and, with an intellectual energy that came from the needs of his starved mind, he had reconstructed his notions of the universe and therefore his theology. He seemed to himself, immediately this great horizon dawned upon him, "suddenly emerging out of the glimmer of twilight into the full sunshine of open day."

Something of the same sort had now happened to Johnson's classmate, Daniel Browne. When the two friends were brought together as the first Yale College Tutors, they threw themselves enthusiastically into the new learning. To the old hidebound Collegiate School curriculum of Dr. Ames and the classics and Rector Pierson's primitive "Physicks," they now added lectures to the Seniors in Locke and Newton, with the books of these new philosophers on their tables to read from. "Till now," writes Johnson's biographer, "the Ptolemaic system of the world was as strongly believed as the holy scriptures; but they soon were able to overthrow it, and to establish on its ruins the doctrines of Copernicus." For some reason or other, the reverend Trustees appear not to have realized this tremendous departure from their School's teachings. If they did, they overlooked it as harmless. But the students received the new learning with alacrity and in one signal instance, at least (in Jonathan Edwards' case), it was to produce important results for an even wider audience than New Haven.

II

And there was another element in the situation that was now forming at the College among this group of young Congregational ministers. We have seen how Samuel Johnson, reading a chance English prayer book at his home in Guilford as a young boy, had come to feel sympathetic toward the Church of England ritual and discipline. Timothy Cutler, arriving at Stratford in 1709, had found several of the leaders in that town leaning toward the Church of England, as the result of the founding of an Episcopal Church there by the missionary Muirson. From later developments, it would appear that Cutler felt himself moving in that heretical direction as time passed, and that the opportunity to leave the Congregational pulpit that the Yale College Rectorship offered him, as well as to read the Dummer books, had something to do with his acceptance. However that may be, these young men (now, with Daniel Browne, the three resident heads of Yale College) were by 1720, at the latest, experiencing the first throes of a seismic intellectual revulsion from the traditional Calvinism of the institution, and of the Connecticut Colony itself, and dimly foreseeing a change of heart toward the Church of England.

I suppose that this change was an extremely important personal matter for that early day in the 18th Century. If it came about very gradually among this small group of scholars, it is certainly true that it resulted, to a very large extent, from their reading of the contemporaneous English divines whose heretical books the Trustees had unwittingly placed on the College library shelves. Little did the contented Trustees, attending to their own flocks' Calvinistic orthodoxy, remote from New Haven, know of this surreptitious proceeding. Into their Garden of Eden, planted with sound Calvinistic vegetation for the orthodox consumption of their Rector and Tutors, the serpent of the Church of England had appeared, and was tempting their Adam to eat of the Tree of Knowledge. Jeremiah Dummer's report of old Governor Yale's offhand notion that a little more learning might bring Puritan Connecticut into the fold of that mother Church which his own career had so adorned, was not so far from a possibility as it might have seemed to the Trustees on hearing of it. And Dummer had lost no chance to plant that tree. The long-winded Barrow, Bishop Patrick, the rather bigoted Dr. Robert South, Bishop Sharp, Dean Sherlock of St. Paul's, Whitby the Arminian, and Archbishop Tillotson,—the great English Churchmen of the decade just passed,—were all on the shelves in the new College hall, and their heretical doctrines open to him who ran. And, as this small group of Congregational ministers read them, their Congregationalism gradually slipped off, and Episcopal robes fell upon their shoulders.

III

The beginnings of Episcopacy in Connecticut had been made some eighteen years before this time, when, as we have seen, the London Society for the Propagation of the Gospel in Foreign Parts had been chartered by William and Mary, and an American missionary sent over in the person of George Keith, the former Quaker. Keith had found the Connecticut of that time a unanimously "dissenting" community. Israel Chauncy's little town of Stratford, however, shortly afterwards had an Episcopal group, and, when the New York Church of England leaders sent one Colonel Heathcote in 1706 on a missionary journey along Long

Island Sound, he had found a hospitable welcome there among them. The orthodox Congregational people, however, fought off further Episcopal efforts. Matters came to such a climax that a staunch deacon of the Stratford council stood out in the public highway and forbade entrance to the Episcopal services, threatening all who went with fines of five pounds. The natural result of such opposition as this was a wave of Church of England interest all through Fairfield County. The immediate successor to old Mr. Chauncy had gone over to the Church. He had been dismissed and young Timothy Cutler, fresh from Boston and highly recommended by the Boston orthodox ministers for his abilities, had been called to that pulpit. In the meantime the Assembly had passed their Act of Toleration, after having tied down the Colony to the Congregational creed and loosely organized the churches in the Saybrook Platform. From that moment Episcopacy advanced steadily and unobtrusively throughout the coast towns, until its famous irruption took place in the very center of the Colony College itself that had been founded for the purpose of carrying on the traditional Congregationalism.

For the result of the private reading of the Dummer books by the small group of Collegiate School graduates whom I have mentioned, had been a revulsion of sentiment among them against the old theology and church organization and toward the ancient Church of England. The new Rector had joined this group and become its leader. But the change on their part was gradual. Rector Cutler, preaching to the General Assembly in October, 1719, was at that time so far from his final opinions that his sermons pleased the most conservative of the Colony leaders and received the unusual compliment of printing. It was through his suggestion, probably, that the Yale College scholars were given regular sittings in the New Haven Meeting-house, where they occupied "the northeast half of the fore gallery" and annually paid a shilling apiece to hear the Rev. Joseph Noyes preach.[1] Throughout the next two years there was no indication, so far as the public and the Trustees knew, of any coming difficulties. But these were brewing.

Tutor Samuel Johnson had resigned his office at the close of Rector Cutler's first year to become the minister of the West Haven Congregational Church. His diary shows that he had scruples over the method of ordination which he received, but that he accepted the situation, near-Episcopalian as he was. His classmate, James Wetmore, had a year before become the North Haven minister. He, also, had shown a disposition not to fall in with the Saybrook Platform method of ordination, and he appears not to have been ordained in the now customary Congregational way.

The coming storm was thus rising. And we find, from Samuel Johnson's manuscript account of these days, that this was due to the following circumstances, of which a hint or two may have been given above. As the small group of readers of the new books had discussed them from time to time, the impression had been growing on them that there was but little resemblance to the Primitive Church in Connecticut Congregationalism. The more they read in the English divines that Dummer had seen to it were included in the College library, the more these young Congregationalists found themselves losing faith in the theology and church methods of their older contemporaries. When they had arrived at this disturbing state of mind (for it should be realized how serious a matter it was in those days for established young Congregational ministers, with their

---

[1] This practice was maintained until the controversy between the two Congregational factions in the "Great Awakening" resulted in Rector Clap's establishment of a separate Yale College Church, which has continued to the present day.

careers before them, to change their church views) they seem
to have set about a rigid reëxamination of the entire subject.
Gurdon Saltonstall, when a young man, had pursued this
same course and come out a "rigid" Calvinist. But Johnson, Cutler, Wetmore, and Browne, with their friends Hart,
Eliot, and Whittlesey to a lesser degree, went through the
process and came out Episcopalians. They reread the traditional Calvinists, such as Hoadly and Calamy, and
they then reread King's "Inquiry" and Slater's "Original
Draught," and Potter's "Church Government,"—all in the
College library. And Samuel Johnson as a kind of committee of one restudied the early Church fathers in the original
tongues and reported his results. The upshot of this intellectual upheaval was the definite opinion on the part of these
young men that the Episcopal Church was the lineal descendant of the Apostles, that the priesthood could only
come down through the Bishops and head of the Church,
and that ordination was unlawful unless given by "a Bishop
at the head of the Presbytery." Shortly after this great decision, young Johnson rode over to Stratford, where one
George Pigot had been settled as the Episcopal clergyman,
talked matters over with him and invited him to meet him
and his friends in the College library at New Haven. The
group which we have named met Pigot there, and listened to
his arguments for Episcopacy. While doing no more than
declaring their keen interest in his statements, they let him
understand (as would appear from the report that Pigot at
once sent to England) that they were prepared to be ordained in that Church as soon as they could find that "they
will be supported at home."

IV

This was sometime in June, 1722. The news of it must
have leaked out, for rumors at once began to spread that

there were heretical tendencies cropping out in the new Yale College. One Joseph Morgan, traveling through the Colony, hurriedly wrote to Cotton Mather about it, reporting that "Arminian books are cried up in Yale College for eloquence and learning, and Calvinism despised for the contrary; and none have the courage to see it redressed." Samuel Johnson had by this time become famous for the eloquence with which he conducted the little Congregational church services in West Haven. So famous had become his prayers that large numbers of devout Congregationalists were attending his Sabbath-day meetings to hear them. It is a bit amusing to read in Johnson's own account of these days that these prayers were not his own, and extemporaneous as was the custom of the day, but were taken from the Church of England ritual.

The rumors which had been flying about concerning the orthodoxy of the College heads must have come to the attention of the Trustees at about this time, as to Governor Saltonstall. Added to the local talk there had come a report from Boston that a money collection was going forward there to build a Church of England house of worship, and that Rector Cutler was expected to be its first clergyman. The Trustees must have been worried, and that worry must have been brought to a head when, closing his Commencement prayer that September, Rector Cutler boldly ended with the well-known Episcopal supplication, *"And let all the people say, Amen."*

Immediately after this ceremony, the Trustees met in the College library.

That they were mystified and astounded by the reports and by Rector Cutler's astonishing departure from tradition goes without saying. And their agitation could hardly have been diminished by the number of people who, it is said, had come to New Haven for the occasion "expecting some strange occurrences." This meeting of the Trustees had been asked, it seems, by Rector Cutler and Tutor Browne, and the others in the group of men who had been coming around to the Episcopalian viewpoint. Rector Cutler introduced Johnson and Browne, Wetmore, Hart, Eliot, and Whittlesey to the Trustees and to the large number of Colony ministers who also crowded into the room. The question was at once propounded by these young men, led by Cutler and Johnson, whether the Connecticut method of ordination was a lawful one, and the announcement made that all of them were considering the matter of going over to the Church of England. The astonished Trustees questioned each of the group in turn as to their views on this suddenly-proposed proceeding, and, instead of accepting the situation (as possibly the applicants had hoped), "expressed the utmost grief and concern." The declaration of views of the young heretics was demanded in writing. This was promptly given, all signing it. The Trustees ordered a special meeting for a month later, gave the young men the opportunity in the meanwhile to change their opinions, and adjourned the meeting, no doubt in the midst of the greatest excitement that they and the Congregational ministers of the Colony present had ever experienced.

Events now came on with a rush.

It is a famous story how Governor Saltonstall, unwilling to believe that a proper statement of the Calvinistic principles to the seceding young ministers would not land them, as it had landed him, on the traditional side, did not wait for this adjourned Trustees' meeting, but called a public debate, with himself as moderator, at which the difficulty could be threshed out; how, at this debate, held in the College library on October 16, Rector Cutler, Johnson, and Wetmore led the argument for the Church of England, and how the Trustees, floundering in unknown waters, were quite

Rector Cutler and the Trustees

unable to meet the standard Episcopal arguments regarding Timothy's "evident superintendency of the clergy" at Ephesus, "of the Angels in the seven churches of Asia," etc. Faced by Samuel Johnson's glib knowledge of all the arguments of the great English divines in the books stacked on the library shelves about them, the astounded Trustees could not meet him at all in his statements that "they must either receive Episcopacy or reject infant baptism and the first day sabbath." It would appear that all the unfortunately-ignorant Trustees could do, met as they were by the words out of the very books they had so unwittingly placed on the College shelves, was to lose their tempers. This they promptly did, no doubt the fiery and orthodox John Davenport leading in the fray. Nothing but "mere rhetorical declamation" coming from the confused Trustees, and "irritating remarks" (which probably young Johnson replied to as heatedly), Governor Saltonstall had to close the debate, with none of the satisfactory results he had hoped from it.

And now the fat was in the fire. The Collegiate School had been founded to be a bulwark against Satan, "wherein youth may be instructed in the arts and sciences, who through the blessing of Almighty God may be fitted for public employment both in church and civil state." It had been, in Cotton Mather's phrases to Elihu Yale, "the seminary from whence they expect the supply of all their synagogues." It had been founded to bring up the oncoming generations of Connecticut youths in the traditional Calvinistic orthodoxy of the settlers. And now, its Rector and chief Tutor had been found to be Episcopalians, and undoubtedly to have been teaching the principles of that ancient heresy to the Colony youth, abetted by a group of its most distinguished recent graduates in the neighboring pulpits. Connecticut orthodoxy had escaped the Scylla of Harvard Latitudinarianism only to crash upon the Charybdis of Episcopacy.

V

How the Trustees took this situation may well be imagined. As President Woolsey later said, "I suppose that greater alarm would scarcely be awakened now if the Theological Faculty of the College were to declare for the Church of Rome, avow their belief in Transubstantiation and pray to the Virgin Mary."

The incident was followed by a small avalanche of letters from the Trustees to their old Boston friends who had supported them in the founding of the Collegiate School. Joseph Webb, of Fairfield, describing how prominent men had become involved in the affair, wrote to Cotton Mather: "It is a very dark day with us; and we need pity, prayer, and counsel." John Davenport and Stephen Buckingham wrote to their Boston friends of the "dark Providence" hanging over Connecticut. It had been a glorious past that the Colony College had had, they said in this joint epistle. "But who could have conjectured that its name, being raised to *Collegian Yalense* from a *Gymnasium Saybrookense*, it should groan out Ichabod, in about three years and a half under its second rector so unlike the first, by an unhappy election, set over it." "In that Rectors election or confirmation or any act relating to him the senior subscriber hereof . . . never came," devoutly thanks John Davenport. And "how our fountain, hoped to have been and continued the repository of truth and reserve of pure and sound principles, doctrine, and education—shows itself in so little a time so corrupt." Old Moses Noyes, writing later to Judge Sewall, puts the case of the astonished orthodox Trustees even more strongly to that original framer of its charter. It had all happened because no leader had followed James Pierpont, thinks Noyes (in which he was doubtless right), and now the simple Colony College, which never should have been set up at a metropolis like New Haven, where troubles of this sort were likely to occur, was in a bad way. "It was an awful stroke of Providence," writes the aged minister at Lyme, "in taking away Mr. Pierpont, . . . and it is much more afflictive because our young men are feared to be infected with Arminian and Prelatical notions. So that it is difficult to supply his place. It was a wrong step, when the Trustees, by the assistance of great men [here a fine rap at Governor Saltonstall] removed the College at Saybrook, and a worse, when they put in Mr. Cutler for Rector. The first movers for a College in Connecticut alledged this as a reason, because the College at Cambridge was under the Tutorage of Latitudinarians; but how well they have mended the event sadly manifests. But God is only wise, and will produce glory to his name out of the weaknesses and follies of men."

Holding these views, the action of the Trustees was prompt and did not wait for the scheduled adjourned meeting.

The day after the great public debate, they "excused" Rector Cutler "from all further service as Rector of Yale-College," accepted Tutor Browne's resignation, voted that all future Rectors and Tutors should accept the Saybrook Confession, and "particularly give satisfaction of the soundness of their faith in opposition to Arminian and prelatical corruptions or any other of dangerous consequences to the purity and peace of our churches," and elected two new Tutors, James Pierpont, the son of the former Collegiate School leader and a graduate of 1718, and William Smith, of 1719, both "staunch Calvinists" of the orthodox type.

Rector Cutler, Tutor Browne, and Tutor Samuel Johnson had alone stood the public test of their new faith before Governor Saltonstall, though Reverend Wetmore was to join them afterwards. Rev. John Hart of East Guilford meekly returned to the Congregational fold, and was to finish out his short life there, in good standing in the Colony churches. Samuel Whittlesey went back, chastened in spirit, to his Wallingford congregation, repentant of his close approach to apostasy, to live a useful life as a good Congregational minister, and publish a number of orthodox sermons of no particular consequence thereafter. Jared Eliot of Killingworth was to become, as we have seen, "the first physician of his day," and a scientific man of international reputation.

Rector Cutler, Samuel Johnson, Daniel Browne, and James Wetmore, however, went over to the Church of England.

Samuel Johnson made some effort to have his West Haven congregation go over with him to the Church, but without success. On November 5, he sailed from Boston with Timothy Cutler and Daniel Browne for London, where he received degrees at Oxford and Cambridge, and was appointed an Episcopal missionary. Returning to Connecticut on that errand, he became the first settled Episcopal clergyman in the Colony, came to know that charmingly-visionary Bishop Berkeley of Rhode Island and was the cause of that eminent clergyman's great gift to Yale (in the curious belief that that College might become Episcopalian). Johnson afterwards was elected the first President of King's (later Columbia) College at New York, and later in life returned to Stratford, where he died in his seventy-sixth year, one of the most noted scholars of his day, its leading American Episcopalian, and one of its best citizens.

As for the other two heretics, Daniel Browne fell sick from smallpox on his journey to England and died there, while Rector Cutler was properly ordained in the Church of England, and returned to New England, settling at Boston, where he lived a long life as

Daniel Browne Jun

Rector of Christ Church, embroiled in a steady series of difficulties with Harvard and the Congregational churches of the town.

There has been a tradition that this defection of Timothy Cutler and his friends was but a part of a much broader movement to turn Connecticut into a Church of England community. Such a scheme, so the story goes, had been broached among several "gentlemen of considerable character among the clergy." Awaiting the outcome of the Cutler-Johnson secession, these plotters had made "no open profession," and now, when the College had promptly stamped it out and "they saw that the people would not hear them, but dismissed them from their service, they were glad to conceal their former purposes and to continue in their respective places." But I imagine that this rather inglorious story was hardly within the facts. The Episcopalian flurry of 1722 was a personal matter with the small group of students of the new College books, and had no Colony-wide importance. A handful of Connecticut Congregational ministers, indeed, became Church of England clergymen,—one of them the Rev. Samuel Seabury, father of the future Episcopal Bishop of that name and Yale graduate of 1748,—but this was a number of years later.

While the episode is not exactly within the limits of these chronicles of Yale's beginnings, the Church of England upheaval in the College in 1722 had a little later development, brief reference to which in this place will serve to tie up the threads of the famous Cutler affair. When the first Episcopal Church was established in New Haven in 1750, there was a great local to-do. President Clap took drastic action. Two Yale students, sons of the minister, were refused permission to attend their father's Church services. Samuel Johnson, then President of the "intended College at New York," took up the gauntlet for the Episcopalian students of his old Connecticut Colony. Writing a long letter to President Clap of Yale, and thanking him for his congratulations upon his own election to King's College, this first Connecticut Church of England leader agreed "to hold a good correspondence not only as Colleges but as Christians," providing the New Haven people would "act on the same equitable, catholic, and Christian principles as we unanimously propose to act upon," by which he meant that Yale College should be free to Episcopalians. "I am prodigiously mistaken," writes Johnson, "if you did not tell me it was an allowed and settled rule with you heretofore." Whereupon Yale's old Tutor proceeds to attack Yale College for excluding "the people of the Church belonging to this Colony from having the benefit of Public education in your College." "Your argument," he writes, "that it is inconsistent with the original design of the founders, which was only to provide ministers for your churches," is untenable. Among the "founders," says Johnson, must be included "the principal benefactors." And he mentions "Mr. Yale," well known to have been a famous Church of England pillar, and Bishop Berkeley, whose purpose he understood to be a "catholic" one in giving his great donation. This Johnson himself had secured, though "You," he says to President Clap, "did not think fit to do me this justice in your History of the College, though humbly suggested." Yale College should not be restricted to Congregationalists. "For God's sake," writes the President of King's College to the President of Yale, "do not be so severe to carry matters to this pass." But President Clap was obdurate. A separate College church was established, and the College laws against attending outside services were rigidly enforced. It was not until a century more had passed that Episcopalian students of Yale were allowed full liberty to attend their own Church services.

Tutor
Jonathan
Edwards

CHAPTER XII

THE END OF AN ERA

I

HE Episcopalian irruption having
quieted down, and Yale College again
under theologically-trustworthy Tutors,
the Trustees proceeded again to make
a new start.

We will recall that the Colony
General Assembly, in the Charter of
1701, had not incorporated the Colle-
giate School, partly because it questioned its power to do
so. Even if the Assembly had felt that it had such a power,
it would not have exercised it. The general inclination of
the Colony leaders was to keep out of sight so far as Old

England was concerned, and to enjoy the privileges they had plucked from the burning and which less fortunate Massachusetts had been deprived of. But the terms of that original document had been ambiguous in language in some places and troublesome in practice in others. Not being incorporated, the Trustees had all along been looked upon by the legislators as mere trustees or "partners" in a private enterprise of general Colony interest. This had been productive of a continued paternal interference on the part of the General Assembly. It had resulted in the acts of the Trustees becoming matters for public revision. As the votes of mere private trustees, these acts had been considered illegal (properly, so we are told on good modern legal authority), unless they were unanimously voted.

We have seen how this legal situation had been a stumbling-block in the settlement of the Collegiate School site, concerning which there had at no time been unanimous action. The Trustees had found it necessary to sign in a body all of the minutes of each meeting. If any of the Trustees were absent from a meeting, it had been considered necessary to send around that paper for their signatures. A Trustee, apparently, could not resign. Nor could an inactive Trustee be succeeded by a more helpful one. The result of this had been that the College had been saddled all these years with old Samuel Mather of Windsor, sick abed, at no time in touch with affairs, apparently not the least interested, of failing mind in his old age, and never at any meeting.

At this juncture Governor Saltonstall was again called to the College's aid. An "Act in explanation of the Addition to the Act for erecting a Collegiate School," was drawn up by him to meet these troubles and passed by the Assembly. It provided that a Trustee might resign or be succeeded by another if incapacitated; that seven of the Trustees should constitute a quorum, and that thirty years instead of forty was to be the minimum age for a Trustee thereafter. The Rector, who legally had previously been but a servant of the Trustees (though Pierson and Andrew had been original members of the board), was now made a Trustee *ex officio*. Armed with this new power, old Samuel Mather was promptly ousted from his place, and the Trustees began proceedings to find some proper minister who would accept the Reverend Cutler's vacant Rectorship. No eligible man appeared on the horizon, however, and for the next four years the College continued without a permanent head, Samuel Andrew again officiating at Commencements, though apparently not with his former title *pro tem*.

II

Just how the College managed, in those four years, to get along as an educational institution, does not clearly appear from the ancient records. Young Pierpont and Smith continued as the only two resident officers until 1724, when their places were taken by Robert Treat, of Milford, grandson of old Governor Treat of Andros' times, and by Jonathan Edwards, both of them well-known subscribers to the Saybrook Confession.

This latter young scholar, the most brilliant Yale College graduate of his time and in due course to become the most distinguished name in the intellectual life of his generation, had remained in New Haven for two years after his graduation in 1720, studying theology under the Rev. Mr. Noyes and by himself. He had then preached for a while to a dissenting Presbyterian congregation in New York, and had then returned to his father's house near Elisha Williams' farm in Wethersfield for further private study. For a year he had occupied various pulpits about the Colony, and refused the ministry at North Haven left vacant by James Wetmore's apostasy to the Church of England. Accepting the senior Tutorship at Yale College in May, 1724, young Edwards occupied the place for the next two years, when he began that long career at Northampton which is one of the great chapters in American theological history.

During Jonathan Edwards' two years as Tutor at Yale College, the conditions were such that practically the entire responsibility rested upon his shoulders alone. And I fancy that if he had not been just the type of man he was,—tremendously energetic intellectually (he was accustomed, later, to spend thirteen hours a day "in close study"), astonishingly brilliant and as astonishingly capable,—the affairs of Cotton Mather's "dear infant" would have gone wry indeed. But he happened to be that kind of man, and, somehow or other, without a permanent and older head,— the Trustees merely taking turns as visitors,—the Yale College of 1724-1726 not only jogged along under his direction, but very decidedly prospered. When Jonathan Edwards' career as senior Yale Tutor was over, some sixty youths had become scholars at the institution.

New England's future theologian, however, did not altogether relish his routine labors as the spiritual head and fountain of knowledge for this large flock.[1] He was in the first phase of that intellectual development which later was to make him famous. He had, as we have seen, had much the same experience in reading the Dummer books as Samuel Johnson, though with opposite results. Reading Locke's "Human Understanding," in the College library, we are told he had found "a far higher pleasure in the perusal of its pages, than the most greedy miser finds, when

[1] Anson Phelps Stokes has gathered what is known of Edwards' Yale career in a chapter of his "Memorials of Eminent Yale Men," published by the Yale University Press in 1914.

gathering up handfuls of silver and gold, from some newly discovered treasure." Already a thinker and incipient philosopher, Jonathan Edwards appears to have found his life *Jonathan Edwards.* among the Yale students somewhat irksome. He writes in his journal, June 6, 1724, at the end of his first week as Tutor: "This Week has been a remarkable Week with me with Respect to Despondencies, Fears, Perplexities, Multitudes of Cares and Distractions of Mind; being the Week I came hither to New-Haven, in order to entrance upon the Office of Tutor of the College. I have now abundant Reason to be convinced of the Troublesomeness and Vexation of the World, and that it never will be another Kind of World."

We have some interesting records of the life of these youths under Sir Edwards. That it was a period of strong religious fervor for the most of them, would have been true, doubtless, had not a Jonathan Edwards been their senior Tutor. It was just before the first warnings of the coming great revival, in which the Yale College students were to be stirred up by a fellow scholar, a religious enthusiast named David Ferris, and which was to be led by Jonathan Edwards himself. The pendulum, that had swung toward irreligion for the past fifty years, was swinging back again. But there were other reasons for this, as well. The Colony had been visited by a disastrous plague of smallpox only three years before; the ravages which this had made had sobered people considerably. And the Trustees themselves had brought a new religious strength to the institution by forcing the two previous Tutors publicly to accept the Colony creed. The life of the College, therefore, was strongly tinctured by a renewed rallying to the traditional faith (however religiously inert the Colony folk, generally speaking, were). For the first time since Abraham Pierson's death, it seems to have again had something of the religious fervor of those early days in the Killingworth parsonage.

And so the daily life of the Yale College youths of this day formed itself about the serious business of their souls' welfare. There are daily prayers in the dining hall, at sunrise of mornings and again late in the afternoon. Private prayer meetings in the students' rooms are held, as they were in Samuel Johnson's day, and students mighty at these functions are looked upon with admiration by the less gifted. "Secret prayer" is also a rule of the institution itself. "Every student," so the ancient code reads, "shall exercise himself in reading Holy Scriptures by himself every day," and hold private prayers for "wisdom for himself" in his room of nights. The leading scholar of the Senior Class, under Jonathan Edwards' eye, asks the blessing thrice daily at meals in the common dining hall. On Sabbath days the whole retinue of students parade, in their scholars' gowns, out of the yard of the College house, through the high board fence that we see in Greenwood's drawing of that building, down the footpath across the Market-place to the squat Meeting-house, where they tramp up into the gallery, and listen to Mr. Noyes' none too interesting though orthodox preaching. The highest fine,—twenty shillings,—for any college dereliction at this time fell upon the scholar who found himself *in extremis* on these occasions and, writhing on his bed of pain (as has been the frequent happening ever since), remained away until the flowing gown of the last of his fellows disappeared within the Meeting-house doors. Nor could anyone attend any other religious meeting. All of each Friday and Saturday appears to have been given to a rigorous preparation for the Sabbath-day services. Wollebius' "Theology," and Ames' "Theses and his Medulla,"

The College Yard
from the
President's House

and "the Assembly's Shorter Catechism in Latin" (so the laws operative at the close of those two years go) were recited on week days, and Dr. Ames' "Cases of Conscience" on Sundays. The College year began in the middle of October, and continued to the middle of the following September, when Commencement was held.

There were some obstreperous youngsters among these serious-minded scholars, and College Laws (which had to be copied by all of the Freshmen as soon as they matriculated) were framed to govern them. Jonathan Ashley's manuscript copy of these, laboriously and fearsomely scratched down as a Freshman in 1726, gives a good picture of the student's life of 1726, in addition to what I have narrated. "Every student shall consider ye main end of his study to wit to know God in Jesus Christ and answerably to lead a Godly sober life," sets down this Freshman. "All Students shall avoid ye profanation of God's Holy name Attributes word and ordinances and ye Holy Sabbath, and shall Carefully attend all public assemblies for Divine worship, and shall avoid all appcarances of Contempt and irreverence." There were injunctions against "lying, needless asseverations, foolish garrulings, Chidings, strifes, railings, gesting, uncomely noise, spreading ill rumors, Divulging secrets and all manner of troublesome and offensive behavior." In their relations toward their parents, "as also magistrates, elders, Rector, tutors," they had to keep "Due silence in their presence and not Disorderly gaynsaying them."

Judging from these College laws of 1726, the quiet little village spread about the borders of the new College yard could have seen but little of the scholars. Sequestered in their new College hall, where they roomed, dined, studied, recited, read the Bible, and met at daily prayers, Jonathan Edwards' youthful charges had little time to look about them in the town, or make acquaintances. As at Harvard, and at the English universities on a greater scale, these young gentlemen were supposed to spend their four years of college life strictly attending to business and their souls' salvation, without many vacations or recreation between-times. They were rigidly kept at work except for a half-hour at breakfast, an hour and a half "att noon after Dinner," and "after ye Evening prayer till nine of ye Clock." As we now look back upon those early Yale days, the life was very much that of a latter-day country boarding-school. During the regular College hours each scholar was expected to "studiously redeem His time," and to observe "both ye hours Common for ye students to meet in ye hall and those yt are appointed to his own lectures which he shall Diligently attend." Except when a student's father came to town to see how his son was progressing, none of the College youths were permitted to look in at any of the town taverns; "victualling house or inn to eat or Drink." Picking up stray town acquaintances of a "Dissolute" sort was naturally regulated against, nor were the opportunities present to make it possible. Even when the great public holidays on "Training Days" or at General Court elections, or the "High Days" came around in the none too generous Colony calendar, the Yale students had to keep their rooms, unless special permission came from the Tutors "to go a hunting or fowling." No lights were permitted in the College rooms after nine at night or "before four in ye morning."

All of the scholars of this day were called by their sur-names, "except he be ye son of a noble man or a Knit's Eldest son." Until President Daggett's time, the students were listed in the catalogues according to their family standing, and no doubt received perquisites on that basis.

The curriculum of Jonathan Edwards' period as senior

Tutor was only a little broader than that with which Abraham Pierson had begun the Collegiate School education at Killingworth. We have seen how Tutors Johnson and Browne had introduced something of Newton and Locke in the upper-class studies. This had been a very great advance, and Edwards, who drew upon Locke for his own brilliant philosophy some score of years later, undoubtedly continued them in his classrooms. So that the Seniors and the post-graduate students who came back to study theology, doubtless had access to the Dummer books and had their eyes partly opened to the intellectual activities of England. Rector Pierson's quaint conception of natural laws, and his undoubted faith in the theory that the sun rolled around the earth, were hardly taught to this second generation of Yale students.

Yet much of the antiquated supernatural rubbish of an earlier scholastic time was still taught, and, indeed, remained for many a year the conservative teaching of the College. One Dr. Daniel Turner, Fellow of the Royal Society of London, for some now unknown reason, had asked for an honorary degree from Yale in 1723, and had been granted one,—an M. D.,—the first New England honorary Doctor's degree after Increase Mather's personally-granted Doctor of Laws in 1692 at Harvard. In return for this,—possibly in purchase of it,—Turner had sent over twenty-eight medical books (several of them by himself), and these must have added considerably to the modern character of the College shelves.

I presume, however, that few of the students read Dr. Turner's collection or the library books, as perhaps a number of the Trustees were now quite willing that they should. The emphasis in the four-years course of this day was still on theology and that acquaintance with the classics which would make the original Scriptures and commentaries intelligible. We have mentioned Benjamin Lord's recollection of the books that he studied during the Saybrook Collegiate School period: "Tully and Vergil"; that ancient Latin manual of "Burgersdicius" that was in the Cambridge course of study of that day; Heerebord and "Ramus's Logick"; the "Psalms in Hebrew"; "Ames' Medulla" and "Cases of Conscience." Homer was not in the list, nor much "Composition and Language" (of course no modern tongue), and the mathematics was elementary. Wollebius and the Assembly's Catechism we have also noted. And we have seen how "the utmost that was generally attempted in classical learning was to construe five or six of Tully's Orations, as many books of Vergil, and part only of the Greek Testament, with some chapters of the Hebrew Psalter. Common arithmetic and a little surveying was the *ne plus ultra* of mathematical requirements." To understand Newton and Locke, Rector Cutler had added "Alsted's Geometry and Gassendus' Astronomy." But, otherwise, the chief business of the College was as of yore,— and rigidly theological. For the Freshman year there was logic and elementary Greek and Hebrew (advanced knowledge of Latin being expected); in Sophomore year the same; Junior year was "principally in Physicks"; and "ye fourth year in metaphysicks and mathematicks still carrying on ye former studies." But for all four classes "ye last days of ye week are allowed perpetually for Rhetorick, oratory and Divinity and in teaching both tongues, and Arts [whatever that was], and such Authors,"—doubtless from the Dummer books,—"as shall be approved by ye Rector." The exercise in translating English and Latin and the Hebrew Testament into Greek "before they begin to Recite ye originall tongues," was incessant throughout the three upper-class years. All of the students had to "publickly Repeat sermons. in ye hall," and all had to prepare their "Disputations" and to "Declaim" once in six weeks before the others. Latin was the only language permitted for "schollars in their Chambers and when they are together," and for all classroom work except in English itself. This conversational Latin was probably not very good. Dankers and Sluyter, visiting the more cultivated Harvard thirty years before this, had been scandalized by the bad manners and illiteracy they found there. They went into Harvard Hall and found ten scholars "smoking tobacco in a room which smelt like a tavern." They tried Latin on these youths and were astonished at the sad result. The Yale students of 1726 probably did no better.

For tuition in this Calvinistic stronghold the scholars paid at this time thirty shillings, and for board in the Commons four shillings eight pence a week. At Commencement twenty shillings were collected for the diploma (paid over to the Rector), and twenty more for the expenses of the Commencement dinner,—thus starting a custom which has come down to the present day.

III

Their charter now legally "defined" by the General Assembly, a set of College laws in force to protect the scholars from temptations and theological backslidings, an increased number of scholars in attendance and the Rector's house ready, the Trustees now made a final effort to find a proper person for the permanent Rectorship.

This position had been offered to Timothy Woodbridge immediately after the Cutler fiasco, probably in a final attempt to smooth over the Hartford dissension. But he had declined, though he officiated at the next Commencement as the presiding officer. During the four years that had since passed, it would appear that no Rector *pro tem* (as

had been the case after Pierson's death) had been appointed.
Young Jonathan Edwards seems to have managed so well
that there was no need for one, though old Samuel Andrew
of Milford again acted in the office at the Commencements
in the College hall and Meeting-house.

Edwards, however, was now considering a call to the
Northampton Meeting-house and the necessity for a decision
was thus forced upon the rather inactive Trustees. Several
efforts to this end, to be sure, had been made before this
time, but without success. One Nathaniel Williams, a Harvard graduate of 1693, and for the last fourteen years
master of the Boston Grammar School, had declined it.
The Rev. Eliphalet Adams, Harvard 1694, now the successor of Gurdon Saltonstall at the New London church,
and just elected a Trustee, was approached; he was willing
enough, but his congregation refused to dismiss him. A
unanimous election had then, in 1724, been offered to the
Rev. Edward Wigglesworth, Harvard 1710, Professor of
Divinity at Harvard, but he had refused. As a substitute
for him the Trustees had elected the young William Russell
of Middletown, the son of little old Noadiah Russell of
almanac fame, and, as we have seen, a former Tutor. At
that same meeting,—it was the one when Jonathan Edwards
had been appointed Senior Tutor,—it had been voted to
call Elisha Williams in case Russell did not want it. Russell
declined and Elisha Williams was formally elected the Yale
College Rector, September 29, 1725.

We have followed this enterprising young gentleman
through his days as the head of the rival Collegiate School
at his Wethersfield farm, his minis-
terial labors at Newington, and his *Eliphalet Adams*
entry into Colony politics as clerk of
the Lower House. During these years he had been Jonathan Edwards' instructor, and I suppose that the latter's

Rector Elisha Williams

firm friendship and admiration for him no doubt had had
something to do with the call now voted.

Yet conditions were different in 1726, so far as the Board
of Trustees was concerned, than they had been during the
long struggle over the College site. The bitternesses had
evaporated that had come from that controversy. Governor
Saltonstall had gone. Of the original eleven Trustees, only
four,—Andrew, Woodbridge, Webb, and Samuel Russel,—
were left. James Noyes, Israel Chauncy, Thomas Buckingham, Abraham Pierson, James Pierpont, and Noadiah
Russell had gone the way of all men, and the decrepit Samuel
Mather had been quietly retired. Their successors,—Moses
Noyes, Ruggles, John Davenport, Thomas and Stephen
Buckingham,—who had taken part in the Hartford controversy, were still Trustees, and to their number had been
recently added Eliphalet Adams of New London and Samuel

Whitman, also a recent Harvard graduate, and now the minister at Farmington. The Trustees were now for peace, and Elisha Williams' election appears to have been satisfactory to all of them. Some little matters had to be adjusted, however, concerning the financial reimbursement of the Newington church people for his loss (as was the regular Assembly fashion of the day) before he could accept. The Assembly finally lifted Colony taxes from the town for four years until a sum could be in hand to settle another pastor, and Elisha Williams turned his back on politics for the moment, rode down to New Haven with his wife and goods, was joyfully received by the Trustees, took the oath of allegiance to the Saybrook Confession, and moved into the new Rector's house, which in turn was to become the home of Presidents Clap, Stiles, and Dwight.

President Clap's "Annals" has a pleasant little account of the installation of this new Rector that was to close this first era in Yale history. "In the Library," he says, "before the Trustees, he gave his Consent to the Confession of Faith and Rules of Church-Discipline, agreed upon by the Churches of this Colony, in 1708. After Dinner he made a publick Oration in the Hall; and the Trustees successively came and saluted him as Rector."

And after this ceremony he no doubt entertained some of the visiting ministers at his new Rector's house. This was a rather fine building for that early day. Standing at the south end of the old Hooke lot at the corner of the present Chapel and College Streets, it faced the latter highway, some twenty feet back from it. It was a large house, two-storied after the manner of the better houses of the day, with a great high-sloping roof with dormer windows and two chimneys, between which was a square-fenced open cupola. Between the great square lower rooms was a broad central hall, extending through to the gardens, broad double doors leading

The President's House * 1722

into it from the roadway.   In the rear was a summer kitchen, surrounded by orchards and meadow running out to the present Chapel Street.   It had been built, finally, from the College funds and £300 received from the Colony imposts on "rhum," and it was to stand until 1834, when, after an interim, it was to be succeeded by the church building, now College Street Hall, still standing on the site.   Sitting at his library window in this spacious "President's House," Rector Williams could look up across his garden, and the street with its slow ox-teams and its square-coated villagers in their knee-breeches passing by, to the cerulean College building where his Tutors and the College library and the scholars were housed, and where, bulwarked on all sides against the insidious approach of any new and heretical theology, the Connecticut Colony leaders of the 18th Century were to be started on the orthodox path.

IV

And so we come to the end of these easy-going chronicles of the beginnings of Yale. Puritan settlers, black-gowned ministers, Colonial Governors, youthful scholars, troop before our eyes out of the musty past, up and down the King's Highway of the Long Island shore, as we recall these early Yale days. But a century before, and the site of the new Colony College, and of New Haven itself, had been a wilderness. Settled by dreamers of a Puritan Utopia, the New Haven theocracy and with it its proposed Puritan college, had faded away in that workaday world which its disillusioned founders came to see existed in New England as it did in Old England. New times had come, and with them that renewed need of a Colony school which should rebuild the shattered religious fabric of the settlers. This had been accomplished, and Yale College, rising out of the all but wrecked Collegiate School, now faced the ancient New Haven Market-place, "mounted in an eminent place thereof," a veritable "Egyptian pyramid" to the memory of Governor Elihu Yale, who had unexpectedly made it possible.

The foundations had thus been laid for the Yale that was to come. Yet these beginnings of the College were more than half a century before the Revolutionary War, and in a period in American history when every social institution was primitive and provincial and in the makings. The keynote of the settlement of New England had been religious liberty. John Davenport and Thomas Hooker had set up their tabernacles in the Connecticut wildernesses with this chief end in view, and their successors had maintained that end. The stern Puritanism of the Colonial settlers, indeed, was to come down through the next century and mould, if not retard, the intellectual character of the

Connecticut people. A survey of 18th Century Yale would show this clearly, if, indeed, a study of still later days would not still find conservative currents flowing, if in less measure, from this early Puritan spring. It was not until the modern scientific period came in, and American nationalism became a fact, that the Yale which developed from these early beginnings came to throw off the intellectual conservatism with which, bounded by its Puritan theological horizon, it started. If religious liberty was the characteristic of the first Connecticut generation, and political liberty that of the Revolutionary period, it was another century before the next step—intellectual liberty—followed. Yet, with all of its drawbacks, the stern Puritanism of the beginnings of Yale has been a mighty force in the upbuilding of the country. It had in it the germs of freedom, just as it itself sprang from the religious and political iconoclasm of its early English beginnings.

But this was all in the future. The first quarter century of the College hardly had been more than a continuous struggle for life itself. Harvard, having thrown off the yoke of the traditional Massachusetts Theocracy, was well on the way toward its second and broader intellectual stage when Yale began as a Connecticut Congregational stronghold on the Saybrook Platform.

Elisha Williams

INDEX

INDEX

Adams, Eliphalet (*Harv. 1694*), minister at New London, 425; elected Trustee of Yale College, 425, 426; declines Yale College Rectorship, 425

Addington, Isaac, Mass. conservative, 137; asked for draft of Collegiate School charter, (*1701*) 159, 164; reply with Samuel Sewall, 166; sends charter, 176; for church-control of Collegiate School, 177; letter to Founders about charter, 178-9; Pierpont's changes from charter of, 179-81

Allerton, Isaac, early New Haven house of, 35

Alling, John, of New Haven, Collegiate School Treasurer (*1702-17*), 203, 250, 287; solicits money for New Haven site for college, (*1716*) 319; New Haven house and public offices of, 203; death of, (*1717*) 338; purchases for Collegiate School, 389

Andrew, Samuel (*Harv. 1675*), called to Milford, Conn., church, (*1685*) 121; career at Harvard, 122, 251; pioneer in Collegiate School movement, 144-7; conservative in church-synod movement, 157; Trustee of Collegiate School, 181, 312, of Yale College, 426; at Trustees' meetings, 196, 284, 319-22, 340; scholarly but unbusinesslike character of, 197, 251, 313, 324; poor administration head for School, 251, 369; sends scholars to Collegiate School, 234; Rector *pro tem*, (*1707-16*) 288, 307, 316, 322,

324; *pro tem*, (*1716-19*) 330, 335, 343, 362, 369, 415, 425; undesirous of Rectorship, (*1717*) 313 (footnote), letter to that effect, 334-5; helping to secure new Rector, 361-2; for Saybrook site for School, 317, 319; for New Haven site, 320, 340; teaches Senior classes, (*1707 ff.*) 250, 318; on College House building committee, (*1717*) 327; relations with Timothy Woodbridge, 335; orders Saybrook books brought to New Haven, 365; and student rebellion, (*1719*) 370-1; and Commons rebellion, (*1721*) 387-8; advises Rector Cutler's election, 372; among few surviving Founders, (*1726*) 426

Andros, Sir Edmund, Governor-General of N. E. and N. Y., 110; effort to absorb Conn., 115, 121; arrives in New Haven, 132; gift of books to Collegiate School, 300-1

Antinomianism, in Mass., 23, 105

Arithmetic, in Collegiate School curriculum, 423

Arminianism, in Yale College, 409

Ashley, Jonathan (*Y. C. 1730*), copy of College laws by, (*1726*) 420

Astronomy, added to Yale College curriculum, (*1719*) 423; Copernican theory first taught, (*1721*) 398

Athenæum (*of 1761*), 354

Atwater, Joshua, New Haven Colony Treasurer, 44; College Street lot of, 325-6; sold to Collegiate School for College House, 326; house torn down, (*1717*) 338